Joni

THE CREATIVE ODYSSEY

OF JONI MITCHELL

Katherine Monk

GREYSTONE BOOKS
D&M PUBLISHERS INC.
Vancouver/Toronto/Berkeley

Greystone Books
An imprint of D&M Publishers Inc.
2323 Quebec Street, Suite 201
Vancouver BC Canada V5T 4S7
www.greystonebooks.com

Cataloguing data available from Library and Archives Canada
ISBN 978-1-55365-837-5 (pbk.)
ISBN 978-1-55365-838-2 (ebook)

Editing by Peter Norman
Copyediting by Shirarose Wilensky
Cover and text design by Heather Pringle
Cover photograph by © Jack Robinson/Getty Images
Printed and bound in Canada by Friesens
Distributed in the U.S. by Publishers Group West

We gratefully acknowledge the financial support of the Canada
Council for the Arts, the British Columbia Arts Council, the Province
of British Columbia through the Book Publishing Tax Credit, and
the Government of Canada through the Canada Book Fund for our
publishing activities.

Greystone Books is committed to reducing the consumption of
old-growth forests in the books it publishes. This book is one step
towards that goal.

"Alas, who knows what in himself prevails.
Mildness? Terror? Glances, voices, books?"
RAINER MARIA RILKE, *Späte Gedichte (Later Poems)*

For my mother, Joan: healer, hugger, creator

contents

Introduction   *viii*

one | LADY LOOKED LIKE A DUDE:
Impersonation and Identity   *1*

two | FACING DOWN THE GRIM REAPER:
Illness and Survival   *27*

three | BABY BUMPS:
Expecting and Expectation   *48*

four | WOODSTOCK:
Myth and Mythmaking   *88*

five | BUSINESS AND BULLSHIT   *104*

six | GODS AND MONSTERS   *136*

seven | LOVE:
The Big Production   *193*

eight | I'M OKAY, YOU'RE O'KEEFFE   *218*

nine | SING SHINE DANCE   *232*

Afterword   *257*

Acknowledgements   *259*

Notes   *262*

Bibliography   *276*

Index   *280*

INTRODUCTION

I WILL BE HONEST. I wasn't a huge Joni Mitchell fan before all this started. Sure, I think *Blue* is probably one of the ten best records ever made, and Mitchell deserves every accolade she's received—as well as all the ones she hasn't. But like so many people who grew up listening to Mitchell's vast catalogue in large part by sonic osmosis, I had a preformed idea about who she was and what her songs were about. To me, the name "Joni" conjured thoughts of earnest heartbreak, wholesome hippie-ness, mournful love songs delivered in high soprano, and, well, macramé plant hangers. These loose impressions were attached to the lattice of her legend, which I learned of as a kid growing up in Canada during the seventies.

My first memories of Mitchell's music go back to early childhood, sitting in my older sister's bedroom: Tracy had the record player, a fancy model that functioned like a primitive jukebox. My mother had given her Joni's 1968 debut, *Song to a Seagull*, wrapped alongside *The Best of Peter, Paul and Mary: Ten Years Together*. Half the fun was watching the records drop with an achingly slow mechanical clicking sound. The rest of the joy was suckled from the tinny tweeter as the milk of seventies rock poured from the grey plastic casing, quivering with each thump of electric bass. When we heard "Night in the City," Mitchell's upbeat single off *Seagull*, we'd giggle until our tummies hurt. Something about the yodelling octave shifts made us giddy, and of course we tried to sing along—if you could call the noises we made "singing."

The rest of the album made my stomach hurt for other reasons. Most of the music sounded so mournful and lonely, it sent a prematurely existential shiver down my six-year-old spine. It certainly wasn't *Sesame Street*. I loved *Sesame Street*, and if there was any real pole star in my early life, it was Ernie, the oddly ageless, somewhat genderless Muppet in a striped jersey. I loved the way Ernie laughed.

After researching this book, I believe Mitchell probably would have dug Ernie, too—because, in some ways, she's an ageless, genderless Muppet with a penchant for mischief. That's certainly one of the sides I've come to know as a result of my Joni voyage, but for most members of Mitchell's generation, the very name "Joni" is spoken with reverence—alongside "Jimi," "Leonard," and "Dylan."

My mother's record collection featured all these names on skinny album spines. It was contained in a cupboard above the stereo with wooden sides, and it did not mingle with the second-hand rock albums my sister and I had lying about the floor or stacked six-deep on her plastic party machine. My mother had Beethoven and Bach, as well as Barbra, Janis, and Nana, but most of the records in her collection were bought for the cover art. She would use the large colourful graphic squares to gussy up her showroom at work, where she tried her best to display silky hectares of fashion scarves without the aid of models, lighting, display equipment, or great amounts of space. She made do with a few Styrofoam heads in berets and, of course, scarves. These Pucci-esque silks and rectilinear polyesters were displayed before a wall of record covers. This added a sense of urbane chic to the otherwise rundown shmatte palace in Chabanel, the needle trade ghetto on the north side of Montreal. When the displays finally came down, the records came home. My mother gave them a chance. She would listen. Sometimes she would dance. She has little recollection of this. Not because she's senile or dead. But because the musical part of her being seems to be something she sees as part of her past—a part of her life she left behind, in the basement, above the now-broken stereo that won't turn off unless you unplug it.

It's when I think about my mother that I feel an urgent sense of purpose behind this book. My mother is, and always was, a highly intelligent and creative woman. Yet most of her artistic energy has been spent on cooking, flower arranging for the church, sewing terry cloth onesies for me and my sister, and pursuing her many business ventures—which led to that novel commingling of gatefold record sleeves and scarves. She had no time to be creative, she would say—like we all say, because we, as a society, undervalue the creative impulse. We almost mock the idea of being "an artist for a living." But as I've come to discover, being an artist is living. Joni Mitchell taught me that.

It was the first of many lessons writing this book taught me, but it was probably the most transformative: it framed the rest of the journey and brought new meaning to the project itself. The closer I came via Joni Mitchell's life to the core of the creative experience, the closer I came to understanding my own creative potential—and the underlying pulse of this book. This is very much a book about Joni Mitchell but, at its heart, it attempts to celebrate the essence of the creative experience. In the end, that's what Mitchell's life odyssey was all about: attaining meaning via the act of making something.

This lifelong drive is unfathomably simple and universally applicable but surprisingly easy to misunderstand, especially when you add thick layers of philosophy, calcified deposits of bad press, and a standoffish relationship with the public.

I soon learned that I'd had a completely inaccurate view of who Joni Mitchell really was—even if I knew the basic outlines of her biography. For instance, I knew that she was raised in Saskatchewan, dated James Taylor, lived in Laurel Canyon, wrote "Both Sides Now," released the universally beloved Blue, and won several Grammys. I also knew she chain-smoked sans apology, had a baby no one knew about, surrendered her for adoption, and reunited with her more than thirty years later in an estrogen-fuelled media circus of attention and awkward, forced intimacy.

Perhaps the most daunting fact of all was Mitchell's noted distaste for the media. As a reporter who once covered pop music, I knew some of her "people." I was aware that Mitchell never liked doing interviews and retired from show business on several occasions because it was too exhausting to be continually misunderstood in the scum pond of celebrity sound bites. In fact, at the dawn of this project, Mitchell was already done with biographers. As one of her last remaining business representatives told me: "She doesn't even want me sending solicitations. Nothing. She will not talk to you."

A huge problem quickly reared its head: How do I add anything original to the already exhaustive amount of Joni material without any new Joni Mitchell musings? The answer was not immediately apparent, but after immersing myself in the Joni Mitchell archive for a few months in the hope of finding a great big hole to fill with a new book, the outlines of a very different Mitchell began to emerge. And she was nothing like the person I thought she was.

She was a lot more complex, more literate, and far more creative—as an entire human being and not just as an artist—than I had ever imagined. She was full of fabulous paradoxes, damning and redeeming herself in the same breath. One minute she would be trashing the status quo with righteous zeal, and the very next, she'd recoil at the idea she sounded badass. Similarly, she hated doing interviews, yet some of the transcriptions are fifty thousand words long. There was an almost amorphous quality to the person emerging between the lines of text and archived interviews. She was not the mono-dimensional Joni monolith I was expecting. She was an evolving force of nature and, most importantly, an ever-questioning creative spirit.

I soon discovered Mitchell's inquisitiveness wasn't limited to the arts. As I pored over interviews, I realized she had a profound interest in philosophy and religion that guided her oeuvre. But she was also self-taught and, therefore, largely unencumbered by the academic posturing that can halt honest learning in its tracks. She pulled ideas together in a novel and entirely personal way. Romanticism, asceticism, nihilism, and humanism seemed to bleed from the same sliced vein of expression without the cauterizing influence of a formally educated intellect. As a result, Joni Mitchell could dance down original paths of enlightenment, going boldly where few musicians could ever hope to go.

She'd traipsed across the hostile landscapes of modern thought, where the likes of Martin Heidegger, Albert Camus, and Friedrich Nietzsche forever ride the metaphysical merry-go-round, chasing the elusive ring of human meaning. Mitchell frequently cited these sources, and many more, to the music journos who poked and probed at her artistic soul. She wasn't always quoting them verbatim, and she often mixed chunks of ideas together, but there was no doubt she grasped the material, internalized it, and expressed it in her words and music. Despite some snide insinuations, she wasn't reading the deep stuff to show off, or to prove herself literate to the frequently phony entertainment community. She was reading to understand herself, and her work. As a result, these big ideas would become compass points on her creative journey, with none other than Nietzsche—the granddaddy of nihilism and the man who killed God—emerging as the central N, her true north, on the map of her life.

Just how much Nietzsche influenced Joni Mitchell's oeuvre was probably the biggest surprise of all. While many writers had noted Mitchell's affection for Nietzsche's most literary work, *Thus Spoke Zarathustra: A Book For Everyone and No One*, usually that analysis went no further than a nod to a handful of songs that Mitchell herself described as Nietzschean. The biographical gap I was seeking stood before my feet, and within hours of rereading *Zarathustra*, I was sucked into what I can only describe as a Nietzschean wormhole where the macramé plant hangers, gingham dresses, and patchouli that once framed my impressions of Joni Mitchell vaporized in a thundercloud of creative power. It did not take me long to realize that this woman had gone far beyond the boundaries of the standard singer-songwriter. She was more of an artist-astronaut, extracting the ore of human meaning from the act of personal creation.

By the time I finished the research, I felt Joni Mitchell might be the only artist on the planet to survive the music industry with her soul intact. Hell, she may be the only human being in modern existence to approach the creative heights of the Nietzschean Superman—an individual who reconciles all his petty human flaws to become a true creator, or what Nietzsche described as "the lightning from the dark cloud of man."[1]

I know that sounds a little inflated and maybe down-right pedantic. But that's the rock I landed on. After walking through the door as an ambivalent observer, with absolutely no ego stake in the narrative or any messianic image to protect, I found myself feeling profound admiration for Mitchell and her unmatched courage in a world where art meets commerce in a head-on collision.

She has created one of the most enduring catalogues in the history of popular music, but she isn't like any other pop musician, folk legend, or celebrity icon I have ever encountered. Her work, her life, and her world view form a unique tapestry in the annals of popular culture because they have complete integrity. She never dropped a stitch of self. There are no holes of compromise, or any moth-eaten patches of pandering commercialism. Due to a confluence of benevolent circumstances, Mitchell was able to call her own shots from the beginning of her career: her first recording deal with Reprise Records gave her full creative control over every album, from internal content to external packaging. I can't overstate how rare, and how important, this piece of Mitchell biography is: it means she was in control of the artifacts from day one. It also means we can look at her career as a pure example of the pop star phenomenon, untainted by the usual peer and commercial pressures. Where most performers are essentially chauffeured around their own lives, driven by trends and an agent's profiteering advice, Mitchell has always piloted her own craft. She did not "show her tits" or "grab her crotch," nor did she suffer through any outsider's attempt to turn her work into focus-grouped sludge. She held true to her fluctuating and often fickle creative muses and managed to emerge as an icon recognized the world over.

Where did Joni Mitchell gain her creative strength and vision? And in this age of just-add-water pop stars on *American*

Idol, what does it mean to be a creator anyway? Do we need artists, or have the suits successfully sold us on the deep meaning of money and all the other abstracts our society assigns as "valuable"?

These are not new questions. Fortunately, the greatest thinkers in history applied themselves to these problems. Better still, Joni Mitchell read their work and transmitted their messages through song.

All I had to do was tease out the tangle. In order to do so, I had to dive into the deep end of a pool I normally waded in. I read a lot of philosophy and psychoanalytic theory. From Martin Heidegger to Rilke, Joseph Campbell to Sigmund Freud, Ellen Levine to Nietzsche, I immersed myself in ancient and contemporary thoughts about the creative process in the hope of decrypting Joni Mitchell's artistic success.

I have endeavoured to integrate these ideas into the text and to show how each golden philosophical thread helped Mitchell through the labyrinth of the artistic process. After all, the creative life offers up a never-ending series of challenges that must be overcome, and Mitchell found strength and purpose at each turn, partly because of her stubborn personality, but also because she had a philosophical grounding that gave her perspective. So there are many skeins of philosophical fleece twisting through this odyssey, but each one leads to the same whole Joni.

From Joseph Campbell, we can glean the importance of myth and mythmaking to the human experience. Campbell believed we crave mythical stories to help us unravel our own mysterious sense of meaning and feel the magic of existence. From Freud and his former student Carl Jung—not to mention Abraham Maslow, Ellen Levine, and all the other psych-types who see the creative act as the most important difference between us and our primate cousins—we can learn to use the language of psychology to describe the creative impulse and its role in personal realization. These thinkers believe that creative activity is a psychic cure for existential angst because it attaches us to the creative power of the universe itself and gives us a sense of belonging to something larger than ourselves.

From Heidegger, we can extract the metaphysical importance of the poet and the singer, mortals who can "reach into the abyss" and "sense the trace of the fugitive gods." It is the artists who can show "their kindred mortals the way toward the turning." In his essay "What Are Poets For?" Heidegger says we "must learn to listen to what these poets say," because they "are on the way to the destiny of the world's age." The poets and the singers (terms he used more metaphorically than literally) represent the very salvation of the human soul.[2]

And from Nietzsche, a man many people sadly believe to be soulless, we can pull on the most important thread of all: the idea of self-creation, as well as self-destruction. In *Thus Spoke Zarathustra*, Nietzsche killed "the vain old god" for one good reason: to free us from the concept of being "smaller than" or "less than" a grand creator. He killed the God concept not because he hated the idea of a Creator—he loved creation above all—but because he figured that as long as we felt inferior to some abstract concept of God, we would never take full responsibility for the good and evil within us, or for our limitless creative potential. Nietzsche believed that to be a fully realized human being, one must overcome oneself: unchain the creator within, even if that means bulldozing the walls of institutional thinking.

I have no doubt Joni Mitchell got there.

Not only did she create herself from scratch on the golden plains of Saskatchewan, but she also turned away from the crucible of celebrity and willfully created art—whether people were inclined to embrace it or not. Sometimes they did. Often they did not.

I hope this book appeals to the avid fan as well as the wary cynic because, forty years after my first giggling encounter with Joni Mitchell's music, I can see the scope of her journey. Moreover, because Mitchell has shared her personal and creative growth so clearly, and so honestly, her life has emerged as a well-painted portrait of experience, illustrating both the universal and the particular with equal skill.

What makes the odyssey all the more impressive is how Mitchell has managed to turn the blink of the music industry into an extended stare-down with the masses. This is the woman who, at fifty-one years of age, picked up the Grammy for best pop album (and best album package) for *Turbulent Indigo*—more than a quarter-century after she won her first statuette for Best Folk Performance with *Clouds*.

My hope in writing about Mitchell is to avoid becoming a "smug fool" who tears apart her life's work—one of the woes she describes in her last recorded song, "If." Instead, I hope to unveil the defining stops of her personal voyage and draw a creative map—a road guide through human experience that anyone can grasp, regardless of how you feel about her music. In fact, the music is something I embrace along the course of this journey but do not spend great amounts of time discussing sonically. Mitchell has always maintained (in a quote attributed to Frank Zappa, David Byrne, and others) that "writing about music is like dancing to architecture." The point I will drive at is the beauty of Mitchell's creative life at every level—regardless of how problematic or selfish it may appear.

In other words, this is not a fawning chronicle of a life, nor is it a comprehensive portrait of an artist. It's simply my take on the woman whose soprano I first heard as a kid, and whose alto I have grown to love as an adult.

I have gathered the material into chapters centred on various creative challenges and life themes. From romantic love to career burnout, Mitchell has survived the human comedy without losing her sense of humour, her compassion, or her will to become a better, more complete person. She did this because she believed in the larger purpose of being, and existing, as an artist.

As someone who's watched the entertainment industry for decades, I've witnessed the creative process debased at an alarming rate in the wake of the so-called "economic crisis." The tougher things get, the less art seems to matter. And yet, at a time when the local entrepreneurial spirit has been steamrolled by offshore manufacturing, franchise shopping, and endless remakes of old movies, the creative impulse may well represent our best chance at a better tomorrow.

Joni Mitchell's creative courage certainly stoked my personal furnace, and changed my life. She put me on a different track, where I found myself questioning the basic geography of being—and remapping the existential terrain. It got a little dark every once in a while, but there was always a great big ball of creative fire to guide the way. Joni Mitchell taught me the only real meaning in life is making something, because by making something, you make something of yourself. I feel incredibly privileged to have had the chance to create this book; my deepest hope is that in reading it, you will feel the same thump of the universe beating in your chest—and release your creative spirit with a fearless cry of freedom.

KATHERINE MONK, *February* 2012

one

LADY LOOKED LIKE A DUDE
Impersonation and Identity

"When the sound and wholesome nature of man acts as an entirety, when he feels himself in the world as in a grand, beautiful, worthy and worthwhile whole, when this harmonious comfort affords him a pure, untrammelled delight; then the universe, if it could be sensible of itself, would shout for joy at having attained its goal and wonder at the pinnacle of its own essence and evolution. For what end is served by all the expenditure of suns and planets and moons, of stars and Milky Ways, of comets and nebulae, of worlds evolving and passing away, if at last a happy man does not involuntarily rejoice in his existence."

GOETHE, essay on Winckelmann

"I WAS THE only black man at the party."

That's the sentence with which Joni Mitchell intends to open her own (as yet unpublished, four-volume) autobiography. And so, in a gesture of homage, I happily surrender the first sentence to her. Not only is it suitable for her own words to kick off this rambling adventure into the creative soul, but the compelling image of "the only black man at the party" also takes us to the doorstep of the fundamental creative challenge: Who am I?

Self-perception is the foundation of identity. But few of us let ourselves defy expectation, and even fewer would have the guts to answer the question "Who am I?" with "I am an artist." We usually let others define us.

We have a bad habit of building our own house with other people's bricks, trapping ourselves in an identity that isn't truly our own. Further limiting our freedom is the notion that all those bricks have to be mortared and arranged in a certain way to match some recognizable, off-the-rack architectural design. The same way neighbourhoods have bylaws to enforce conformity among houses, society has unwritten expectations about the reasonable boundaries of behaviour and personality. You can be a little different, but you have to fit in. This means that from the moment we are conscious of our place in a larger universe, we're essentially moving into one prefab box of identity after another—and frequently resenting it.

Joni Mitchell never did that. When she asked herself "Who am I?" she came up with the only right answer: "Anything I want to be."

After all, she was the only black man at the party.

In an enigmatic phrase that she said in 1998 to New York Times journalist Neil Strauss,[1] Mitchell asserted a self-created, self-assigned identity that did not match a single brick of public evaluation. She constructed her own house and she lived in it—at least for one day, and one very memorable Halloween night. When Joni says she was the only black man at the party, she doesn't just mean it as a metaphor to suggest she's been ostracized, undervalued, oppressed, and misunderstood—which she has been. (She told Alice Echols of L.A. Weekly in

1994: "I write like a black poet. I frequently write from a black perspective."[2]) She also means it literally: Mitchell actually showed up at a swanky Hollywood shindig in blackface.

"I WAS THE ONLY BLACK MAN AT THE PARTY."

Before we get to the *Guess Who's Coming to Dinner* moment, it's important to note Mitchell's album covers. Those familiar with her catalogue know most of her twenty-seven releases feature a self-portrait created by her own hand. This was the result of her first record deal with Reprise, which gave her full creative control over content and packaging, but it also gave her a chance to freely experiment with optics, perception, and her own public identity. Every cover shows a different side of Joni Mitchell, a different public face, but the one she offers up on the cover of *Don Juan's Reckless Daughter* is easily the most different of all.

On the cover of the 1977 release, there's an image of a black dude strutting in full peacock mode. Standing nearby is Mitchell, recognizable in a Mickey Mouse–inspired robe and top hat. A boy in a tux watches in awe as she releases doves from thin air. They stand on paprika-coloured plains, and a text bubble coming from the man in the chapeau reads, "Don Juan's Reckless Daughter." If you bought this album, you probably stared at the cover a good long while, before no doubt giving up on its cryptic meaning. I owned the record, and until I wrote this book, I didn't know the black dude was Mitchell.

For a white woman to take on the guise of a black man is an extreme makeover. So what image did Mitchell feel the need to blow up? Judging by the bout of press that preceded this incident, Mitchell may have felt caged by male expectation. As *Melody Maker*'s Michael Watts wrote of her 1974 show at London's New Victoria Theatre: "Joni Mitchell is disturbing in a very real way because after watching and listening to her for a while you start thinking she's not just a woman, she's WOMAN, embodying all male desires and expectations." No wonder she wanted to shed her pale skin and female form: the false image was hemming her in.

Mitchell explained the role play like this: "I was walking down Hollywood Boulevard, in search of a costume for a Halloween party, when I saw this black guy with a beautiful spirit walking with a bop," she told Angela LaGreca of Rock Photo in 1985. "As he went by me he turned around and said, 'Ummmm, mmm ... looking good, sister, lookin' good!' Well I just felt so good after he said that. It was as if this spirit went into me. So I started walking like him," she said. "I bought a black wig. I bought sideburns, a moustache. I bought some pancake makeup. It was like 'I'm goin' as him!'"[3]

When she showed up for the Halloween party at the sprawling Topanga Canyon home of Betsy and Peter Asher (a former Sony Music executive who would eventually manage Mitchell's career), no one recognized her—not Cheech, not Chong (both of whom cameoed on Court and Spark's "Twisted"). Not even former lover J.D. Souther could see past the faux 'fro and dark pancake that was getting oilier with each cocktail. He assumed the Ashers' interloper was a pimp, but politesse stopped anyone from asking who he/she was. It was only once the black man removed his hat, sunglasses, and, finally, wig, that people realized the black man at the party was Joni Mitchell.

Her walk on the wild side was a complete success, an experience so empowering she would make a mental note of it as the opening line of her own life story. One gets the feeling that for the first time, Mitchell escaped the exterior facade of the "winsome bittersweet blond"[4] with the high cheekbones and big Canadian teeth that haunted her from the moment she became a star. Her liberator was the alter ego she originally dubbed "Claude" but would eventually become known as "Art"—Art Nouveau.

This urge to flee her old folk persona was matched in her music, which by the time of *Don Juan's Reckless Daughter* was beginning to shift towards jazzier structures, unusual orchestrations, and new backup players. Mitchell says the gender-bending getup was just a Halloween necessity inspired by a fortuitous encounter with a complete stranger. But given the parallel shift in her artistic production, it seems something deeper was taking place at a creative level: she escaped not only the now-iconographic image of long blond Joni but also her own race and gender on a visual level. Mitchell talks about "feeling like a black man in a white woman's body"[5] on a regular basis, but by making the internal external, she consummated a long-gestating belief that she had to use her yin *and* her yang. As Mitchell summed it up in a 1994 interview with *Mojo's* Barney Hoskyns: "I started in the business kind of ultra-feminine, but as I went along I had to handle so many tough situations for myself—had to be both male and female to myself."[6]

Somewhat surprisingly, Mitchell's black and butch experiment didn't raise all that many eyebrows in 1977. Drag was strutting into the mainstream thanks to the cult success of *The Rocky Horror Picture Show*, the theatrical side of David Bowie (who had already given us Ziggy Stardust), and the increasing visibility of gay people in rock 'n' roll—Elton John was a *Billboard* juggernaut and Freddie Mercury's black leather fetish accessories were becoming fashion. I don't think Mitchell donned the *Don Juan* disguise because she thought it would open up new audience demographics, or because it made her trendy and hip. I don't think she was even making an overt political statement on gender or race in North America. I think it's a reflection of the un-gendered creative soul that can accommodate both male and female energy—what Jung called the anima/animus dynamic—as well as the magic of the creative impulse. It's a theory I believe is backed up by the presence of Mitchell as both magician and black man on the album cover.

Mitchell told Angela LaGreca that she wasn't all that aware of what was actually going on in her mind at the moment she gave birth to "Art." "A lot of it is instinct—the important point is the chain of events," she said, "I was just going on the hottest impulses I had, the creative ideas."[7]

This absence of forethought, intellectualization, and self-criticism is an important piece of the creative puzzle and one Mitchell clearly mastered early—over the course of her career, she would don multiple identities. "I feel like I belong to everything and nothing," she told Barney Hoskyns. "Sometimes, that's lonely."[8]

With Art Nouveau, Mitchell set herself up as outsider and social pariah, given she was "the only black man" at a party where the rest of the guests were affluent white people. She took on the identity of a man who was systematically disenfranchised by the establishment—which describes Mitchell's feelings about her position in the music industry, especially when she attempted to experiment with her own style. She was getting into jazz and traditionally "black" structures, but industry types were only too eager to keep her in the little enamelled Joni box, a pretty white folksinger with a guitar and a pristine soprano.

Mitchell enjoyed the role playing. She's often described herself as a frustrated actress, or filmmaker, who "writes roles" for herself. Over the course of her career, she's assumed countless identities and surrendered to what she calls a bad case of "multi-phrenia." She's highly aware of the game and even called herself on it when she declared to the *Toronto Star*'s Marci McDonald in 1974: "Will the real me please stand up?"[9]

This ability to play with identity is the foundation of the creative process, for a variety of reasons. Not only does it affirm the importance of self-creation; it spurs a sense of dynamic tension between who you are and what the world expects you to be. Each individual has the innate ability to subvert expectation, to recreate the world at the drop of a plumed chapeau, but very few of us try. All of which makes Joni Mitchell's creative journey so compelling: she did it without even thinking about it. She did it on instinct, as though the creative impulse was mapped into her DNA.

FROM CRADLE TO CREATOR

Psychologists, evolutionary biologists, philosophers, and all variety of scientists have spent a great deal of their own creative energy trying to understand the creative impulse—and most of them believe it's the reason for our rise to the top of the species totem. *Homo sapiens* is the only creature to question and to seek answers to abstracts. We make connections between what is and what could or should be, and that's the ignition button on the creative engine.

According to Sigmund Freud, the creative self is kick-started in infancy. It begins as a way to reconcile the nihilistic forces in the universe by giving us a sense of meaning through the assertive power of self. Early child psychoanalyst Melanie Klein applied Freud's concepts to her own research, and in her 1932 book *The Psycho-Analysis of Children* she said it all came down to the life-affirming power of the "good breast" versus the destructive presence of the "bad breast." The good breast is nurturing, loving, and accessible whereas the bad breast is dry, unpredictably unavailable, and emotionally cruel. For an infant to reconcile these two conflicting realities, she engages the power of creation to gain a sense of control over her environment and the goodness/badness of the breast.[10]

For Freud's colleague and follower Carl Jung, creativity is everything that "flows from the living fountain of instinct" and connects us to the deeper sense of self that is the "collective man" and our shared subconscious.[11] Artistic man lives in a higher realm, in harmony with the timeless, echoing gong of experience. These ideas, contained in his 1919 essay "Instinct and the Unconscious," assert the spiritual value of the artistic impulse. Jung believed the creative act puts us in direct contact with truth by building a bridge to the collective subconscious—the chorus of human souls we can all hear at a primal level and desperately need to connect with in order to achieve full psychic integration.

Nietzsche distilled the notion of self-creation and identity down to the word "I." He separated this word into two components: the intellectual notion of self and the physical reality of being. "You say 'I' and are proud of this word," says Nietzsche in *Thus Spoke Zarathustra*, calling our attention to what Freud would later call ego. "But greater than this—although you will not believe in it—is your body and its great intelligence, which does not say 'I' but performs 'I.'"[12] Identity isn't just a function of the words we speak and the image we hope to put forward; it's a matter of what we actually do. He says our body has a way of knowing that operates independently of words, language, and ego. This "body" of instinct is the seat of the creative soul.

Semiotician and psychologist Jacques Lacan picked up on this notion of the performed "I," and distilled it further using the image of the mirrored self. Lacan, a name typically batted around by top-shelf academics whose ideas can be so hard to reach, said that once a kid sees himself in the mirror, there's a schism between the reflected self, which seems ideal, and the true self, which seems vulnerable. For the rest of our lives, we try to resolve these two images into one whole "Me."[13]

There is no simple trick to personal integration, which is why there's an entire industry devoted to self-help, creative emancipation, and spiritual awakening. We all sense there's something more to existence, but we often can't access it because we're trapped in that house of mistaken identity, built from bricks that didn't come from our own oven.

How do we find the key to our own true house? First, we have to recognize that other house we built, then pull it down brick by brick. Dissecting meaning, component by component, is called "deconstruction." Joni Mitchell constructed, and deconstructed, her meaning through identity several times over. It's one of the reasons why she's such a realized creator.

If we're to take the experts' word for it, Mitchell's central strength in this endeavour was her ability to achieve safe distance. She had enough perspective on her identity that she could play with it. She literally did this through "Art" and, in so doing, gave us a human case study in what art therapists have been scribbling about for decades. According to psychologist Ellen Levine, the creative act allows us to gain distance from our core self and, in turn, gauge it and transform it from a healthy perspective. "Distancing allows for the capacity to separate and externalize, not to detach but to maintain a connection without fusion," she says. "[The artifact] can be seen as a crystallization of feelings in the form of the art work, not the actual feelings themselves. There is comfort in this kind of distancing," she continues. "It creates a space within the psyche for understanding and re-incorporation." She says that role play can be a good distancing technique and explains, "Here, through words, actions, or movements, a radical shift in perspective takes place in which the roles are reversed and reversed again. Enacting the point of view of the other and feeling what this is like involves new information, and on a deeper level, a new bodily experience."[14]

Levine's words echo Nietzsche and Lacan as they affirm the importance of the physical and the concrete, but she also asserts our potential to scale these brick walls with a little imagination and a sense of play. "By creating an as-if situation in play, there is the possibility for exploration and, as always, surprise," she says. "There is a significant felt difference between talking about a difficult ... relationship with another person or part of the self, and being the other for a discrete period of time—talking, walking, and feeling the experience of otherness."

A HISTORY OF SELF-CREATION

The gatefold sleeve for Don Juan's Reckless Daughter certainly wasn't the first time Mitchell slapped an image of herself on her own package. The tradition of self-representation—and, in turn, self-creation—began with her first album, Song to a Seagull (1968): the cover featured Mitchell's own pen and ink doodling as well as a small photograph of herself.

The artwork grew more ambitious with the 1969 release of Clouds, successfully setting in celebrity cement the image of Joni Mitchell as hippie chick earth goddess: the self-portrait on this cover is a close-up of the singer holding a red lily in one hand with Saskatoon landmark the Bessborough Hotel, built by the Canadian Pacific Railway and designed to look like a Bavarian castle, looming alongside a snaking river in the background. Mitchell's face is almost beatific; her blue eyes gaze at the listener with an open expression. The near-random designs of Seagull are abandoned in favour of a complete and carefully painted portrait. This speaks to a creative confidence in Mitchell's artwork that's matched by the music: Clouds contained the proven single "Both Sides Now," which had already charted thanks to Judy Collins's smash cover version, as well as "Chelsea Morning," which Mitchell would turn into a hit on her own.

Ladies of the Canyon followed in 1970, and here Mitchell's line drawing of herself is incorporated into the Laurel Canyon landscape, suggesting her identity is now literally integrated into the scene—which was probably the most interesting and creative community in Los Angeles at the time, home to every noted musician and artist in the area, from Jim Morrison to Frank Zappa.

At first glance, the cover art for *Ladies of the Canyon* may feel like a return to *Seagull's* singular dimensions, but the line drawing is assured and created from just a handful of pencil strokes. It also places Mitchell in geographical context once more—demonstrating an unspoken understanding of the relationship between the artist and her environment. As Mitchell says of this period: "[It was] like falling to earth... It felt almost as if I'd had my head in the clouds long enough: Shortly after that time, everything began to change. There were fewer adjectives in my poetry. Fewer curlicues to my drawing. Everything began to get more bold and solid in a way."[15]

Blue (1971) and *For the Roses* (1972) followed, but unlike Mitchell's previous releases, they featured photographic covers. The first was snapped by Tim Considine at a concert; the second was taken by Joel Bernstein on a bluff overlooking Mitchell's home on British Columbia's Sunshine Coast. These photographic covers are certainly of the moment, and show a very attractive female, but the music beneath the covers was equally "realistic" as it explored two significant disillusionments: heartbreak and the realization of romantic love's limitations on *Blue*, and the emptiness of the music industry on *For the Roses*.

The cover for *Court and Spark* (1974) signals a return of Mitchell's artistic energy with a rather abstract sketch called *The Mountain Loves the Sea*. Minimalist in form and colour, the sketch features a strange, hugging, Madonna-like wave cresting before mountains. Mitchell says she created the drawing, at one time owned by Rosie O'Donnell, in a "moment of whimsy" on her land in B.C. "It's a metaphor for the way the waves met up with the mountain; the way they embraced one another," she said.[16] Interestingly, this visual fusion of ocean and mountain—water and earth, chaos and order—graced the cover of Mitchell's most successful album of all time. *Court and Spark* is the only Mitchell release to hit the number one spot on the *Cashbox* chart in the U.S. and on the Canadian sales charts (it hit number two on the U.S. *Billboard* album chart), and it contains Mitchell's only Billboard Hot 100 top-ten single, "Help Me"—which peaked at number seven.

The live concert album *Miles of Aisles* was released in the same year and features a photograph Mitchell snapped as she was viewing the empty stage in the Pine Knob Music Theater outside Detroit. It's taken from the point of view of a spectator, which tickled something in Mitchell, who said it "appealed to me as an abstract painting—the blue blobs where the knees are, the checkerboard grid at the top. I like the way it looks, but more than that, it was just impulse."[17]

A significant creative shift took place on *The Hissing of Summer Lawns* (1975) as Mitchell moved away from standard pop/folk forms and embraced jazzier structures and syncopated beats. (The album was also declared by *Rolling Stone* to have the "worst title of the year.") The cover reflected the change; it showed a group of tribesmen holding a snake outside a sprawling city skyline. The colours are black and lime green, and the lines are either curvilinear (the natural world of the tribesmen and the snake in the foreground) or entirely linear (the urban architecture of the First World in the background). The tension between these two worlds splashes all over the album. Raw, primal energies mingle with the rarified fumes of intellect, and although some embraced this new sound (Prince has repeatedly talked about his debt to Mitchell and *The Hissing of Summer Lawns* in particular), many more rejected it.

Unfazed, Mitchell continued to experiment with both her art and her image, and her following release, *Hejira* (1976), ushered a return to the photographic cover. This time, it was a composite collage showing Mitchell in black and white as a highway rolls through the middle of her body, the vanishing point of the road ending right around her heart.

Up to this point, all the photographic covers feature Mitchell as she is, and as her fans would recognize her, so the next album marked a definite turning point: *Don Juan's Reckless Daughter* was proof that Joni Mitchell wasn't just an artist on a creative odyssey; she was entirely self-aware of her personae, her place in the universe, and her innate potential for recreation. After all, if we're going to decrypt the cover featuring Art Nouveau, Joni as magician, and a little kid with doves, we could say Mitchell has been her own pimp; transcended race and gender lines; maintained a respectful, childlike sense of wonder in the face of creation (the boy in a tux); and learned to embrace the magic inner peace and winged spirit of the truly artistic stance (doves).

MANIFEST DESTINY

Mitchell's comfort with myriad identities speaks to her experience as the chameleon and, in turn, an innate trust of her creative impulse. It was entirely "incorrect" for a white woman of privilege to assume the identity of a black man from the streets, but she did it without fear. This fearlessness could have come from a sudden revelation that forced her to rebel against her old familiar sense of self. More likely, Mitchell's foray into gender-bending role play was merely the culmination of a long personal history with a shape-shifting identity and a strong propensity for self-creation.

Does this mean Joni Mitchell was born to be an artist and her life's journey was cast in stone before she even exited her mother's womb? Maybe, but that makes creativity sound like an almost Calvinist enterprise, where only the select few will find salvation through the expressive process—and that just doesn't seem fair, nor does it resonate as truth. I believe we all feel the tickle of the creative spirit.

Jenny Boyd, a music fan who ended up in the midst of the psychedelic explosion as a result of her attraction to sexy rock stars, eventually wrote her PhD about the creative experience. In her book, *Musicians in Tune*, she says, "a creative person's drive determines whether or not he will be able to express himself, no matter how much talent he has."[18] Given that most psychologists believe we all have innate creative abilities to help us reconcile life's nagging conflicts and "actualize our true nature," it seems Mitchell is simply a brilliant example of someone who figured out the importance of self-creation early.

Boyd says most successful artists are possessed by a sense of "destiny" or a "calling." Mitchell believes in these mysterious forces: in the 2003 PBS documentary *Joni Mitchell: Woman of Heart and Mind*, she says, "Bad fortune changed the course of my destiny… I became a musician."[19] The "bad fortune" was getting pregnant, but the idea of destiny is clearly present. More importantly, Mitchell had the strength to surrender one vision for another; she could roll with the waves of destiny. And a lot of us can't do that. We hang onto the debris of broken dreams until we drown, believing fate has cheated us of a shot at personal happiness.

THERE'S AN "I" IN JONI

Joni Mitchell built her ark of "I" at a young age. Roberta Joan Anderson was born on November 7, 1943, and for those nearest and dearest to her, she remains "Joan." How did Joan become Joni? Easy: she made it so. Mitchell adopted the name Joni at the age of thirteen after admiring the jaunty look of her art teacher's name on his canvases. Henry Bonli was an abstract expressionist who followed the Barnett Newman school of hard-edge colour fields, and he signed his work with a lower case i—a detail that impressed Mitchell far more than any large swaths of applied pigment. She told Timothy White: "I admired the way his last name... looked in his painting signatures."[20]

That "name-changing" event took place in 1957, back when "you had to dance a foot apart." Did Mitchell have any clue then that her bold little i—which stands entirely alone and completely disconnected to the loopy J and the rather pedestrian o-n—in her own signature would be the beginning of a great big I?

Maybe, but if so, she's kept it to herself. It smacks of self-importance, at least to the Canadian psyche, which is infused with a socialist sensibility of equality and an unfortunate case of "tall poppy syndrome"—you can't stand too tall, lest you be cut down to size by jealous colleagues and peers. In Canada, it's best to keep quiet about your suspicions of personal greatness, because most of us find it distasteful. Those who don't feel uptight about tooting their own horn move to the United States, where they can be embraced for their moxie and self-confidence.

Joni made the big move to the U.S. in the wake of her brief marriage to Chuck Mitchell, a folksinger who lived in Detroit and helped Canadians land gigs in the U.S. It was Chuck who gave Joni the other half of her now-legendary stage name, and it's because of Chuck that Joan Anderson fully became the character of Joni Mitchell—or, at least, the person she imagined Joni Mitchell to be.

Joni has suggested that Chuck Mitchell's shortcomings as a husband made her a musician, but she takes ownership of her own talent for self-creation. She creates her own mythology—a fact not lost on the *Toronto Star's* Marci McDonald. "She writes her own press releases," McDonald said, depicting Mitchell as a "myth spun in vinyl and remembered spotlights. In swirling soprano self-portraits and worshipful press clippings, all cornsilk flashes and free-spirit poetry. There's no myth in the top of pop quite like it."[21]

Indeed, there's no myth like it because no other artist—to my knowledge—entered the music business with the ability to write her own narrative. Most biographies accompanying a record's release are written by PR people at the label or impoverished rock writers looking for extra cash. Mitchell is one of the few—in fact, before the age of blogging, I knew of none other—who wrote her own bumph. McDonald saw this piece of self-penned biography, written in "her child-like loopy longhand," as "a little short on details and little long on preserving the mythology."

"I was born in Fort Macleod, Alberta, in the foothills of the Canadian Rockies—an area of extreme temperatures and mirages," writes Mitchell. "When I was two feet off the ground I collected broken glass and cats. When I was three feet off the ground I made drawings of animals and forest fires. When I was four feet off the ground I began to dance to rock 'n' roll and sing the top ten and bawdy service songs around camp fires and someone turned me on to Lambert, Hendricks and Ross and Miles Davis. And later Bob Dylan." The self-penned history continues: "Through these vertical spurts there was briefly the church choir, grade one piano, bowling, art college, the twist, a marriage, runs in the nylons and always romance—extremes in temperature and mirages."

PLANTING A SEED

That's a rather hasty take on a rather extended career arc, even up to that early point, so let's fill in the details while we're still talking about the creation of personal identity.

Roberta Joan Anderson was born under a blue Alberta sky. Her father was a flight lieutenant with the Royal Canadian Air Force. Her parents—who were clearly expecting a boy they could name Robert John—had met a year earlier, when the thirty-year-old Myrtle McKee was working in a bank in Regina. "Mickey"—as she was known to her girlfriends, and is credited in the liner notes for *Clouds*—didn't think she'd find any men in town, since the war had vacuumed up all the good specimens. But after a tea leaf reading, Myrtle was told she would fall in love, marry within the year, and die of a long, slow disease. (The first two were correct but not the third: Myrtle died in her nineties without protracted pain.) Myrtle thought Bill looked cute in his uniform (as Joni sings in her filial tribute "The Tea Leaf Prophecy"), and they were married after a quickie courtship. Joan remembers her crib and watching the dust swirl in the beams of light poking through an old plastic blind. She has since described herself as "born materialistic" and "like a crow" because she enjoyed picking up shards of broken glass and holding them up to the light— back when parents allowed kids to handle sharp objects and blow stuff up.

Stints in small-town Saskatchewan followed as the Andersons moved from Fort Macleod to Maidstone, then North Battleford, and eventually the "big city" of Saskatoon.

Mitchell's childhood was rather charmed: she played outside and roughhoused with the fellas, whom she tended to identify with more than the girls.

A HISTORY OF DEFYING GENDER

Mitchell says she's always considered herself "one of the boys." She's moved back and forth across the gender divide most of her life, even when it was considered cultural taboo. When she was growing up on the wheat fields of the Canadian prairie, her playmates would choose a new Roy Rogers stand-in to lead the day's play agenda. Joan wanted to be Roy, but the boys wouldn't let her, so she begged her parents to buy her a Roy Rogers shirt and hat for Christmas. Her father finally relented, but when Joan showed up ready to lead the boys in her red shirt and hat, complete with "Roy" stitched on the pocket, they told her she couldn't be Roy. She could only be Dale. And Dale stayed home and cooked.

A lot of girls have this earth-shattering experience at a young age, when they're suddenly denied the chance to do something because of their sex. For Mitchell, whose father had raised her in many ways like a boy, encouraging her to build things and go outside in the fresh air, there was a sense of betrayal and frustration that would linger into adulthood. "I had a good relationship with my father. He taught me a lot of things that, had he had a son, he would have taught a boy. How to make bows and arrows and so on," she told the *New Musical Express* in 1985. "I enjoy men's company, and I grew up enjoying it."[22] Mitchell says she has female friends, but she tends to relate better to men because she's driven. "Sometimes I remind [women] of their inability to get going." That's on the good days. The bad days look different: "I'm a little afraid of women," she told Cameron Crowe in a 1979 *Rolling*

Stone interview. "In my observation, what passes for feminine camaraderie is conspiracy."[23]

This distrust of other women is proof of Mitchell's gender alienation. She doesn't feel like she belongs to either camp, and although this no doubt amped up her existential angst, it freed her from a singular perspective calibrated to the status quo. She could dress up as a pimp in blackface. She could wear a Roy Rogers shirt. And she could own her sexual power, sharing her body with the men she wanted, and at times even objectifying them sexually. When she dated percussionist Don Alias, she painted his portrait. This isn't such a big surprise, considering Mitchell painted a lot of her partners—as well as her cats. What made the Alias painting so unique was the decision to paint him wearing a bathrobe, with a full erection. "It was me, with my bathrobe open with—bang!—like this hard-on sticking out," Alias told Sheila Weller, author of *Girls Like Us*, before his death in 2006.[24] The musician was embarrassed, especially when Mitchell hung the portrait in the middle of the living room. He must have felt a little used, maybe even a little exposed and dirty, because he demanded Mitchell perform an artistic castration: he wanted his genitals removed from the canvas. Mitchell refused, eventually compromising on a semi-excited schlong. While this may be the only documented case of Mitchell compromising her artistic integrity, it proves once more how willing she is to step outside the box of expectation.

"I believe that I am male and I am female," she once told Crowe. In 1987, Bob Dylan echoed this take on Mitchell. When asked by *Rolling Stone* reporter Kurt Loder what he thought of women onstage, Dylan said: "I hate to see chicks perform. Hate it… because they whore themselves." When asked if he thought the same thing about Joni Mitchell, Dylan replied: "Well, no. But then, Joni Mitchell is almost like a man. I mean, I love Joni, too. But Joni's got a strange sense of rhythm that's all her own and she lives on that timetable. Joni Mitchell is in her own world all by herself."[25]

Leave it to Dylan to place gender in a musical context, where time and metre are the ticking social rules measuring out gender expectation and success. It's a very workable metaphor, and one that parallels a relatively new landmark in gender studies: Judith Butler's 1990 book, *Gender Trouble*. Butler is a professor of rhetorical studies and comparative literature at UC Berkeley, and one of her central concerns in *Gender Trouble* is untangling the many strands of personal and public identity.

From uprooting the potentially sexist foundations of language itself to deconstructing the forces that shape our current reality, Butler tries to understand gender "outside the box"—or, in Dylan's terminology, she tries to hear the beats as entities separate from the time signature. Butler's book is a dense read, but her conclusions are mind-altering—and for our purposes highly relevant—because she comes to believe gender is a function of performance. Gender is not a noun as much as it's a verb—a series of actions that are socially equated with one sex or the other.

Gender "is always a doing… the 'doer' is merely a fiction added to the deed—the deed is everything," she writes, echoing Nietzsche's idea that "I" is an act of performance. "There is no gender identity behind the expressions of gender; that identity is performatively constituted by the very 'expressions' that are said to be its results"—in other words, there is no solid, immutable, universal force defining human beings as one or other. We are what we do.

I was heartened to discover that someone else had made the link between Judith Butler and Joni Mitchell. When I found Stuart Henderson's 2005 essay "Gendering Joni Mitchell" online, I felt a wave of relief—I wasn't the only one to look at the creative importance of gender-bending, especially as it applies to Mitchell. Henderson draws detailed observations to apply Butler's theory to Mitchell's life. He argues that Mitchell's identity is not solid and that "Joni Mitchell" is a function of performance—a mix of performances so vast and varied, it defies classification at every level: musically, stylistically, instrumentally, or even in terms of gender.

"Once critics were forced to take her more seriously, her woman-ness became conflated with an apparent maleness," Henderson notes. "It was undeniable that [Mitchell] was never merely a pretender to the male role—with every record, Mitchell was demonstrating her idiosyncratic vision of the art of composition."[26] Mitchell transcends gender because she's become a creative force unbound by thick black borders. Henderson's essay is undeniably thorough, but it only covers 1966 to 1974 and so omits Mitchell's truly adventurous gender explorations, such as the cover of *Don Juan's Reckless Daughter* and, more recently, her support and appreciation for John Kelly, the Obie-winning performer who's earned fame playing Mitchell in a one-man show. Kelly tried on Mitchell's identity for size at the Wigstock drag festival in the late 1990s, donning a long blond wig, flowing dresses, and an acoustic guitar. "Really, it's the idea of [Joni] that I present on stage," he told Brian Jewell of *Bay Windows* in 2007. "This clever, sometimes seemingly spacey goddess. She tells crazy, outrageous stories that have you wondering where she's going with it. She's a riot."[27]

In one of the last published interviews Mitchell granted, with Matt Diehl for the *Los Angeles Times* in April 2010, she shared the spotlight with Kelly and described herself as a big fan of the show. A friend of hers had told her she might not like it, but when she decided to check it out for herself at New York's Fez, she was pleasantly surprised. "It was really a fun, unique experience—more homage than a normal drag show. It was like being a ghost at your own funeral," she said. "The audience responded to John as if he were me."[28]

Mitchell's words reaffirm the two central points of this chapter. First, personal identity is an act of self-creation and performance: Kelly can conjure Mitchell's soul by "doing" what Mitchell does, and Mitchell herself recognized the performance aspect of her identity in the same interview when she said, "I'm a method actress in my songs, which is why it's hard to sing them." Second, Mitchell is a happy gendernaut, content to veer over the double yellow line on the gender highway, peering over the edge of the abyss with a giggle in the back of her throat. After all, what could be more threatening to an iconic artist such as Mitchell than a drag queen appropriating the repertoire and making it his own? I mean, it could have been hissy mockery—a queen lip-synching "A Case of You" with a bottle of Stoli—but the fact that Kelly is a man seems to have no effect on Mitchell's psyche. He could play her as easily as any woman could. "I'm usually the playwright and the actress," she said, giving the performance-based theory of identity an added punch in the arm. "But in this case, with John, we now have a new actress! Right?"

FAKING IT, BEING IT, AND THE IMPOSTOR SYNDROME

It was in the same interview with the *Los Angeles Times* that Joni Mitchell accused Bob Dylan of being "a plagiarist"—a comment that eclipsed the rest of the content and set off a chain reaction of anti-Joni comments from the legions of Bobby faithful.

Citing Mitchell's assumption of persona on the album cover of *Don Juan's Reckless Daughter*, as well as the name change from Joan to Joni, Diehl probably thought he was navigating safe waters when he said: "You've had experience becoming a character outside yourself. The folk scene you came out of had fun creating personas. You were born Roberta Joan Anderson, and someone named Bobby Zimmerman became Bob Dylan."

Mitchell's response is now destined for the annals of rock 'n' roll history: "Bob is not authentic at all. He's a plagiarist, and his name and voice are fake. Everything about Bob is a deception. We are like night and day, he and I."

By calling Dylan "fake" and insisting that she and he are "like night and day," Mitchell asserts her authenticity—and, in turn, her superiority over the iconic tambourine man with the nasal drawl.

Many people who enter a creative field are steeped in self-doubt about the depth of their ability. What made Mitchell different?

In 1978, two psychologists coined the term "impostor syndrome" to describe professionals who believe their success is accidental, or even unearned. In the opening salvo of their landmark paper, "The Impostor Phenomenon in High-Achieving Women," Pauline Rose Clance and Suzanne Imes declare the phenomenon to be largely female: "In our clinical experience, we have found that the phenomenon occurs with much less frequency in men and that when it does occur, it is with much less intensity."[29]

According to Clance and Imes, the crippling effects of impostor syndrome tend to affect women because female talent isn't reinforced in our society. Men feel entitled and deserving of their success, even if they score much lower in ability than a woman with low self-esteem. Society reads confidence at face value until undeniable failure, sheer incompetence, or violent defensiveness forces a shift of opinion—and even at that, the problematic evidence is often overlooked because the man is able to rebound quickly with an assertive ego and defend his greatness. Moreover, we want him to rebound because it puts the universe back in its normal order.

Women are not typically infused with a reservoir of confidence, and the authors of the study blame society's low evaluation of female creativity as well as family dynamics for this unfortunate cycle:

> We have observed that our "impostors" typically fall into one of two groups, with respect to early family history. In one group are women who have a sibling or close relative who have been designated as the "intelligent" member of the family. Each of the women, on the other hand, has been told directly or indirectly that she is the "sensitive" or socially adept one in the family. The implication from immediate and/or extended family members is that she can never prove that she is as bright as her siblings regardless of what she actually accomplishes intellectually.[30]

By comparison, the members of the other group of "impostors" have been told the opposite: they are gifted and can do anything they set their minds to. This can backfire, though, once the female child discovers she is human and is not capable of "perfection with ease": "Because she is so indiscriminately praised for everything, she begins to distrust her parents' perceptions of her. Moreover, she begins to doubt herself. When she goes to school her doubts about her abilities are intensified. Although she does outstanding work, she does have to study to do well and... jumps to the conclusion that she must be dumb. She is not a genius; therefore, she must be an intellectual impostor."[31]

Clearly, from what Mitchell said about Dylan, she's not suffering from any brand of impostor syndrome—and probably never did. From the beginning of her career, Mitchell seems aware of her foibles—"I'm selfish and I'm sad." But she believes in herself and her bona fide ability.

Self-confidence is one of the hallmarks of a realized creative soul. However, the source of Mitchell's certainty remains somewhat mysterious. Perhaps it was the result of being an only child who was never forced to compete with a sibling for parental affection or wear an inappropriate label that scratched and bled. Perhaps it was the result of another absence: a lack of gender stereotyping growing up. According to Clance and Imes, "the high-achieving women in our sample escaped, at least to some degree, the societal sex-role stereotyping in the preschool years that can be transmitted through the parents."[32]

The other defining element of the impostor syndrome is self-awareness of "intellectual flattery": the subject wins over authority figures and those she respects by gushing false and insincere remarks. According to the study:

> She believes, "I am stupid," but at another level she believes she is brilliant, creative, and special if only the right person would discover her genius and thereby help her believe in her intellect. She first finds a candidate she respects and then proceeds to impress that person. She studies the person carefully and perceives very accurately what that person will be responsive to. She uses her friendliness, charm, looks, humor, sexuality, and perceptiveness to win the person over... If the candidate is in a difficult situation,

the woman listens with understanding and concern. She may volunteer to assist a professor with his/her pet research project. She may even become sexually involved with her mentor.[33]

I'm sure we've all encountered at least one woman who matches this description to a T. But for all her efforts, her attempt to solve the impostor riddle fails, no matter what kind of forced ego reinforcement comes her way, because the entire relationship is based in artifice, and she knows it.

In the end, impostor syndrome is based in fear—easily the most destructive force to the creative soul. Mitchell's ability to take on alternate personae (even controversial ones) and her deep belief in herself make her the fearless and potent creator she is. Exactly how Mitchell found her courageous will, and rode it to the top, will become clearer in the following chapter.

two

FACING DOWN THE GRIM REAPER
Illness and Survival

"What does not kill me makes me stronger."
FRIEDRICH NIETZSCHE, *Twilight of the Idols*

ART NOUVEAU, Mitchell's pimped-out blackface alter ego, made his public debut in November 1977, the same month legendary jazz musician Charles Mingus Jr. was diagnosed with amyotrophic lateral sclerosis (ALS, or Lou Gehrig's disease), a progressive neurodegenerative disorder that reduces muscle function to the point of paralysis. It is terminal and has no cure, and because it's relatively rare, it's considered an "orphan disease"—one that lacks an international infrastructure for research and support. It was a cruel twist of fate for the man who wrote in his stream-of-consciousness biography: "I am Charles Mingus—I am nothing. I am Charles Mingus, a famed jazz musician but not famous enough to make a living in society, that is in America, my home."[1]

Goethe said "the first and last task required of genius is love of truth"[2]—and Mingus spoke his truth, regardless of the consequences. He expressed himself as honestly as he could, not only in his words and music but also in his entire stage presence. He famously sacrificed one of his own instruments in a moment of ire, destroying a bass at a Village Vanguard show when the audience wouldn't shut up—which earned him the nickname "The Angry Man of Jazz."

Passion is often mistaken for anger, and Mingus was passionate about finding the most honest mode of expression: "In my music, I'm trying to play the truth of what I am. The reason it's difficult is because I'm changing all the time."[3]

Mingus, like Mitchell, never felt he had to cement himself into one pair of shoes. He had a love of experimentation and pushed the very boundaries of his own identity in order to come closer to the truth of his own art, yet until that November, the two were complete strangers to each other, creators from opposite ends of the universe. Mitchell was a middle-class Canadian girl who entered the business via the folk circuit, while Mingus was of mixed racial heritage (white, black, and Chinese), grew up in Watts, and, according to his autobiography, once worked as a pimp before settling into a career in jazz.

Maybe Mingus recognized something of himself in Art Nouveau's rakish grin and manly bop, because when he picked up *Don Juan's Reckless Daughter* and saw this white-bread chick prancing around with a pimp's strut, he was rapt. Apparently, Mingus thought Mitchell had real "balls"—not just a faux masculinity as a result of her drag conquest; he was impressed by her musicality. "Mingus was intrigued by that disguise," Mitchell told *Impact's* Mary Dickie in 1994. "*Don Juan's Reckless Daughter*, which was very unpopular in the white community, was understood by the black community, and I picked up a black following with it. World beat had not yet happened, and white people were just not ready, especially in pop music, for this. I was dressed as a black man on the cover, and because of that I was reviewed in black magazines, and when they discovered the error they didn't seem to turn back," she said.[4]

The black man in Mitchell struck a chord with the black man in Mingus, igniting a deathbed collaboration between the two artists that would eventually redefine them both.

Mingus wasn't impressed just by Mitchell's boundary-busting music and her ability to don the costume of a black Don Juan. When he listened to the piano tracks on "Paprika Plains," he figured Mitchell was on her very own planet: the tuning was entirely off.

"I finally flew to New York to meet him, and he was in a wheelchair with his back to me, but when he turned around he had a real mischievous look on his face and I thought, 'Uh-oh, he's really going to fuck with me, this guy,' but in the best way!" In 1983, Mitchell told *Musician* magazine's Vic Garbarini: "One of the first things he said to me was, 'Those strings on "Paprika Plains" are out of tune!' And this was true!"[5]

The dissonance was the result of a protracted recording period. "We went in the studio and cut this thing four times. It was a trance-like situation," she said. "In the meantime the piano had been retuned a number of times. Then I gave the piano piece with lyrics to an arranger who added strings. The strings begin in the January section of the piano piece, but when they hit the October part, the piano tuning has changed, so the strings have no chance to retune as they cross over. That really infuriated Charles," Mitchell said. "The orchestra's out of tune... they're in tune, they're out of tune! Well, that drove him crazy (laughs). So he thought I was a nervy broad."

Despite these imperfections—or more likely because of them—Mingus asked Mitchell to work with him on a project based on T.S. Eliot's *Four Quartets* with a full orchestra. The bassist and composer wanted Mitchell's voice as a narrator—which immediately upset Mitchell's former beau, jazz drummer John Guerin, who was a huge Mingus fan. "You unconscious motherfucker," he told Joni. "You don't even like his music," Guerin said, according to her 1994 interview with Alice Echols in L.A. Weekly.[6] As Mitchell told Leonard Feather of the Los Angeles Times, "[Mingus] wanted me to distill Eliot down into street language, and sing it, mixed in with this reader."[7] She was intrigued by the idea but, after mulling the material for a while, couldn't commit to the creative endeavour, because reconfiguring Eliot felt like a violation of a creator's code. "It seemed like a kind of sacrilege," she said.[8]

Mingus let the Eliot go but told Mitchell he'd written six melodies just for her, and he wanted her to pen some lyrics for each. Flattered by his attention and excited by the risk, she pushed herself into the unknown: "Immediately... the project became challenging and fun. I knew it would be difficult, but this was an opportunity to be pulled through the die of black classical music with one of the masters," she said.

When she saw Mingus again, his condition had deteriorated. "He had become very seriously ill, he and his wife, Sue, went to Mexico, to a faith healer, and during that time I spent ten days with them," Mitchell told Feather in 1979. The two musical pioneers had a lot to talk about, but Mingus's muscle control was seriously affected. He was in a wheelchair, largely unable to move. Most importantly, "his speech had deteriorated severely... every night he would say to me 'I want to talk to you about the music,' and every day it would be too difficult. So some of what he had to tell me remained a mystery."

Mitchell says the whole experience rearranged her creative approach and pushed her to explore. "The funny thing was I wasn't a huge fan of Mingus; he was too rooted in the blues for me," she said. "I had to be pulled through jazz blues with more complex melodies before I could appreciate the simple blues that were the roots of his composition. It opened me up to another block of music. So it was worth it, but it cost me my airplay. I was excommunicated," said Mitchell, the rebel saint. "From that point on, I was considered a jazzer by the rockers and a rocker by the jazzers, except the great ones. They are less bound by boundaries, as a rule."[9]

Mitchell, like many successful artists, is comfortable in the chaos of the unknown, and so was Mingus, who said: "Making the simple complicated is commonplace; making the complicated simple, awesomely simple, that's creativity."

To psychologists, the complicated, the chaotic, or what we've called the "unknown" or "mystery," represents the "unconscious"—the wellspring of creativity, at least according to Jung. Great artists seem capable of turning off their rational mind just long enough to access the formless energy beyond our understanding. Musicians constantly talk about how their best songs seem to come to them whole: "The last time this happened was when I wrote 'The Boys of Summer,'" Don Henley explained to Jenny Boyd in *Musicians in Tune*. "It was incredible. It was just coming to me, and I don't know where it was coming from."[10]

Mitchell echoed Henley's feelings. "With one particular song I wrote, when it came time to write about my experience, it was so dense with imagery that... it was hard for me to sift through it... There came one line, though, that was like a gift. It flowed out. I drew back and said 'thank you' to the room... I'd been grinding the gray matter trying to get this thing to come and maybe I then just relaxed or something. Whatever it was, when it poured out it did seem like it was a gift," she told Boyd. "There are pieces in a song that just seem to pour out in spite of you. I mean, you're the witness but the language does seem to come from someplace else."[11]

These gifts arrive when she allows the gurgling fount of the unconscious to do its work. "Oh, yeah, I work from intuition, so I'm always flying blind and looking to be thrilled. I think it's easier to recognize the truly spectacular from an intuitive position than from your intellect, which is linear, dealing only with knowledge of the past projected into the future."[12]

Mitchell says she relied on this creative autopilot while recording *Mingus* because the central creator, Mingus himself, was unable to communicate. Mitchell had to find the confidence to speak for him and create her own melodies to fill out the album. At the same time, she tried to maintain the original Mingus vision, and at his urging, she read a passage in his autobiography that dealt with his philosophical stance, particularly the god concept. "It was his own metaphorical description of God and relationship to God," she told Leonard Feather. "I just couldn't lift that literally and make it adhere to his melody. That threw me into my own confrontation with my own metaphors about God and it boggled my mind—it fried my brain."[13]

I like the idea that Mitchell's circuits sizzled when she tried to reconcile her own creativity with the idea of an outside, almighty creator. It suggests she was questioning something fundamental and profound through the act of creation itself. From a very practical, real-world point of view, Mitchell was moving through the definitive metaphysical process—death—from a distance. She was observing the downward spiral of the organic body. It was becoming a cruel cage for a creator who could no longer use his hands, make music, or use his voice. This loss meant Mitchell had to find her own way through the creative thicket.

The album was greeted with barbs, but Mitchell says her skin had thickened after *Summer Lawns* was trashed. She had no regrets. Eager to capture the essence of Mingus and the creative courage they shared, she marched into the darkness of the unknown without fear—a key component of what Nietzsche saw as the true creator. "Live dangerously!" he urged. "Build your cities on the slopes of Vesuvius! Send your ships into uncharted seas! Live in conflict with your equals and with yourselves!"[14]

Both Mitchell and Mingus loved dancing on the edge. It's this passionate desire that unites them. "He had a very wide emotionality. He cried easily, he fought easily, and he was an angry man," she told Leonard Feather. "There was a lot of mojo in his life—there's a lot of mojo in my life, too. Charles was a very complex person, and when it came down to finish the album, I felt that we didn't have a complete portrait. I wished that every song had been dedicated to a certain aspect of his personality. But in a way, this did happen indirectly. The four [Mingus melodies] I did complete were all in some way inspired; they came to me in mysterious ways."

If Mitchell felt uncharacteristically insecure about *Mingus* during its creation, she used her creative will and inner belief in the creative "mystery" to overcome the doubt. In fact, when she talked to the media about the record, she actually sounded a little—um—overconfident: "I'd be surprised if it wasn't well accepted in the jazz world, because it contains all the best elements of that music: It's very spontaneous, creative and fresh. As for the pop field, I dare not make any predictions. I hope people will find it accessible, but I know how intimidating great musicianship is to a lot of people."[15]

David Crosby once said Joni Mitchell is "as humble as Mussolini." This makes for a delicious sound bite, but it also points to one of the biggest misapprehensions about the artistic process—and that concerns ego. Mitchell loses patience on the topic: "I am an arrogant artist! And I'm sick of the false humility in this business!" she told *Details* in 1996.[16]

> And I get really arrogant when they start pitting me against people and saying something or someone's like me when that something is mediocre! And talk about arrogance— Crosby has no right to call... I mean, I'm fond of Crosby. In fact, when I thought he was gonna die I actually prayed for him. [But] when Crosby says I'm as humble as Mussolini, let us please put it in context that he's always ready to take credit where it isn't due, and that's typical—get a man within four feet of me and he's gonna say he did it.

Yes. Joni Mitchell is one nervy broad, and her creative *cojones* were big enough to go toe to toe with a recognized jazz master. Regardless of what the outside world said, or continues to say, about *Mingus*, Mitchell sees the album as an unmitigated creative success because it achieved a level of musical symbiosis: "Even the great jazz vocalists tend to be fronting a track, whereas in this music, we're all mimicking each other," she told Leonard Feather. "We're really entwined."[17]

The very word "entwined" is interesting because it conjures another passage from Nietzsche about the ability of the creative process to reconcile day and night, life and death—or the world views of a willowy blond Canadian and a black man from Watts: "My world has just become perfect, midnight is also noonday, pain is also joy, a curse is also a blessing, the night is also a sun," reads Nietzsche's "Intoxicated Song" from *Zarathustra*. "You will learn: a wise man is also a fool. Did you ever say yes to one joy? O my friends, then you said yes to all woe as well. All things are chained and entwined together, all things are in love."[18]

EROS VS. THANATOS:
THE GREAT LIFE-DEATH DYNAMIC

If there is one truism to extract from the Mingus sessions, it's that opposites do attract—and often result in surprising creative chemistry. The mother of all binaries is life versus death. It informs every level of our existence. It has perplexed philosophers for millennia and propelled the first shoots of psychoanalytic theory. Once Sigmund Freud got over his fixation on the libido as the central force shaping human behaviour, he wrote *Beyond the Pleasure Principle* (1920) in the hope of explaining certain destructive neuroses and the desires of some victims to repeat unpleasant and even death-affirming experiences. He came up with an earth-shattering revelation: the urge to repeat such experiences comes from a desire to return to "an earlier state of things," which in turn suggests a state of "non-being," or death. Once we recognize death as an undeniable reality, the only way we can regain any sense of control is to steer the car over the railing—or at least feel like we are. Freud had a hard time reconciling the death wish theory and admitted he may have "gone astray" in his desire to understand this human contravention of the natural law. But he stuck with it, and balanced it against the life wish (and all our desire for pleasure) to come up with the creative dynamo that defines the psyche: "Eros vs. Thanatos"—Life vs. Death.

In Freud's observation, the creative impulse allows us to form bridges between these two states in order to soothe ourselves. In his famous example, he saw his grandson drop a wheel on a string from his crib and pull it back up again, saying the words (primitively in German) "*fort*" (gone) and "*da*" (there). The game allowed the child to reconcile separation anxiety by playing out a drama of lost and found in his own mind. He could make the wheel appear and disappear at his whim—thereby giving him an illusion of control over the negative force of "gone." As Ellen Levine puts it in her book *Tending the Fire*, Freud believed that "the basic tension of organic existence is between the regressive force of the death instincts and the progressive force of the life instincts." In the process, he redefined the creative act, and all fantasy, as an almost backward way of gaining a better grasp of reality. He didn't win a lot of friends with this suggestion, even though most psychologists now agree the fort-da game is part of "normal development."[19]

At the time, his peers felt the constant wrangling between Eros and Thanatos was an untenable equation. Moreover, they felt *Beyond the Pleasure Principle* was too abstract and non-clinical—an anomaly for the famed clinician. Quite ironically, they rejected what is largely considered to be Freud's most creative essay dedicated to creativity itself. He held fast to his belief, despite the naysaying, because he felt what he had written resonated on a deeper level that defied empirical proof. And in doing so, he changed the dimensions of the entire psychoanalytic endeavour, which now has plenty of time for Freud's life-death struggle as the central creative spindle that gives our lives meaning.

POLIO

Mitchell remembers the flight from North Battleford to the polio ward of St. Paul's Hospital in Saskatoon. It was October 1953, and Mitchell was nine years old. She had collapsed that morning, unable to walk. The day before, she looked in the mirror and noticed the dark rings under her eyes. She looked different. She thought, "You look like a woman today." Mitchell still remembers what she was wearing: "grey pegged slacks, a dark gingham blouse and a blue sweater." Not only does this prove a particular brand of self-awareness but it also suggests how deeply the memory of sickness etched itself into Mitchell's young mind. The comment "You look like a woman today" also hints at an early level of separation between her inner self and the reflection she saw in the mirror. Her use of "you" points to a schism—and proves Mitchell was already standing outside herself, watching her personal evolution from a subjective—potentially creative—place. The face that looked back at her was changed, and she interpreted it as being "a woman," a grown-up. Yet this empowerment was betrayed the next day when she couldn't stand up. As she watched the ground beneath her fall away on the plane ride, she thought it resembled "topaz brooches on the black velvet land," she would later say. "Or something cornball like that."[20]

Her moments of creative inspiration would continue, even in the hospital. Her descriptions of the polio ward conjure Little Nell in Bleak House. The sound of wheezing, squeezing machines echoed through the sterile hallways. Mitchell remembers being wheeled past the room with the iron lungs and seeing little heads popping out from the gigantic metallic cocoons. Once the disease reaches the lungs, constant ventilation is required—otherwise it's a fast death. And many kids did die—more than three thousand from poliomyelitis in the U.S. alone. Mitchell remembers the nuns carrying cauldrons filled with scalding hot towels they would place on her body, blistering her skin. "The heat was meant to do something to the muscles," she said. "The disease only rampages for two weeks and then you're left with the disaster. I was unable to walk or stand. I was train-wrecked. My spine looked like the freeway after an earthquake. An adult male doctor could put two fists under the arch of my back."[21]

For weeks, Mitchell would be forced to face the very real possibility she might never walk again. To cope with the crisis, she sang, painted, looked at the little Christmas tree her mother brought her, and prayed to no particular god, or maybe no god at all. She can't remember. She thinks she prayed to the dwarf conifer. Whatever she was doing, it worked. Despite a significant curvature to her spine, Mitchell ditched the crutches and the corrective shoes and pushed forward, one foot in front of the other, with a stubbornness that marks her still. "I walked. I went home for Christmas," she says. "So polio, in a way, germinated an inner life and a sense of the mystic. It was mystical to come back from that disease."[22]

NEIL YOUNG

Two years before Mitchell made the flight from North Battleford to Saskatoon, a kid from Omemee, Ontario, named Neil Young discovered he couldn't touch his chin to his chest. He was six years old and feverish. The local doctor was all too aware of what it probably was and sent Young to the Hospital for Sick Children in Toronto. Splayed out in the back seat of the family car for the ninety-mile trip, Young wore a mask and hugged the toy train his father had given him that morning. Six days later, little Neil was back home—skinny and unable to walk properly. Apparently, the moment he saw his family, the first words he uttered were: "I didn't die, did I?"[23]

Young's early confrontation with death defined the rest of his life. It changed him physically, rendering him "fragile and delicate" at a time in a boy's life when toughness and athleticism are key ingredients to masculinity. "His legs were like toothpicks, and one day I just asked him [if he'd suffered from polio]," Young's friend Donna Port told biographer Jimmy McDonough, recalling a conversation with the adult Young. "The look of terror gave me the answer. Then it just flowed out. He was wrapped up in a blanket at the time, crying. It was a huge emotional scar to him. We talked about how cruel kids are when you're growing up. It explained a lot."[24]

The polio infection also stunted his sense of belonging and made him feel like an outsider for most of his life. By the same token, it nurtured his creative drive. Young was forced, quite literally, to use muscles he never would have used before. He says he's ambidextrous because the polio paralyzed his dominant left side and forced him to use his right hand, ensuring he could reap the most from both the logical left side of his brain and the creative right side. More importantly, he discovered that the pain of being an outsider could be assuaged by the mere act of creating and being surrounded by creative people.

"I always liked building things," Young told McDonough. "I like having crews working, stuff going on. Creativity. People working and getting paid and creating something—feeling good about what they're doing."[25] From a purely pragmatic perspective, polio also made Young incredibly stubborn. "When Neil makes up his mind he's going to do somethin', he does, y'know—and nothing could stop him," his mother, Edna "Rassy" Young, told McDonough.[26]

Joni Mitchell clearly saw a reflection of herself in the kid from Omemee. They met for the first time in 1964, at a coffee house just outside Winnipeg called the Fourth Dimension. "Polio survivors—Neil Young is another one—are a really stubborn bunch of people," Mitchell told McDonough. "Neil and I have a lot in common: Canadian, Scorpios, polio in the same epidemic struck the same parts of our body; and we both have a black sense of humour: Typical Canadians."[27]

Mitchell and Young orbited each other from that moment on. Both eventually headed to Toronto, what Mitchell calls a "wannabe city," in search of folk fame and fortune. They hung out in the same haunts and hovels, and both were looking for an open door to the U.S. This proved difficult for both artists, but Mitchell negotiated it through her marriage to Chuck Mitchell. Young says his earliest performances in the States were probably the result of Joni and Chuck. Later, Mitchell and Young shared a manager in Elliot Roberts, a business relationship with David Geffen, and a friendship with Graham Nash. For Mitchell, the connection with Nash was largely romantic. For Young, it was creative, as the eventual formation of Crosby, Stills, Nash & Young would prove.

From the outside, and certainly to fans of the era, Young and Mitchell became key pieces in a sprawling folk-pop-rock musical puzzle that was quickly redefining the very essence of youth culture. Yet, according to Elliot Roberts, who watched the entire scene unfold from the front row, Young remained an outsider. "Neil never dealt with anyone ... he will go a year without talking to you, 'cause he doesn't initiate phone calls," Roberts told Jimmy McDonough. "Even then, you knew he was his own person. Neil didn't hang with the band [at this point in time Buffalo Springfield], wasn't friendly with the band, wasn't nice to the band—'cause they weren't cooperating with him. They were always afraid of Neil. He had this vibe like Clint Eastwood," says Roberts in the Young biography. "He was like death."[28]

If you look into Neil Young's eyes, you can feel the stark edges of the existential void, and it pierces a tiny hole right through you, somewhere near your solar plexus. The first time I met his spacey brown gaze, I thought this shiver was the result of feeling star-struck. But the second time, at the Sundance Film Festival for the release of Jonathan Demme's concert film Heart of Gold, I knew it was something different. Young had just emerged from his second great stare-down with the Grim Reaper in the wake of an emergency brain aneurysm operation. The chill was with him still. I asked him if the recent near-death experience spurred his creativity. He gave me a glance that spoke a silent "duh," stared at me for about twenty seconds, and didn't answer.

ALIENS

Neil Young, Joni Mitchell, and Charles Mingus have all been described as being different—to the point of being "alien." In fact, the descriptive pops up in regards to great creators quite frequently. Oscar Wilde's epitaph carries the stanza: "And alien tears will fill for him / Pity's long-broken urn / For his mourners will be outcast men, / And outcasts always mourn." On a more literal—but far less credible—note, Leonardo da Vinci and Beethoven have been labelled "alien spies" by the conspiracy theorists and the late-night radio hosts who cater to their collective paranoia.

I think this is a tad insane, but understanding the symbolic importance of UFOS and the "alien presence on Earth" was a subject that obsessed none other than Carl Jung. "In the visionary mode, the creative person is more conscious of an 'alien' will, or intention beyond his comprehension—a detached portion of the psyche that leads an independent life," he says. [29] Fascinated by the collection of anecdotal data about alien visitations in the advent of the atomic age, Jung started collecting stories about alien sightings as early as 1946. "I'm puzzled to death about these phenomena, because I haven't been able yet to make out with sufficient certainty whether the whole thing is a rumor with concomitant singular and mass hallucination, or a downright fact," Jung wrote in a letter to a friend in 1951. By 1959, he published the short book *Flying Saucers: A Modern Myth of Things Seen in the Sky.* As the title suggests, the Swiss psychologist wasn't writing a proof of such phenomena but a treatise on why we seem to create mass myths. He concluded that alien sightings were examples of synchronicity where "external events mirror internal psychic states." He also suggested that the cult surrounding alien lore "may be a spontaneous reaction of the subconscious to fear of the apparently insoluble political situation in the world that may lead at any moment to catastrophe. At such times eyes turn heavenwards in search of help, and miraculous forebodings of a threatening or consoling nature appear from on high."[30] Before technology gave us the capacity to imagine shiny flying discs, human beings saw dragons, gods, angels, and other inexplicable beings in the skies that they assumed to be gods.

Mitchell's familiarity with Jungian theory is part of the historical record. At her publisher's urging, she read Jung's autobiography, *Memories, Dreams, Reflections*. But I'm not going to assert the theory that Mitchell and her highly creative cohorts are beings from another planet. I've already declared my skepticism. However, at the very least, I do believe there's a significant connection between the creative creature and the collective unconscious, and this renders artists a brand of alien because they can see, hear, and feel things the rest of us cannot. They live in an alternative universe, where they can find the creative distance required for truly original thought.

Joni and Neil have both used alien and spaceman imagery to articulate their feelings, in interviews as well as in their lyrics. Listen to the words for Young's "After the Gold Rush" (1970) and you will hear a whole story of humanity's next exodus into space, a tale that prompted Linda Ronstadt, who covered the tune with glass harps, to say: "I would think, 'This is the future. Neil's humans leave the planet and go off to start a new space colony.' I've always felt Neil had a great deal of really uncanny prescience in his writing."[31]

"Well, I dreamed I saw the silver space ships flying in the yellow haze of the sun," read Young's lyrics. "There were children crying and colours flying all around the chosen ones. / All in a dream, all in a dream, the loading had begun. / They were flying Mother Nature's silver seed to a new home in the sun."

The year before "Gold Rush," Mitchell penned the anthem for a generation in the song "Woodstock," which contained the lyric fragment, "We are stardust / Billion year old carbon / We are golden." A little over four years later, she wrote "The Same Situation," which contained a reference to astronauts: "Still I sent up my prayer, wondering where it had to go / With heaven full of astronauts and the Lord on death row / While the millions of his lost and lonely ones call out and clamour to be found / Caught in their struggle for higher positions."

In his Neil Young biography, Jimmy McDonough uses the word "aliens" in his description of the first meeting between Mitchell and Young in the aptly named Fourth Dimension club: "Mitchell and Young were kindred souls of a sort; both young, intense and painfully unique. It must have been like two aliens recognizing each other out on the open prairie... Both are essentially loners."[32] A half-century after Young and Mitchell first laid eyes on each other, we can safely say they're both musical legends and widely regarded as two of the most talented artists to ever strut across the planet, even if their legs didn't work that well as a result of polio. Both have been scrutinized, idolized, and dissed for taking artistic risks that baffled their fans, but each time they just get back in their creative capsule and blast off.

As Mitchell put it to Alice Echols in 1994, "I see like an alien. I don't have the soul of a white woman. I have the soul of a Martian, because I wander through this world as if I'm not of it, which I suppose is the perspective of an artist in the first place—the alien outlook.[33] Years later, she reiterated the spaceman metaphor when she appeared on MuchMusic's *Intimate and Interactive* with Jana Lynne White in 2000: "An artist is born. They're born with an artistic attitude. They're born to be the axe for the frozen sea within us. They're born to be in conflict; they're born to be an alien and an outsider."[34]

MORGELLONS SYNDROME

> "The net with which you capture [creativity] is made up of
> the threads of your alertness."
> JONI MITCHELL

You may have had your doubts, but there was a purpose behind the preceding alien tangent—and not just as an exaggerated way of saying that artists are outsiders. I felt it was important to set up this section and give it creative context, because if there's one single story in the Joni Mitchell annals that really perplexes people, it's the one you're about to read.

In 2006, a number of people in the Los Angeles area complained about a mysterious skin condition they dubbed "Morgellons syndrome." The cluster of cases prompted news attention and a public statement from the L.A. County health authority, which dismissed any health risk to the general population. Victims of the condition described their symptoms as "bugs crawling beneath the skin" and "threads and fibers" wriggling around under their dermis. Such "unexplained dermopathies" have been recorded throughout human history and largely written off as delusional, but when Joni Mitchell told the media she suffered from the mystery ailment in 2009, Morgellons syndrome hit the mainstream.

Mitchell described her condition in detail to the *Los Angeles Times*: "I have this weird, incurable disease that seems like it's from outer space, but my health's the best it's been in a while." She said,

> Two nights ago, I went out... I don't look so bad under
> incandescent light, but I look scary under daylight. Garbo
> and Dietrich hid away just because people became so upset

watching them age, but this is worse. Fibers in a variety of colors protrude out of my skin like mushrooms after a rainstorm: they cannot be forensically identified as animal, vegetable or mineral. Morgellons is a slow, unpredictable killer—a terrorist disease: it will blow up one of your organs, leaving you in bed for a year. But I have a tremendous will to live: I've been through another pandemic—I'm a polio survivor, so I know how conservative the medical body can be. In America, the Morgellons is always diagnosed as "delusion of parasites," and they send you to a psychiatrist. I'm actually trying to get out of the music business to battle for Morgellons sufferers to receive the credibility that's owed to them.[35]

Mitchell did exactly that. She spent several years lobbying various organizations and speaking publicly about the disease. She even bowed out of performing for the opening ceremonies of the Vancouver 2010 Olympics, citing her medical condition.

In 2010, the Centers for Disease Control and Prevention in Atlanta launched a formal study. They examined 108 reported cases of Morgellons and found every single case could be explained as entirely normal. Every fiber was put under the microscope, every scab examined, and the only parasites found were on a patient suffering from pubic lice.

I haven't seen any reaction from Mitchell to this study, but I'm sure it hasn't miraculously cleared up her condition. If she's feeling it, it may as well be real, because our bodies and our brains are one and the same system. In fact, early on in utero, brain cells and skin cells are the same thing—just a mass of undifferentiated nerve cells. Moreover, as an artist, Mitchell's body is essentially the corporeal "space ship" that contains her creative soul. Like Captain James T. Kirk, Mitchell feels an innate responsibility to "boldly go where no man has gone before."

Mitchell told Iain Blair of Rock Express that if artists are doing their job well, they are "the antennae of the planet—[and] they should be more sensitive to change, and by their very nature and predilection and interest should wade in where others fear to tread."[36] This brings up another central set of metaphors in Mitchell's "Martian" medical files: "sensitivity" and "antennae." These two words speak to the organic interface between Mitchell's mind and the physical reality around her; they speak to the skin, the nerve cells that form the corporeal barrier, the personal body envelope. When Mitchell talked about her work with Mingus, she emphasized their common ground as artists and she used a prophetic metaphor: "Well, let's make an assumption here that an artist has a fine nervous system, okay? Now there are also a lot of people with fine nervous systems, more sensitive spinal columns or whatever, who are not artists, who have no outlet of expression. I think the nuance-y observations an artist makes are going to get picked up first by these sensitive people. Eventually they'll be picked up by people intellectually and then passed down through the culture," she told Vic Garbarini. "There's a sensitivity lag. Some statements that are made by artists in their desire to look at the world in a fresh way have traditionally come up against a shocking reception," she said. "When Stravinsky first played, people jumped up out of their seats and booed and hissed. People were infuriated by even less dramatic changes, like Dylan going electric."[37]

Couple this fully articulated image of the artist with the "fine nervous system" and the "sensitive spinal column" with Mitchell's frequent use of adjectives like "nervy" and "sensitive"—or, less frequently, "thin-skinned"—and we see a common thread concerning the notion of "skin." Symbolically, it's the physical manifestation of Mitchell's relationship to the outside world.

When Susan Sontag was diagnosed with cancer, she attempted to channel the anxiety and face her disease through her art: writing. In the resulting book, *Illness as Metaphor*, Sontag quotes lines from W.H. Auden's poem about terminal illness, "Miss Gee." I think it speaks directly to Mitchell's condition, so I will end the chapter here:

> [Illness is] like some hidden assassin
> Waiting to strike at you.
> Childless women get it,
> And men when they retire;
> It's as if there had to be some outlet
> For their foiled creative fire.

three

BABY BUMPS
Expecting and Expectation

> "For the creator himself to be the child new-born
> he must also be willing to be the mother and endure
> the mother's pain."
> FRIEDRICH NIETZSCHE, "On the Blissful Islands,"
> *Thus Spoke Zarathustra*

MOTHER-CHILD DYNAMICS have an undeniable impact on any creative experience, because "mother" is "the mother of all creation." We've already talked about the fort-da game witnessed by Freud and seen how a child learns to cope with a mother's absence using his or her own powers of imagination. Pediatrician and psychologist D.W. Winnicott took this idea a step further. He braided bits of Freud, Jung, his instructor Melanie Klein, and personal observation to create a detailed theory about the relationship between mother-infant bonding and the creative experience. Picking up on the work of Klein, who described a "depressive position" for an infant as one where he/she has to accept the fact that he/she and the mother are no longer one, he asserted the creative importance of the split—which is typically associated with weaning.

Separation is both terrifying and exciting for the young mind, but it forces conflicting feelings to coexist—and that marks the birth of the creative dynamic. For that potential to be truly nurtured, Winnicott asserted, there had to be a "good enough mother" and a "good enough facilitating environment." In short, the kid has to feel there's a fundamental level of safety in order to move forward and evolve creatively.

"The good enough mother is relatively successful at adapting to the infant's gestures and needs... The good enough mother provides the child with a feeling of omnipotence," writes Ellen Levine, paraphrasing Winnicott. "At the very beginning, the mother fosters the illusion that her breast is part of the infant and under the infant's magical control, that the breast is created by the infant out of his/her capacity to love and to need," she continues.[1] Or, as Winnicott says, "The mother places the actual breast just where the infant is ready to create, and at the right moment,"[2] leaving the child with the impression that the external world corresponds to his or her own creative capacity.

Indeed, like so many things, it comes down to the boob almighty, and in this particular narrative, there are two big boobs to consider: the breast that nurtured Joni Mitchell, and the breast that Joni Mitchell couldn't use to nurture the child she birthed but did not raise.

BREAKING THE PLASTIC BARBIE MOLD

Before we address the issue of Mitchell's maternity, it's worth exploring the expected contours of the female experience at that particular moment in history, because things were changing quickly for women. The image of the stay-at-home mom was beginning to shift after the Second World War, thanks to the wartime integration of women in the workforce, as well as the publication of Simone de Beauvoir's *The Second Sex* (1949). Right before this "second wave" of feminism crested in the sixties and seventies, a new doll with grown-up curves and long blond hair was introduced to the masses, establishing a new binary for the expression of womanhood.

Barbara Millicent Roberts was born on March 9, 1959. She was of German extraction but found loving parents in Ruth and Elliot Handler, two Americans from California who were into toys. She was born wearing a zebra-stripe swimsuit and had enormous breasts protruding from a plastic toothpick body. "Barbie" would go on to mold as many young minds as there were molded Barbie bodies. A year after Barbie's unreal frame was placed in the hands of an entire generation, the oral contraceptive pill was introduced to women in North America.

For Mitchell, as for other members of her generation, trying to straddle the incredible distance between burgeoning notions of femininity and traditional, sexist values would prove challenging. But that's only once self-awareness kicked in. When Mitchell first entered show business, cradling her baritone ukulele at a moose-hunting show in Prince Albert in 1962, she had no problem with—let alone any awareness of— female stereotypes and the so-called hegemonic structure we live within.

Joni was a pliant participant—in the beginning. Over time, she started to question her place in the bigger picture and her relationship to established gender roles. She became more assertive in every aspect of her life. But most changes that are deep and profound aren't all that visible from the outside unless you're looking for them. So with that in mind, it's time to survey the exterior and get a good look at the Joni facade.

In the beginning, Joni looked like a Barbie. Even through the grainy buffering strains of a YouTube stream, her early TV appearances are compelling because she's got natural charisma. She also had ownership of the material. These were her songs. This was her voice. This was her real face. And what a mug it was! Glowing under the scorching TV lights, her blond hair picking up the hot glint with every cock and spin, she looked like the fairest maiden folk music had ever seen. Oscar Brand of the CBC's *Let's Sing Out* pointed out the obvious in his introduction to an October 1966 broadcast: "The young lady's been writing songs since she moved here [Ontario—the show was shot at Sudbury's Laurentian University] from Saskatoon a few years ago. She writes them beautifully, and she sings them beautifully, and she looks beautifully at the camera, too... [snigger] Here's Joni Mitchell with her own song 'Just Like Me.'"[3] As Mitchell sings her tune, which never made it onto an album, she smiles. She engages with the camera as it captures her gaze. Once in a while, you get a hint of the doe-in-the-headlights stare. It's hard not to: she looks like Bambi up there, with her big dark eyelashes and her wide-open, fragile face. The audience, filled with college kids in cardigans, was mesmerized.

Joni Mitchell was brokering her good looks, and it was working. Just about anyone who came into contact with her during these early years would talk about how stunning she was, how otherworldly, how haunting. Rock promoter Joe Boyd remembered the first time he saw Mitchell onstage in London: "In her miniskirt and long straight hair, she stole the show completely... She dazzled the crowd."[4] In one of the early show reviews, *Washington Post* critic William Rice could barely contain himself in the opening paragraph: "A girl in a flowing long gown with long blonde hair and a magically flowing voice cast a spell at the Cellar Door Monday evening that will not soon be forgot. Her name is Joni Mitchell."[5] Calgary club owner John Uren remembered the day she walked into his newly opened coffee house, the Depression. "She looked just tremendous... with all that blond hair. I brought Peter Elbing in from Toronto to open the place. And he listened to Joni and said she should sing [instead of him]."[6] Mitchell became known as the "winsome bittersweet blonde from Fort Macleod, Alberta."[7]

According to Leah Cohen Kunkel, who was part of the Laurel Canyon scene as the wife of drummer Russ and the sister of Mama Cass Elliot, when Mitchell "would sing over that guitar, men were riveted—they stopped what they were doing, they were absolutely enamored... She was drop-dead beautiful." Cohen Kunkel went on to say, "Before that, it was always women [of the Canyon] riveted by the male guitarist—this was the first time it changed."[8] It changed because Mitchell had a physical billboard that drew attention right off the bat. And once she had people's attention, she blew them away. The voice and material hit it out of the park, but those first impressions, a crucial anchor point in the Mitchell mythology, were largely based on looks.

There should be no judgement here: that's the way the world worked in the 1960s. More importantly, Mitchell's understanding of appearance—and how to play it—was one of the many tools in her creative tool box.

She may have been perceived as an otherworldly earth goddess, but she sincerely loved fashion. She still does. It's an integral part of her personality and a means of expression. Her worldly style was one of the first things that made her stand out from the crowd in humble, grain-fed Saskatoon. As her old French teacher Robert Hinitt told biographer Michelle Mercer for *Will You Take Me As I Am*, Mitchell was "very popular with the boys" but "she was very popular with the girls, too. I remember she worked at a lady's clothing shop on Saturdays, she wore a red plaid skirt and red sweater and brown and white saddle shoes, and the ankle socks. The other parents used to complain about her beautiful wardrobe, and I used to say she earned that money by herself, so, you know, don't blame me for her clothes. She was very style conscious. Yes, dressed to the nines."[9] Mitchell became the fashionista of her high school. She wrote a column called "Fads and Fashions" for the school paper, and she financed her closet through her after-school job at Ricki's Ladies Wear.

"My identity, since it wasn't through the grade system, was that I was a good dancer and an artist. And also, I was very well-dressed. I made a lot of my own clothes," she told Cameron Crowe for *Rolling Stone*. "I had access to sample clothes that were too fashionable for our community. I would go hang out on the streets dressed to the 'T,' even in hat and gloves." While Mitchell perfected her sartorial taste, she discovered her penchant for partying, dancing, and playing with the "rowdies" on the wrong side of town. "I was always in trouble," she said. "I flunked math and was held up to terrible ridicule for the way I danced in bars. The local folks said it was downright wicked. I was always involved in a constant war to liberate myself."[10]

Mitchell had no problem accommodating the idea of looking great and being a strong, independent woman, but when the school guidance counsellor suggested she become a hairdresser, she was deeply upset. Mitchell might have played into feminine expectation on one side of her life, but when it came to her long-term future, she saw a very different picture. She was determined not to end up a small-town matron like the ones she saw stroll into the clothing store on weekends, urgently seeking some big-city sophistication in the changing room. She spoofed such women in the high school yearbook: "I am a chronic sufferer of bargainitis—a disease with which every red-blooded female is afflicted," she wrote. "For instance, last week I bought a brown-shantung dress at Blanche Buchanan's for $28 (a fraction of its former price!) At home, I surveyed myself before my vanity mirror. 'Tres chic,' I muttered, although, somehow, without the cooing of the vendeuses, the creation seemed to give me the distinction and interesting contours of a large bran muffin." This comic blurb reveals Mitchell's awareness of the socially affirming aspect of fashion, as well as her expert knowledge of fabric and textiles. She loves beautiful weaves, and she's even compared her music to the finest fruits of a loom: "My music is not designed to grab instantly. It's designed to wear for a lifetime, to hold up like a fine cloth," she told Alice Echols.[11]

We often make the mistake of equating fashion with shallow concerns and ugly, vain men with ponytails, but for Mitchell—as it is now for the likes of Lady Gaga—the fashion world was one place that gave her licence to be free and establish a singular identity. "I'm a clothes horse," Mitchell told *Washington Post* reporter Carla Hill in 1979. "I love fashion."[12]

She's repeated this in several interviews. The former beauty pageant contestant talked about her early fascination with couture in an interview she did with Morrissey.[13] The art rocker asked her about the perceived genre divide between her music and that of the Sex Pistols. She said there was no divide; it was all media manipulation. "When I met Johnny Rotten—I met him in Jamaica, and again I looked at him and I thought—I liked him immediately. He was a lot like I was— he was younger—but he was a lot like I was in high school: fashion conscious. There he sat, you know, in his red suede shoes and his black woolly... plaid jacket in the Jamaican heat all kind of pale and pimply, you know, like avoiding the sun," said Mitchell, capturing the central paradox of the punk movement. Punk had the burning desire to set old values ablaze in a post-consumer pyre, but for all its piss and vinegar it spent a lot of time checking itself out in the mirror. After all, it was another art school fashion victim named Malcolm McLaren who created the punk look at the London clothing store he owned with Patrick Casey called, simply, SEX. The King's Road retailer was where Rotten auditioned for the band and where fetish items such as dog collars, harnesses, and studded leather made it out of the back room and onto the catwalks of Vivienne Westwood galas. The mixture of counter-culture and safety-pin couture gave young people in the 1970s a potent and highly visible identity to adopt via fashion, and Mitchell could relate: "I'm a punk. I've always been, you know—that irreverence. I've always been on the outside. I've never really been in the mainstream."

It might sound petty to suggest that Mitchell's commitment to truthful expression is merely an offshoot of her clothes-consciousness, but we have to remember how few creative outlets women had at this time. Clothing was the most tangible manifestation of self, and Mitchell seemed to understand its importance. She broached the subject with Mary Dickie, who asked Mitchell how she found the strength to be herself in a small-town environment. "I think it started with fashion!" she replied.

> When I was a child you had to wear the same clothes for two or three years. There was a girl who lived kitty-corner to us, and it seemed like she'd wait till I got my winter coat and then get the same one. Somewhere at a very early age I developed a contempt for copycat-ism. In the coffee houses when everyone was raving about Bob Dylan,

I was saying, "Oh, he's just a Woody Guthrie copycat." So very early I was fiercely interested in originality. I can't remember the origins [of that interest] unless it was this winter coat syndrome.[14]

WEATHERING THE WINTER
OF CHANGE AND THE SPRING OF GREEN

The story of how Mitchell wound up "barefoot and pregnant" as a young, unmarried woman living in Toronto's Yorkville district is hardly original. In the summer of 1964, Joni and a fellow art student named Brad McMath bought one-way train tickets from Calgary to Toronto— the "Big Smoke"—to attend the Mariposa Folk Festival. They wanted to see Buffy Sainte-Marie—the Canadian-born, Maine-raised folksinger with the debut smash "Universal Soldier" ticking up the charts— who would one day record Mitchell songs "The Circle Game," "Both Sides Now," and "Song to a Seagull."

Mitchell couldn't have known what would happen to her life in the space of the next few months, but she began her journey with a creative bang. En route, inspired by the rhythm of the steel wheels, she penned what she called her first "real song," "Day After Day." The trip across the vast Canadian landscape took three days, and when the young, reportedly "affectionate" couple arrived in Toronto, they headed to the fairgrounds, only to discover the site had been moved at the last minute as a result of a "not-in-my-backyard" revolt by the citizens of Orillia. All the staging and sound equipment had to be moved overnight to the Maple Leaf baseball stadium. Brad and Joni helped load the trucks, then passed out from fatigue in a nearby field. They had no money. They had no prospects. For McMath, a tall, handsome guy who was clearly revelling in the picaresque hippie moment, the lack of responsibility was probably the realization of a boho dream. Joan Anderson, on the other hand, was just beginning a brand new nightmare.

Exactly when Joni discovered she was pregnant is not clear, but she figures she lost her virginity and got pregnant in the same breath. Either way, on the outside, she carried on as if nothing had changed. She continued working at the local Simpson's department store to earn enough money to make it into the musicians' union, and she continued playing gigs until her belly got too big for her to hold a guitar—somewhere around her seventh or eighth month. The people around her knew she was pregnant, but they said nothing because everyone in her peer group had left home to escape the tyranny of parental judgement and the establishment rules of the status quo.

First Nations poet Duke Redbird lived across the hall from Joni and gave her apples—because she didn't look all that well nourished, and she would later admit that her diet had been "atrocious."[15] Redbird says the young Anderson could be heard composing songs behind a closed door. She and Redbird talked about art and spirituality, as well as the injustices suffered by Canada's First Nations community—such as the tragedy of foster homes and "residential schools," where children were removed from their ancestral homes, stripped of their language, and often molested sexually. Mitchell touches on these themes in the song "Cherokee Louise": "She runs home to her foster dad, he opens a zipper, and he yanks her to her knees."

Joni had a lot on her mind as she entered her final term, and when she walked into the Toronto General Hospital maternity ward in February 1965, at the age of twenty-one, she was no doubt focussed on what was best for the baby. McMath was long gone. He bolted back to the west, first to Saskatchewan and eventually to San Francisco to be a part of the boho mother ship hovering over the Haight like communal smoke rings—wait, those were communal smoke rings. McMath heard things were warmer in California. But for Joni, things were hospital cold. She was surrounded by medical equipment in a sterile environment where even the people were unfriendly. She says because she was a charity patient, and because she was a young, unwed mother who was about to give up her baby, the staff was curt.

According to adoption advocacy groups, Mitchell gave birth during what was called the "baby scoop" era, when women were placed in maternity or "wage homes" as a sort of "punishment" for engaging in sexual intercourse before matrimony. The women were dubbed "inmates," and if a biological father was still part of the picture, contact with the villainous inseminator was forbidden. Ever since legal adoption started in Ontario in 1921, the main objective was to ensure that the biological parents had no lasting connection to the baby, thereby sparing the child from what was considered a dangerous moral example. The secrecy aspect of adoption became law in 1927 at the urging of adoptive parents, who believed the bonding process demanded exclusive parenting roles.

On February 19, 1965, Joan Anderson gave birth to a daughter she named Kelly Dale—after the bright emerald green that defines the fertile Canadian landscape in summer. After the birth, the nurses bound Joni's breasts to stop her from lactating—a practice she would later call "barbaric."[16] They probably would have booted her out the door a day or two after delivery, but there were complications so she was allowed to see and hold the baby, who was, go figure, really cute. Suddenly, the young mother started to envision a future that could contain, and maybe even support, another life. But reality dug in. "I have no money. I have no home. I have no job. When I leave the hospital, I have no roof over my head," she told the *Los Angeles Times* in her first in-depth interview after she revealed her secret to the public in 1997. "But I kept trying to find some kind of circumstance where I could stay with her that wouldn't be malforming to her and to myself."[17]

She thought she found the answer when she met Chuck Mitchell, a nice-faced folksinger from Detroit with a mild degree of fame. Chuck played the headliner's lounge on the main floor of the Penny Farthing, the Toronto club where Joni Anderson was playing the less glam room for nobodies upstairs. Chuck Mitchell had never brought his bag of tricks to Toronto before, but chances are the crowd had heard a lot of his repertoire, which consisted of his ode to the Weimar era: plenty of Brecht and Weill to guarantee theatricality. When Chuck and his accompanist, Loring Janes, started butchering "Mr. Tambourine Man," a song Joni had been struggling to learn, she ran downstairs to catch it. "He'd rewritten some of it, and badly, too... so we immediately got into a conflict," Mitchell later said.[18] When the boys went to catch Joni's set upstairs, Loring noted her playing, musicality, and fretwork. Chuck noticed her gams.

Chuck and Joni were engaged within thirty-six hours of their first encounter. And they may as well have already been married, since Chuck intimates they slept together—and Joni says they argued—from their first night together. The dynamic seems to have continued over the course of their brief, nearly two-year marriage. As Joni walked down the aisle a few months after accepting Chuck's spontaneous proposal (he says he was shocked when she said yes), she told herself: "I can get out of this."

She did get out of it, but for the first month of that hastened and maybe-not-so-sacred union, she was thinking about the baby. The young couple even went to the foster home to visit her, but Chuck wasn't the one with the latent parenting plans.

He says he left the decision up to her. She says he didn't want to bring up another man's baby. The argument continues, but chances are they're both right. "One month into the marriage, he chickened out, I chickened out. The marriage had no basis, except to provide a home for the baby,"[19] Mitchell told the *Los Angeles Times*, rendering any notion of genuine romance null and void from the beginning.

Chuck Mitchell—the man she describes in "I Had a King" (on *Song to a Seagull*) who dressed in "drip-dry paisley" and "carried me off to his country for marriage too soon"—still tours as Chuck Mitchell. The name has cachet, thanks to his famous ex-wife. They toured as a duo for a while and scooted across the country in the Porsche (a 1956 356A coupe) Chuck bought himself with the wedding-gift cash, but eventually Joni was looking to go solo—both onstage and in life. She tried to do the domestic thing. She was a good nester. In public, she nodded and supported Chuck. Drawing on her deep reserve of textile, artistic, and fashion skills, she turned their walk-up apartment in Detroit's student ghetto into an antique-filled pad worthy of a spread in the local daily. They were, or at least appeared to be, a hip couple who entertained and put up a stream of touring acts. Chuck could probably see the bitter scrawl on the bar wall: Joni was going to be bigger than he was. He didn't want to separate—at least not onstage or as business partners. (The two formed Gandalf Publishing together, a nod to their shared *Lord of the Rings* fascination; the name was formally approved by the famed author after the Mitchells made the request in writing.) As she told the BBC's Mary Black in 1999, Mitchell saw Chuck's reluctance to separate as only logical: "He made more money with me than he did without me. He held the purse strings completely."[20]

Chuck says he was feeling trapped under a wave of contempt, then finally did the manly thing and admitted he was

"scared." Mitchell replied to this gesture of masculine vulnerability with her unique brand of sympathy: "You're bringing
me down." Chuck says he responded in silence, mouthing the
word "Bitch!" under his breath. Things soon disintegrated
to the point where Chuck started getting jealous, and Joni
enjoyed the power. When Chuck felt the only way to control his wife was to turn her over his knee and give her a
spanking—literally—that was the end of the marriage, but
not before Joni received her green card allowing her to work
in the U.S. "She was very ambitious, very calculating and
very self-centred—and so was I," Chuck Mitchell said in an
interview with David Gardner of the *Daily Mail* in 1996.[21]

Shortly after Joni received her coveted work visa, she was
on tour and playing poker somewhere in Michigan when she
turned to the complete stranger next to her and said: "I'm
leaving my husband tonight. Will you help me?"[22] As Mitchell
explained in *Motion Picture* magazine in 1975, her impulse to
bolt had been building. "Chuck Mitchell and I were husband
and wife for about nine months. That's all it took to end," she
said. "He was seven years older than me, and I married him
about thirty days after I'd met him for the first time."[23] That
stranger said yes—so apparently there's a man out there with
the best moving story ever. They rented a U-Haul, drove back
to Detroit in the middle of the night, and lugged half the con-
tents of the apartment down five flights of stairs. That was
the end of Mrs. Chuck Mitchell. But by the time she hit New
York City hours later, she had given birth to a new creation
with a catalogue all her own: Joni Mitchell—single, and singular, artist.

Mitchell wrote about this chapter in her life in the lyrics
for "Little Green," a song that seemed to the general public
more like an empathetic portrait of a lost woman than any
brand of personal biography when it first appeared as the

third track on Blue. According to Mitchell, she first penned the tune in 1967, then rewrote it several times before recording it for posterity as a natural extension of the emotional catharsis Blue represented at that moment in her life. The song was both personal therapy and wishful prophecy, as it helped a mourning mother cope with the surrender of her child. It also asserted hope for a better tomorrow and a "happy ending." This type of magical optimism in the face of sadness was a key feature of Mitchell's oeuvre at this time. Early on, she learned that the best way to cope with emotional hardship was to transform the destructive energy into something constructive. She turned to her career as the central creative project in her life, and she reaped a different brand of reward.

When Mitchell spoke with Cameron Crowe in 1979, long before she told the world about Kelly Dale, he asked her about children and whether a life without them might be too lonely. She said, "That's the part about it ... I don't know, really, what your choices are. Obviously, that's a constant battle with me. Is my maternity to amount to a lot of black plastic? Am I going to annually bear this litter of songs and send them out into the marketplace and have them crucified for this reason or that?"[24]

Mitchell didn't have a whole lot more hope for a flesh-and-blood baby. She told Crowe, as she told several other reporters, that she didn't think the world was a nice enough place for a new life. "I wouldn't frivolously get pregnant and bring a child into this world, especially a world that has such a difficult future as the one we're facing. Also, the children of celebrities have been notoriously troubled," she said. "But when it comes to the business of raising children, I finally feel emotionally stable enough to deal with it. It's taken me this long, but it may be something that's denied me."

Mitchell was thirty-five when she said those words, and to some degree they were prophetic. She conceived again with her second husband, Larry Klein, but she miscarried—a sad event that began the amicable unwinding of the eleven-year relationship. Mitchell would only realize her "motherhood" in 1997, when she decided to look for Kelly Dale. Rumours about a Joni love child had been circulating ever since she told Michael Watts of the *Sunday Times* in 1983 that she'd given birth to a daughter and given her up—raising hopes among many young women that Mitchell might be their long-lost matriarch. The only way the reunion could be fruitful was if Kelly Dale—now called Kilauren Gibb—was seeking her birth mother. Turns out, Gibb had been eager to learn the truth about her biological parents since learning at the age of twenty-seven that she was adopted. (Explaining the late revelation, her adoptive parents said they thought she already knew and never saw any point in making her feel like an outsider.) It was only when Gibb became pregnant with her first baby that she finally learned the truth and filled out the requisite paperwork to start the search process.

The rest of the story reads like the final act of a Hollywood movie: Gibb gets an information package from the adoption registry that describes her mother as someone who left Canada to become a folksinger in the U.S.; Gibb's friends tell her about Mitchell's quest for her kid, but there's no biographical material in the library for her to peruse or compare notes with; she turns to the Internet, where Wally Breese and, now, Les Irvin, have created an exhaustive Mitchell archive. Before long, she's on the phone with Mitchell's Vancouver-based manager and there can be no doubt: their voices are identical.

The mother-daughter reunion took place in March 1997 in Los Angeles, at Mitchell's Bel Air home. The two women compared faces, looked at photos, and attempted to bridge the chasm between sameness and strangeness. "She has my mother's stature," Joni told Bill Higgins of the *Los Angeles Times* in April of the same year. "We've got cheekbones galore. She's got cheekbones down every part of her family."[25] Meeting her daughter filled "the hole" that the adoption had left inside Mitchell, but the latent mother-daughter relationship has gone through its share of turmoil. Mitchell allegedly slapped Kilauren after she sassed back on some unsolicited parenting advice. The police were called, but no charges were ever laid. The two were estranged at one point, and it's not clear where the relationship currently stands. In a Facebook video posted by Gibb in December 2010, she plays out a rather pathos-laden family drama with nutcrackers and tequila bottles. It seems to be a slap in Mitchell's face for being "an absentee" parent. In one of her last interviews, Mitchell didn't want to discuss the matter, saying only that it was "a work in progress."[26]

MOTHER LOAD

Joni Mitchell never told her mother she had a baby. She kept the secret for decades, suggesting a sensitive relationship. Myrtle McKee Anderson and her daughter, Joan, had their own mother-daughter dynamic, with the perceived threat of shame and embarrassment running as a central theme. When "Joni's Big Secret" was splashed across newsprint in 1997, Mitchell told Bill Higgins of the *Los Angeles Times* she'd concealed the episode because "the scandal was so intense." She also said: "A daughter could do nothing more disgraceful. It ruined you in a social sense. You have no idea what the stigma was. It was like you murdered somebody."[27] To compare an unwanted pregnancy to homicide might seem melodramatic in these days of delivery-room DVDs and eat-your-own-placenta parties, but North America was on a very different cultural page in 1965. This was before the landmark 1973 *Roe v. Wade* case pulled abortion out of the back alleys and into the medical system and Madonna redesigned the modern crèche as a testament to single motherhood. Fear of parental rejection was a clear factor in Mitchell's decision-making process, and despite some hindsight revisionism in the wake of the 1997 reunion with her daughter, it was probably justified. A decade before she passed away on March 20, 2007, at the age of ninety-five, Myrtle acknowledged the hard edges of the Anderson parenting style. "We were very strict about [Joan's] upbringing," she told Reola Daniel of *Western Report* in 1997.[28]

Myrtle and Joni had discussed the possibility of an unwanted pregnancy before she left for art school in Calgary. "We had talked about this type of problem beforehand," Myrtle told Daniel. "I think [Joan] thought we would be quite disappointed... In retrospect, we're sorry she had to have a baby without our support. If we had known, things would have been different." Myrtle was described by a friend as "very Calvinistic," and is on the record as a person who did not believe in abortion—a position she shared with her daughter, who said it "wasn't an option." It also wasn't legal. Myrtle told Laila Fulton of the *Calgary Sun* in 1996, "It's Joni's fault this is coming out now; she's too open and frank about it. This is really embarrassing."[29] Myrtle was red-faced with shame several more times, even though Mitchell talks about trying to hold back and be good: "If I'm censoring for anyone, it's for my parents," she told Cameron Crowe. "They are very old-fashioned and moral people. They still don't understand me that well."[30] This idea of being a source of shame for her parents seems to stretch back to Mitchell's youth, when the typical locus of rebellion was clothes—whether it be a boyish Roy Rogers shirt or the rhinestone-studded getup she put together for her first concert, a Ray Charles show. To attend the show,

Mitchell told *Rolling Stone*'s David Wild in 2002, she bought some rhinestones and clipped them to her "slim jeans," then donned her father's jacket. "My mother wasn't going to let me go out of the house dressed like that," she said.[31]

Beyond the guilt, the embarrassment, and the possibility of disappointing her parents, there was another factor that played a role in Mitchell's decision to surrender the baby for adoption, and that was a legacy of lost female potential. When *Inside Connection*'s Steve Matteo spoke to Mitchell in 2000, he asked her where her fount of creativity originated. She answered:

> I assume there must be some kind of genetic thrust. My two grandmothers were very different, but both of them were frustrated musicians. My paternal grandmother had a hard life—baby after baby after baby. She was not a martyr, but she was a total self-sacrificing animal to her many babies. She cried for the last time in her life when she was fourteen, I'm told. The last thing she cried for was that she wanted a piano, and she told herself, "You silly girl. You'll never have a piano. Dry your eyes"... if that was the main turning point in her life—'I want to play this thing so bad, but I can't; it's not my destiny'—then there's a possibility that that urge went into the genetic pool. She had a lot of children who then had smaller families, maybe three or four children. One of them has got to get that gene, don't you think?[32]

As for Mitchell's other grandmother, Sadie, Joni told Matteo: "She came from a line of classical musicians... She had an organ in the farmhouse and she played classical piano and wrote poetry, mostly celebrating her father. And she was a tempest. She always felt she was the opposite of the other long-suffering, good-natured ones. She was always having fiery fits that she was too good, that she was a poet and a musician stuck on a farm. Perhaps [I inherited] the thrust of those two women."

TUNINGS

Mitchell's gifts would not linger around the milk pail. She took possession of her musicianship, and through her many instruments learned to express her many truths—often inventing a language of her own in order to do so. "At seven, I begged for a piano," she told Jenny Boyd. "I was given piano lessons. The lessons used to coincide with the television broadcast of *Wild Bill Hickok*, this was bad timing, plus the piano teacher used to rap my knuckles because I could memorize and play by ear quicker than I could read. So she made the education process extremely unpleasant." As a teenager, Mitchell quit the lessons and focussed on creating original music: "I still used to sit down and compose my own little melodies; that's what I wanted to do, to compose. In that town, it was unheard of, considered inferior. The thing was to learn the masters and play them. I knew I could make up music; I heard it in my head." When she was ready to turn her attention from piano to guitar, her parents balked. "Since they weren't really supportive, I had to buy my first instrument myself," she said.[33]

Mitchell bought a baritone ukulele for $36—money she earned at Ricki's. She wanted to bring music to the prairie bonfire and beer-chugging parties, and, eventually, she moved on to guitar. She taught herself to play using Pete Seeger's *How to Play Folk-Style Guitar*. It wasn't easy for the polio survivor to find the hand strength and dexterity to make the chords ring, but she improvised and, in the process, developed a unique style—and a tuning scheme that baffled just about everyone.

"I went straight to the Cotten picking," she told Jeffrey Pepper Rodgers of *Acoustic Guitar* magazine in 1996. "Your thumb went from the sixth string, fifth string, sixth string, fifth string… I couldn't do that, so I ended up playing mostly the sixth string but banging it into the fifth string. So Elizabeth Cotten definitely is an influence; it's me not being able to play like her. If I could have I would have, but good thing I couldn't," she said. "Because it came out original."[34]

Original, indeed. Only two songs in Mitchell's catalogue are written in standard tuning: "Urge for Going" and "Tin Angel"—two of her earliest compositions. After that, she adopted the open tunings that were first introduced to her by fellow musician and friend Eric Andersen—at the time a relatively successful act on the folk circuit who hung out at the Mitchells' boho-chic digs in Detroit. Tom Rush was another musician who heard something compelling in Mitchell's nascent songwriting. "She knocked my socks off!… My colleagues and I at that time were mainly doing traditional folk tunes, which in my book, is the only kind of folk tune there is," he told Karen O'Brien, author of *Joni Mitchell: Shadows and Light* in 2000. "[Joni's songs] had a folk sensibility to them yet they were fresh and had a literate veneer… They were very exciting, they had a voice that had universal appeal," Rush continued. He liked "Urge for Going" so much, he recorded it himself and turned it into a hit. Encouraged by Rush's appreciation, Mitchell recorded a few more songs on a demo, including "The Circle Game," which she issued a disclaimer for right up front: "It sucks and you're going to hate it and I don't know why I'm putting it on."[35]

Clearly, the confidence in her inner voice had yet to be cemented, but this was a Joni just emerging from her own creative uterus—all wet and soft and needy. Rush's validation of her music gave her the strength and conviction to continue her explorations. He also taught her the fine art of open tunings.

"The moment I began to write, I took the black blues tunings which were floating around," she told William Ruhlmann. "Tom [Rush] played in open C. Eric Andersen showed me an open G, which I think is Keith Richards' tuning, he mainly writes in that. Then there was D modal. Buffy [Sainte-Marie] had a couple of original tunings. But I began to experiment because my left hand is somewhat clumsy because of polio. I had to simplify the shapes of the left hand, but I craved chordal movement that I couldn't get out of standard tuning without an extremely articulate left hand. So, to compensate for it, I found the tunings were a godsend," she said of the open formations. "Not only that, they made the guitar an unstable thing; an instrument of exploration."[36]

People noticed her "non-standard," "California kitchen" tunings. Musicians, in particular, were baffled because they weren't like anything anyone had ever seen, or heard. Mitchell calls her results the "chords of inquiry"—unique palettes of sound to paint each song. She's created more than fifty tunings for her guitar over the years, earning her the dubious honour of being the "James Joyce of tunings," according to ex-husband Larry Klein. Former beau John Guerin was kinder and said she was a "whole orchestra" with one guitar. The same way Mitchell played with her physical identity, she played with her musical identity.

The desire to experiment pulled Mitchell into strange places—not just creatively but literally. Briefly, Mitchell recreated herself anew with an identity she dubbed "Mademoiselle Oink." The name was a nod to the police—a gentle coda to the "sunset pig" she describes in the song "California"—but

Mademoiselle Oink had a specific job title and duty. According to Mitchell's 1988 interview with Q's Phil Sutcliffe, it was "liaison officer between rock 'n' roll and the cops."[37]

One of Mademoiselle Oink's favourite pastimes was to finagle police paraphernalia from officers using her fame and feminine wiles. When she got to Memphis, Mademoiselle Oink was sitting on a small trove of badges and hats, tie clips and jackets. She was looking to expand her collection when she talked up a cop, who was happy to trade a badge for a record. They decided to meet on old Beale Street, the once-thriving spawning ground for Memphis blues that now lay derelict, with the exception of pawn shops, a statue of W.C. Handy, and an old movie theatre playing a Blaxploitation double bill. It was 1976, after all.

As Mitchell cruised the empty streets—which she swears actually had rolling tumbleweeds—a pawn shop owner recognized her. "You Joni Mitchell?" he asked. Mitchell was gobsmacked: "Culturally, this is impossible," she told Sutcliffe. "This guy should not know my name." They struck up a conversation, and Mitchell asked him about a largely forgotten blues legend named Furry Lewis. The man said he was a friend of the reclusive player and set up a meeting, instructing Mitchell to bring a bottle of Jack Daniel's and a carton of Pall Malls. "It was quite a nice visit," said Mitchell, "until I said to him, meaning to be close to him—meaning 'we have this in common'—'I play in open tunings too.'" The comment was entirely benign and friendly, but Lewis immediately became defensive. "He leaned on the bed and said 'Ah kin play in Spanish tonnin'...Somehow or other I insulted him," Mitchell said. "From then on, it was downhill. He just said, 'I don't like her.'"

The experience haunted Mitchell. She felt she was a kindred spirit with Lewis, but he blew her off. She was just a well-intentioned white lady chatting with a one-legged black man living in a hovel. He didn't understand her mission, but Mitchell felt like a pioneer. She was "discovering" her music like a scientist fiddling with flasks in the lab, attempting to decipher the alchemy of her own existence, as well as her own expression. There was mystery to the exercise but also a deep sense of purpose.

"My chords are inverted; the natural order of the scale is altered and twisted," she told Divina Infusino of the *San Diego Union-Tribune* in 1988. "My chords are like questions. They are a depiction of complex emotions. Most major chords are a depiction of well-being and happiness. My major chord will have a dissonant note leading to sorrow, then another note leading back to joy. There is always the possibility of the opposite emotion in my chords."[38]

This internal play of opposites reaffirms the notion of the creative process as a reconciliation of opposing natural forces, and it's one that music PhD James Bennighof discusses in technical detail in his tome *The Words and Music of Joni Mitchell*. In a discussion of Mitchell's tunings, he explains: "A particular tuning usually implies a particular tonic note." The tonic—or keynote—is essentially the core foundation of a chord and the note we want to hear in order to feel resolution at the end of a song. Mitchell's tuning has a tendency to resist the expected tonic, and as a result, her songs immediately feel different. Bennighof goes on to say, "The fact that Mitchell often relocates a single finger configuration along the neck of the guitar to create different chords often gives rise to 'parallel motion'—all notes moving in the same direction from one chord to another," and "the fact that many of her fingerings let some open strings ring often results in several complex chords sharing several pitches."[39] The devil lurks in such complex details: many of the blues chords Mitchell plays were once considered "godless"—or "devil's music"[40]—because they were so different from the orthodox approach to western scale.

Her lexicon of tunings made live performance awkward, since the instruments had to be retuned for practically every song. Electronics simplified matters later in her career, when she embraced the body of a Fender Stratocaster hooked up to a Roland VG-8—what Mitchell described as "a computerized brain with foot pedals into which are programmed a whole palette of sounds."[41]

Before the Roland translated the sounds Mitchell heard in her head to the guitar, she says session players would give her grief and argue over the root of a given chord because she didn't compose or play by the established rules of musical tradition. She was often ridiculed for her independent ear—but it never stopped her. In conversation with KCRW's Chris Douridas in 1998, Mitchell talked about pushing the boundaries of scale and harmony, with specific reference to *Taming the Tiger*:

> Some of the things I told myself to do and tried were pretty strange on this record... I worked my way down from what was considered strange upper harmony anyway. I had a strange harmonic sense. So I was asking the bass to do things on the bottom. [Session players] would say, "Well, that's not the root of the chord." I was asking them to do rhythmic and harmonic things that they thought were not hip. I was... asking people to go against the vogue, and people don't like to stick out. There aren't that many people that like to take chances. They're afraid to be unhip, you know, to take [a risk], to be the leader of the next hip, you have to be willing to be unhip.[42]

Despite what the professional musicians were telling her, Mitchell listened to the sounds in her own head instead of the flapping of the paid hands, and strangely enough, it worked. She created music that was aurally satisfying despite its so-called theoretical flaws. More fascinating still, even the music that Mitchell wrote in standard tunings found a note of difference.

In his examination of the undeniably mournful "Tin Angel," Bennighof introduced me to a musical term I had never heard before to describe how Mitchell undermines expectation: "Replacing an expected final minor chord with a major chord in this way is a centuries-old technique—the raised third of the chord, in this case G♯ rather than G♭, was first dubbed a 'Picardy third' (*"tierce de Picardie"*) in print by Jean-Jacques Rousseau in 1797… to express [the idea that] hopefulness might seem unremarkable, or even clichéd."[43] In other words, the Picardy third is the cliché of a "happy ending," and one Mitchell uses to close her seemingly earnest, and altogether mopey, song about losing one lover and moving on to another. The Picardy third arrives on the lyric "I found someone to love today," suggesting Mitchell is internally aware of romantic love's inability to provide true happiness but, gosh darn it, it's a nice illusion all the same.

TAKING OFF WITH A BIG BYRD

In October of 1967, a burnt-out rock star named David Crosby walked into a small club in Coconut Grove, Florida, called the Gaslight South. He had just quit one of the biggest bands of the era, called the Byrds, after running into trouble with his bandmates Roger McGuinn, Chris Hillman, and Michael Clarke. (Original member, drummer Gene Clark had already flown the coop in 1966, citing anxiety problems. Clarke would exit in the same breath as Crosby.) The boys in the band thought their long-haired rhythm guitarist was bossy and full of himself. Crosby, meanwhile, thought the band that charted with a jangly-guitar cover of Bob Dylan's "Mr. Tambourine Man" had hit a creative plateau. He needed time to consider his next move, and he was about to head offshore on his newly acquired seventy-three-foot double-masted schooner called the *Mayan* (purchased with a $22,500 loan from millionaire Monkee Peter Tork) to think things over. He was thinking he'd spend half his time sailing and the rest of the time producing new talent. When he walked through the front door of the narrow storefront and spotted Joni Mitchell through a diaphanous blue curtain, he knew he'd spotted someone special.

She was playing a simple acoustic set consisting of "Michael from Mountains" and "Both Sides Now," and Crosby was seduced immediately by the woman onstage with the long blond hair and lyrical poetry flowing from her sultry lips. "I was just floored. I couldn't believe that there was anybody that good," he told Mitchell biographer and archivist Wally Breese for an online interview published on the jonimitchell.com website. Of particular interest to Crosby were the bizarre tunings Mitchell played in, which he called "fascinating" because he, too, was experimenting with open tunings. "I'm sure we learned things off each other. We used to play songs to each other all the time. But I think she just outgrew me ... she has since gone further with it than I have. I think she's gone further with it than anyone," Crosby told Breese in 1997. "And I also fell ... I loved her, as it were."[44]

Although Crosby would eventually tell *Mojo's* Sylvie Simmons that falling in love with Mitchell is "like falling into a cement mixer... turbulent,"[45] a relationship blossomed in a cloud of sweet smoke and jasmine-scented salt air as Mitchell looked into Crosby's twinkling sapphire eyes and saw the face of Yosemite Sam and the soul of a lion. The lion also had a lot of clout—and scandal rag notoriety. Crosby was a seminal figure at the dawning of the Age of Aquarius and everyone wanted a piece of him, from the record labels to the ladies. His long, shaggy hair and beard became his trademark, as well as a look adopted by the youthful masses looking to free themselves from the stiffness of Brooks Brothers collars and the establishment expectations their broadcloth represented. He knew what he was doing, and Mitchell could feel it. In fact, the moment she and Crosby started their brief but pivotal romance, she called her manager, Elliot Roberts, and, according to Roberts, told him: "Listen, I'm fucking a Byrd."[46] This may sound a little shrewd, crude, and maybe even exploitative, but for a woman to use her wiles this way was proof of personal empowerment and levelled the field of sexual play. And so, in a THC-infused homage to Henry Higgins, Crosby did his best to transform Mitchell, the fashionable, high-end clothes horse, into his own psychedelic Eliza Doolittle.

Crosby was really the first person to set the myth of Joni Mitchell in motion. It was easy for him. David Van Cortlandt Crosby was the son of an Oscar-winning Hollywood cinematographer named Floyd Delafield Crosby, an active participant in the golden age of cinema with credits that include *Tabu*, *High Noon*, and *The Old Man and the Sea* (with famed cinematographer James Wong Howe)—as well as a curious Canadian documentary called *The Champagne Safari*, which chronicles French Nazi collaborator Charles Bedaux's voyage to northern Canada with casks of bubbly—but that truly is another story.[47] What seems clear is that both father and son were self-styled adventurers and accomplished sailors with a strong sense of creative power.

The younger Crosby started with the all-important externals and gave Joni a hippie makeover. He told her to lose the fake eyelashes and mascara and man-made fibers. He pushed her to ditch her beautiful designer purse in favour of a woven pouch, and even though Mitchell wasn't all that fond of the formless sack or the "natural look"—as opposed to Carnaby Street sexy—she cunningly agreed. Her willingness in the role of Eliza earned her a trip to California, where Crosby was the dude du jour. He introduced her to the L.A.-based music scene, including key disc jockeys, such as Crosby's pal B. Mitchell Reed, known as "the fastest tongue in the west." Ever the showman and impresario, Crosby set up private showcase sets for Mitchell with the musical cognoscenti swarming in the warm cracks of Laurel Canyon. One of his "favourite tricks" (according to Crosby) was to give the friends and guests in attendance a hit of intolerably strong marijuana before asking Mitchell to play a tune or two. "They would walk out stupefied," said Crosby.[48]

The noted session player Russ Kunkel remembers that Crosby's early showcase sets for Mitchell cast a spell. "Most of the women [of the Canyon] were magical then 'cause there was this incredible feeling of freedom that was enhanced by various things, including drugs, but Joni was drop dead beautiful," Kunkel told Sheila Weller. "And she had this amazing voice: her voice register and her guitar tunings, which no one had heard." According to Peter Fonda, Mitchell attracted attention because she was beautiful—and because she had a habit of playing around with the tuning pegs. He said Mitchell frequently took Crosby's guitar and "de-tuned the fucker." Crosby would later credit the musical adjustments to "Martians."[49]

The Crosby-induced buzz surrounding Mitchell grew stronger just as Judy Collins's rendition of "Both Sides Now" started climbing the charts. For Mitchell's relatively green manager, Elliot Roberts, the stars were in alignment for a once-in-a-lifetime coup. He headed to California, met with

Mo Ostin at Warner/Reprise, and walked out with the keys to the creative candy store: he negotiated full creative control for Mitchell's first record deal, from the music in the grooves to the cover art. The deal had only one caveat: David Crosby had to be part of the whole shebang. The former Byrd was seen as being on top of the modern sound, and the label saw the collaboration as crucial. The first test of the mentorship took place within the storied, acoustically imperfect walls of the Sunset Sound complex in Hollywood.

A FLAPPING OF WINGS: *SONG TO A SEAGULL*

"Hey, Joni. I have an idea: Why not sing into the piano, man!"

I have no idea if that's how Crosby said it, but that's what happened when he and Mitchell headed into the studios on Sunset Boulevard to lay down tracks for Mitchell's debut, *Song to a Seagull*. Crosby had assigned himself production duties on the album—and no one was going to argue, including the headstrong Mitchell. She sang into the piano because she could, and because the creatively inspired—and probably somewhat stoned—Crosby thought it would be a good idea. Crosby, who confesses to struggling over songs, whereas Mitchell would create with awe-inspiring ease, said their romance was cooking—until they got into the creative kitchen. "I did bring [Joni] around to everyone I knew...it was a lot of fun. It only stopped being fun when I started producing her first record," he said.[50]

For Mitchell, the Henry Higgins treatment was becoming irritating. She told Estrella Berosini (one of the Ladies of the Canyon quoted in Karen O'Brien's biography) that she really did love David. "But when we get together," she said, "we just don't get along." Crosby saw the collision coming: "Joni is not a person you stay in a relationship with. It always goes awry,

no matter who you are. It's an inevitable thing. We were starting to have friction and at the same time I was starting to
produce her record and I didn't really know how," he admitted
to Breese.

Indeed, Crosby didn't know how to produce a record, but
he was powerful and experienced enough in the music industry to sell his production skills to the Warner executives, who
thought he might have the sonic vision to be the folk-rock version of an era-defining sound designer in the tradition of Phil
Spector. But the last thing Crosby wanted to build was a "wall
of sound" that would stand around Mitchell's oeuvre.

Crosby set out to strip Mitchell down and keep her vocals
as pure as they had been off the coffee-house mike the first
time he heard her. Mitchell understood this was a significant
stand to make at a time when the music industry was shifting away from prefab band models toward the more organic
singer-songwriter who could sell entire albums—and not just
singles. "The record company was going to 'folk-rock' me up
and David thought that would be a tragedy, that my music
should be recorded the way I wrote it," Mitchell is quoted
as saying in Crosby's biography. "He appreciated it the way
it was and since he had been in the premiere folk rock group,
he could go to the record company with some authority and
say 'I'm going to produce her' and the trick was that he was
not going to 'produce' me at all! Anything we added would be
minimal; that's the way we proceeded."[51]

It was in the spirit of minimalism that Mitchell found herself singing into the body of the Sunset Sound grand piano.
Crosby and the veteran sound engineer Art Cryst were the
only knob-turners on the console—and they were unafraid
of experimenting. Fertile vibes were all around them. In fact,
down the hall in the strip mall complex of studios, members
of Buffalo Springfield were putting tracks together for a new

record. Mitchell told Elliot Roberts that he and Neil Young had to meet because they were both funny. Mitchell's intuition was bang on: Young and Roberts would forge one of the longest-lasting artist-manager partnerships in the history of the music industry. The Sunset sessions also laid the keystone to another piece of rock history, because it brought David Crosby together with Stephen Stills and Young, who would all go on to create CSNY with Graham Nash just a short time later.

At this particular moment, however, Mitchell was focussed on singing her highs and lows into the curved body of a grand.

Said Mitchell in a 1968 interview with a Philadelphia radio station: "One of the things we did that was kind of fun: [David] had me sing a lot of it into a grand piano with the ringing pedal down. So every note repeated itself in the strings... [they] reproduce the sound of your voice... It was so beautiful. He had so many ideas. He had the idea too of doubling my guitar part so some of the guitar sounds like twelve-string."[52]

For all the creative will, the technical skills in the booth weren't ready for the challenge. Crosby says he used too many mikes and created an almost cataclysmic system hiss on the masters. "I had allowed too much signal-to-noise ratio... too much hiss," he told Wally Breese. "I wanted to try and get the overtones that happen from the resonating of the piano and of course, it recorded at way too low a level. It was just an idea and it really didn't work."

Art Cryst, the engineer, died shortly after the sessions were finished, leaving Crosby and Mitchell looking for an emergency fix for the masters. They found John Haeny, an engineer for Elektra Records, who stripped off the hiss—but at a price: the audio lost a chunk of range on the high end, and as a result, it feels flattened and condensed. To Judy Collins, it sounded like the whole thing was recorded "under a bell jar."

Despite the sonic traumas that went into its creation and the budding romance that blew apart under the strain, *Song to a Seagull* did what it was supposed to do: it got Mitchell noticed and started the scribblers scribbling.

Rolling *Stone*'s Les Brown reviewed the album on July 6, 1968. The opening paragraph reads: "Here is Joni Mitchell: A penny yellow blonde with a vanilla voice. Influenced, or appearing influenced, by Judy Collins, gingham, leather, lace, producer David Crosby (the ex-Byrd), Robert Herrick, North Battleford (Saskatchewan), New York (New York), Sgt. Pepper's Lonely Hearts Club Band, Chuck, seagulls, dolphins, taxicabs, Dairy Queen floats, someone named Mr. Kratzman, 'who taught me to love words,' the Lovin' Spoonful, rain, sunlight, garbage, metermaids and herself." When Brown describes the production—which was everyone's biggest worry—the session troubles don't come up. "The Joni Mitchell album, despite a few momentary weaknesses, is a good debut. Her lyrics are striking. Her tunes are unusual. Her voice is clear and natural," Brown writes. "One of the major new departures of this album may at first appear atavistic. Joni Mitchell uses no orchestration ... Her main studio trick is to dub in her voice a second time as a choral answer on certain songs."[53]

As Joni is quoted by Brown: "If I'd recorded a year ago, I would have used lots of orchestration. No one would have let me put out an acoustic album. They would have said it's like having a whole paint box and using only brown. But today is a better time to be recording. It's like in fashion. There's no real style right now. You find who you are and you dress accordingly. In music today I feel that I can put down my songs with an acoustic guitar and forget the violins and not feel that I need them."

RUNAWAY BABY

Joni Mitchell has often referred to her songs as children, and the first-born were clearly loved by everyone: *Song to a Seagull* was a creative and commercial success for the first-timer. Nearly thirty years later, she said the oldest kids got all the attention: "[Now I find myself] dismissive of my early songs in favour of championing my underdog children," she said in a 1996 *Los Angeles Times* interview.[54]

Nonetheless, the image of Mitchell as the California earth goddess was cast, and it didn't matter whether it was manufactured at the hands of David Crosby's magic wand or the supremely astute and ambitious woman with the killer voice. It was gaining a life of its own—for better, and for worse.

Says Timothy White in his 1991 book *Rock Lives*: "Mitchell began by embodying the archetypal fair-haired hippie-chick singer, ornamenting the male folk-rock enclave."[55] She fit the part perfectly, but for Mitchell, it really was a performance. She enjoyed the laid-back blue jean style, but she missed dressing up—and she resented the peer pressure to root herself on the seedy side. "The whole hippie thing was a relief in a way—we were all so fresh scrubbed and in jeans," she told Carla Hill. "But [it was also] an inhibiting time, peer pressure. You couldn't dress up. Well, I succumbed to some of that. If anything I'm coming out now."[56]

Joni's facade became synonymous with the flower power generation. To this day, she's seen as the icon for the whole era—not just among music writers and pop culture mavens, but for the fashion world as well.

In 1998, the *Sunday Telegraph* published an article called "Joni Chic," itemizing a look that was being rediscovered by a new generation of performers. "Joni Mitchell was the consummate 'hippy [sic] chick', Annie Hall meets urban-cowgirl,

with a haunting beauty that intrigued many famous lovers,"
waxes the intro. "But Joni's style was also ahead of her time.
While Joni's contemporaries... festooned themselves with
every bead, feather fringe, and bit of patchwork they could
lay their hands on, Mitchell never sought attention with her
style." The piece goes on to describe the look:

> Hair: Long, blonde, parted in the centre or loosely plaited.
> Face: High Faye Dunaway cheekbones, fresh-faced slightly
> tanned complexion with freckled nose. Make-up: Barely
> there. Even if it takes hours to apply, it should still look nat-
> ural. Accessories: Beret or a soft straw or floppy linen hat;
> ethnic, Navajo-style turquoise and silver belts, necklaces
> and cuffs, cameo rings. Clothes: Homespun knits, linen
> shirts and wide-leg trousers, suede jackets and boots, Ikat
> prints and Guatemalan scarves.[57]

The specifics of the description prove how fully realized
Mitchell's "hippie chick" persona was, and because it was so
complete—and so timely—it attracted an automatic following. Mitchell was offering women a completely new type of
role model that negotiated the distance between traditional
femininity and the changing pop culture landscape, where
women were suddenly in charge of their own sexuality and
creative power. Actor Edie Falco (*The Sopranos, Nurse Jackie*)
was one such young woman. Falco said Mitchell's music just
"clicked" for her. "I can't tell you how much I respect her. I'm
in awe, really," she said. "She was there for me at every significant moment in my life. I hear her music in my head. She
provided the soundtrack for my life."[58]

Though she'd been nudged into the role by Crosby, the
ensuing manifestation of Mitchell as folk goddess turned

out to be the right image at the right time. In the wake of the pill, Barbie, the 1963 publication of Betty Friedan's *The Feminine Mystique*, and the 1968 release of Roman Polanski's *Rosemary's Baby*, young women were looking for a female role model who could accommodate so many different dynamics. Mitchell's combination of ethereal good looks, long blond Barbie hair, and wholesome sexuality had its own power. Together with that big, round, octave-spanning vocal box, it vaulted Mitchell to the very top of the pop culture wave as the ultimate California girl—a small irony for a prairie kid from Canada.

Chuck Mitchell recognized later what deeper forces were at play in his ex-wife's rise to fame: "What I didn't understand at the time was this business of identification," he says in Sheila Weller's book. "The guys loved Joni because she looked great. The girls were identifying with her in droves."[59]

This phenomenon of identification did not go unnoticed by executives at Reprise Records, where Stan Cornyn devised a series of print ads for the release of *Clouds* and *Ladies of the Canyon* that exploited Mitchell's enigmatic sexuality as well as her appeal to young women. These minimalist promos featured simple text on a white background and appeared in *Rolling Stone* and other youth-targeted publications. "Joni Mitchell is 90% virgin," read the first marketing salvo. The line, based on the joke that you can't be a partial virgin, was referring to the fact that most of her material was still unheard—even though Judy Collins had a *Billboard* hit with Mitchell's "Both Sides Now." That ad was followed by two more: "Joni Mitchell Takes Forever" (referring to the long-awaited release of *Clouds*) and "Joni Mitchell Finally Comes Across" (referring to the "full release" of the record). Mitchell may have had complete creative control over her recordings, but she had no control over how the record company marketed her—resulting in these hilariously dated, sexist, and altogether shallow yelps of money-grubbing hype.

The gist of the Mitchell marketing angle switched for *Ladies of the Canyon* as the target demographic changed gender. The new ad was a story about a fictional character named Amy Foster, "23 years old and quietly beautiful," suffering the ache of failed romance. Amy "was sitting in her orange inflatable chair listening to Neil Young's second album... toying indifferently with the enormous antique ring on the index finger of her left hand" as she thought about tie-dying some curtains for her '64 Chevy camper. Amy wanted to split for Oregon to "get her head back together," but when the grocery boy arrived with fresh food and the RIT (dye for those curtains), they sat down to smoke a "concise little joint" and to listen to the new Joni album, *Ladies of the Canyon*:

> By the time "For Free" was over they were both quite mellow indeed. As much as they downed her by reminding her all too vividly of her now-irrevocably-consummated relationship with David [Amy's recent ex she'd met at the Jeans West shop], "Willy" and "Conversation" were somehow reassuring—there was someone else, even another canyon lady, who really knew. Amy began to feel a little better. By the time "Circle Game" had finished, Amy was no longer dejectedly contemplating splitting for Oregon. In fact, she could scarcely wait for the sun to get through setting so she could drive up to the top of Lookout and watch Los Angeles twinkle beneath the indigo April sky.

They just don't write them like that anymore, do they? Frankly, I found it a bit shocking that a corporate entity like

Warner Bros. would talk about marijuana and pre-marital sex in an ad campaign, but that was then. And back then, Mitchell clearly represented a novel force in the world of pop music— not only for being a woman who wrote her own material but for being her own woman, as well. That's why she's a role model for the fictional Amy Foster as well as the very real Edie Falco.

Mitchell was aware of the marketing manipulation in the name of profit, and for a time, she submitted, because she was not questioning the basic assumptions behind the status quo: "We're talking about a business that is not as much musical as it is physical. The image is, generally speaking, more important than the sound, whether the business would admit it or not," she told Mary Dickie in 1994. "When I was contracted to Reprise, they didn't know what to do with me. There was no overt sexuality, and I think the executive mentality found that difficult to market," she said. "Always women have had to burlesque it up, and I had no penchant for that, and I didn't think it was necessary. I thought we were liberated, and I guess I bought a lie and proceeded accordingly."[60]

THE F-WORD

Mitchell didn't question the dominant belief system from a gender perspective until later in her career because she didn't have much time for the feminist rhetoric of her day. She says she never even heard the word "feminist" until she went out for dinner with Jack Nicholson and Warren Beatty. Her beer and taco buddies couldn't believe she'd never heard the word, which explains why she allegedly had a brief romance with Beatty, the conquistador of California. Mitchell's tacit acceptance of traditional gender stereotypes allowed her to be part of the guy posse while still owning her own sexual power. She says she resisted feminists and feminism because they felt too "divisive" and she always saw herself "as one of the boys." In a 1998 interview with singer-songwriter Ani DiFranco for the Los Angeles Times, Mitchell's apparently paradoxical views on feminism prove too much for the younger artist, who turns the piece into a feisty meditation on the merits of feminist thinking. It's also, unfortunately, a complete bore— and only seems to prove Mitchell's beliefs about feminists being arrogantly self-righteous and rigid. DiFranco's words say everything: "Either you are a feminist or you are a sexist/ misogynist. There is no box marked 'other.'"[61]

Mitchell couldn't identify with the rhetoric. And despite becoming the reigning royal in a new breed of sisterhood, she felt rather removed from the "hippie" and feminist movements, as well as the marketing. "A lot of hippie politics were nonsense to me," she told Rolling Stone's Steven Daly in 1998. "I guess I found the idea of going from authority to no authority too extreme. And I was supposed to be the 'hippie queen,' so I had a sense of isolation about the whole thing."[62]

She knew she wasn't "fitting in," but her truth demanded expression—even on the surface level. "I remember showing up at a Carole King concert in Central Park [in 1973] in a pair of Yves St. Laurent pants. And a good shirt," she told Cameron Crowe. "They were simple clothes, but they were good quality. And I felt... really uncomfortable... I was outside the uniform of rock 'n' roll and it was annoying to some people." Mitchell was still part Barbie inside. She even bought herself a Barbie car with her first royalty cheque—no, not a pink plastic Corvette, but a brand new car: a Mercedes 280 SE convertible she called "Bluebird." (The car was stolen in the late eighties, prompting a fit of mourning for the 1969 Teutonic symbol of success. Bizarrely, over the course of writing this book, I not only saw the same car on the streets of Yorkville, but I also encountered someone who said they stole it as a lark.) Mitchell was still grappling with her prairie roots, her mother's moral judgement, and her swelling will to make an impression. She was keenly aware of the difference between the package and the content, between her truth and the constructed image of who she was supposed to be, but she was finding a way to make the dissonance feed her creativity—at least for now.

four

WOODSTOCK
Myth and Mythmaking

"People have the need to set people above themselves.
The stage is the illustration of that—the demi-gods.
The god thing is an illustration of that very need
of greater power. In lieu of finding out what that
greater power is, people set up on their own earthly
version of it in order to express it. I stand on stage
and I'm thinking, What are you looking at me for, a
damn junkie hacking away at the guitar, what is this?
This must be a primal need."

KEITH RICHARDS

JOSEPH CAMPBELL SAYS we need myth to help us "feel the
rapture of being alive" by giving us perspective and the sense
of being attached to something larger than ourselves. "When
a story is in your mind, then you see its relevance to something happening in your own life," he says in *The Power of
Myth*. "These bits of information from ancient times, which
have to do with themes that have supported human life, built
over civilizations, and informed religions over the millennia,

have to do with deep inner problems, inner mysteries, inner thresholds of passage."[1] The human experience has been well mapped by the countless other souls who have moved through its myriad hallways. By tracing the steps of others through stories, we can gain a better sense of our place in the universe. Myth, therefore, isn't just the result of a collective act of creation, it's a well-worn and accepted shortcut to the life-affirming creative flame. In the same way the individual can feel the "rapture of being alive" through artistic expression, the masses can access the same feelings of wholeness through resonant storytelling.

Much of what we understand Joni Mitchell to be is more myth than reality, but as we've already seen, she was a willing participant in the creation of her own iconography. She and Crosby created a false idol that would soon be worshipped by the masses. Yet, in the hot carnal sweat of the Summer of Love, Mitchell seemed to catch a glimpse of her own mythologized reflection, stand back, and question. In the very same breath, she created the anthem for the collective myth of her generation.

WOODSTOCK

They say that if every person who claimed to be at Woodstock had actually attended the event, the five boroughs of New York City would have been empty—and more than eight million people would have huddled together en masse. People like to be a part of history, even if their narrative is not entirely true, because it gives them the ephemeral gloss of glamour—and the illusion that an entirely average life is noteworthy. Hey, we all want to feel special, and Woodstock may well have been the most remarkable pop culture event of the twentieth century.

As it was for every other soul on the planet—save the approximately 500,000 spectators and hangers-on who actually made it to White Lake in the town of Bethel, New York, for "3 Days of Peace & Music" in August 1969—the mythology surrounding Woodstock was transmitted to my brain from two sources: the documentary film about the event and the song written by Mitchell containing the chorus: "We are stardust, we are golden, and we've got to get ourselves back to the garden." I don't really know how, but these two emblems fused in my brain, and when I first started working on this book, I was under the impression that Mitchell was actually in Bethel and *at* Woodstock. I could even conjure the image of the youthful chanteuse, sans *maquillage*, sitting in front of a sea of people.

This personally manufactured image would prove to be my next lesson in the fallibility of perception and the seductive power of myth, because Mitchell never did take Woodstock's rough-hewn, unpainted stage. Despite a YouTube video mistakenly labelled "Joni at Woodstock" (it's actually the Isle of Wight Festival), which features the singer-songwriter at a piano singing the signature tune inspired by the event, Mitchell watched the whole happening unfold in the all-too-safe confines of David Geffen's leased apartment on Central Park South.

Mitchell was originally booked to play Woodstock the Sunday night—alongside other attractions including the Band; Jeff Beck; Blood, Sweat & Tears; Iron Butterfly; Joe Cocker; CSNY (Crosby, Stills, Nash & Young); and Hendrix—but her business mentors Roberts and Geffen felt it was too dangerous for Mitchell to make the commute into the chaos unfolding upstate. The roads were jammed, bus service had been cancelled by order of the police, and the only way to get in was via helicopter. Roberts was terrified of flying, and when he heard his newest act, CSNY, battled a rainstorm in the chopper only to land outside the grounds and subsequently hot-wire a pickup (a hidden talent of Neil Young's, apparently) to make it to the plywood stage, he was nervous about getting Joni there. But Geffen and Roberts weren't really afraid for her physical safety in the midst of half-a-million kids huddled together in the mud. It was more of a career-based decision: they believed her show business interests were best served by staying in the city so she could attend her national TV date with talk show host Dick Cavett. This may sound foolish now, but at the time neither Geffen nor Roberts really recognized the event as anything more than just another festival, and not such an important one at that. Newport was already an established event, and the first Monterey Pop had come and gone without incident. Risking a national TV audience for a muddy love-in seemed like a bad idea, and even worse business. They weren't clued out. The fact is, no one really realized what Woodstock would become, including the organizers of the festival itself.

John Morris, production manager at Woodstock, said they were counting on 75,000 attendees, but when he and his crew stood onstage for a sound check and saw the actual crowd swarming in the breaking dawn, the scale of what was about to happen sank in—prompting Morris to utter the two famed words that christened the first live microphone at the festival: "Holy shit!"

"There were so many more than we guessed," Morris recounts in Pete Fornatale's book *Back to the Garden*. "The Beatles had drawn 50,000 people to Shea Stadium. Monterey, which was a year or two before, was 35,000 people over three days. The idea of putting 100,000 people in the same place is normal to us now, but the idea of putting something like that together then and having that many people was beyond the pale."[2]

Journalist Mike Jahn was assigned to cover the festival for the *New York Times*. He was reluctant to go, believing it would be a disappointment compared to Newport, but hopped into a car and headed to Bethel for what would become a life-altering adventure. "I got about halfway there in my rented car and it was trafficky. You just couldn't get anywhere," he said. "I called the *Times* and told them what was going on. I said, 'Look, you better send a hard news team here. I cannot do this myself. This is a major story.' They sent a helicopter for me and that's how I got in."[3]

Richie Havens was supposed to play on the final day of the festival but ended up being cajoled into the opening spot when no one else was available, or coherent enough, to perform. He calls Woodstock "a cosmic accident."[4]

Joni Mitchell watched this "cosmic accident" unfold on television at Geffen's deluxe duplex at 230 Central Park South, a property owned by Helen Noga, the woman who made Johnny Mathis a star. Spellbound by the sight of so many young people converging on Max Yasgur's six-hundred-acre dairy farm, Joni began composing the soundtrack for the rapidly evolving Woodstock myth: "I came upon a child of God. He was walking along the road. And I asked him where are you going? And this he told me: I'm going down to Yasgur's farm. I'm going to join in a rock 'n' roll band. I'm going to camp out on the land. I'm gonna try and get my soul free."

Stephen Stills, who was still buzzing from CSNY's first show in Chicago a few days earlier, got onstage at Woodstock and announced, "This is only the second time we've performed in front of people. We're scared shitless." It's always good to show a little vulnerability onstage. It makes you human, and if Woodstock set out to celebrate anything at all, it was the simple pleasure of being outside, listening to music, and being a human being surrounded by other like-minded souls. CSNY lapped up the attention and the hippie vibe, but they also set the wheels of wishful revisionism in motion.

According to an erroneous Woodstock legend perpetuated by Stephen Stills and David Crosby, Mitchell penned the song "Woodstock" after hearing about the event from her then-lover, Graham Nash—as though she was so impressed by the returning crusaders, she needed to mythologize the event and their participation in it. It's a story that's been told, and retold, and chronicled, and re-chronicled. It's now such a standard part of the Bethel narrative, it's considered digital gospel and appears in the Wikipedia entry for the song, which reads: "Joni Mitchell wrote the song from what she had heard from then-boyfriend, Graham Nash, about the festival."

When Mitchell received the Billboard Century Award for outstanding musical achievement in 1995, Crosby and Nash retold the story—prompting a fit of pique from Mitchell. "When I got my recent Billboard honorary award, I'm sitting in the audience and there's David going (in a nasal, mocking tone), 'I'll tell ya, man, what a great songwriter she is: We came back from Woodstock babbling about it and she wrote that song from our babbling,'" Mitchell relates in a 1996 *Details* article. "I thought, 'You bastard!' I had that song written before they got back."[5]

Mitchell attributes these false memories to male ego and the insistent need to take credit for significant events. Fittingly, when she made her acceptance speech at the Billboard Awards, she raised a flag for her fellow sisters: "I've been thinking a lot about arrogance and humility, trying to find some genuine humility to bring to this situation. But I feel like I'm emerging from the McCarthy era in a certain way. I never thought of it as difficult being a woman in this industry, but it has been pointed out to me… how few women there really were."[6]

The Woodstock saga was one moment when Mitchell did feel her gender. She "felt like the girl in the family"[7] when the boys were given carte blanche for their adventure in Bethel, and she was forced to stay behind.

In a taped TV interview featured on the Dick Cavett DVD box set, Mitchell describes how she had opened for the newly formed CSNY for their first two shows as a "supergroup" but never made it upstate. "What had happened was that Crosby, Stills, Nash & Young had formed… On a Saturday night we played in Chicago, [and] on Sunday we were supposed to go to Woodstock. The boys were taken in and I was told I couldn't go because I had to do a television show the next day and there was a possibility we could get in but they didn't know how we could get out," she says. "I felt, you know, [Woodstock] was an amazing thing that occurred, and to me that was an important event and I think I knew that was as good as it was going to get."[8]

In the actual footage of the post-Woodstock Dick Cavett broadcast, Mitchell is wearing a flowing, floor-length emerald dress as she sits around Cavett's psychedelics-inspired in-the-round set with Grace Slick, Marty Balin, and other members of Jefferson Airplane. One's never really sure if Cavett is even aware that Mitchell never made it to the gig because he introduces the whole show as something of a Woodstock after-party, and he never asks her how she felt about being forced to miss the event of her generation.

By the time Stills and Crosby show up for the last segment of the show, still clearly buzzed from the trip to Bethel, Mitchell has settled in as quiet observer—and good Canadian.

Cavett asks his guests about the intersection of celebrity and politics, given Woodstock's highly politicized peace message in the face of Vietnam.

"Have you ever been asked to endorse a political candidate the way actors and certain singers do?" Cavett asks. Crosby answers: "We usually try not to. How many of them have you ever seen that you would endorse?" Cavett wears a self-effacing grin as Mitchell pipes up with a mention of our sexiest prime minister: "I would sing for Pierre Trudeau." Cavett finds this quaint: "I guess everyone knows you're from Canada. Your work is sort of unpolitical, in general. Isn't it?" Mitchell seems to ignore the diminishing comment about the content of her work. "Well, yeah. I sing mostly about love and things that I can understand. I don't understand politics, mainly because in Canada, we never do anything that political. The biggest political news that I can remember ever there was the choosing of the flag," she says. "That took three years and they finally chose one that none of us like...oh well." Cavett comes back with a global-political quip: "But we're still here... South of you, protecting your border."

Cavett seems a little lost for the better part of the broadcast, but few people in show business could wear befuddlement—or, for that matter, a safari shirt—with as much charm. He wades into a discussion of the concert by asking Stills and Crosby how it felt. For a few seconds, they talk about fatigue and weather, and then Stills—famously (because everything around Woodstock seems to be famous at this point)—gestures to his pant leg and proclaims: "I still have my mud."

In subsequent interpretations of this broadcast—and there are many—Mitchell is described as "envious" as she looks over at Stills's still-dirty jeans.

Envy is a strong word, and despite the emerald green dress she wore for the occasion, she doesn't look all that green with it. She looks like the iconic folk hero who won over the masses with her earnest emotion and masterful, image-laden lyrics.

In an interview with Dave Zimmer, author of *Crosby, Stills & Nash: The Authorized Biography*, Mitchell says she was forced to sit on the other side of the performer/audience divide for the first time in years: "I was one of the fans. I was put in the position of being a kid who couldn't make it. So I was glued to the media."[9]

Marshall McLuhan said the spoken word was the first technology by which man was able to let go of his environment in order to grasp it in a new way; language was our creative means of finding distance and building order from the chaos of existence. He extended the same thinking into the age of the electronic narrative, so when Mitchell says she was "glued to the media" because it represented her only portal into what would prove to be an historic event, she was able to grasp it in a way that people who actually made it to Bethel could not.

"The deprivation of not being able to go provided me with an intense angle on Woodstock," she told Zimmer.

At the time I was going through a kind of born-again Christian trip, not that I went to any church, I'd given up on Christianity at an early age at Sunday school. But suddenly, as performers, we were in the position of having so many people look to us for leadership, and for some unknown reason I took it seriously and decided I needed a guide and leaned on God. So I was a little "God-mad" at the time, for lack of a better term, and I had been saying to myself 'Where are the modern miracles?' Woodstock, for some reason, impressed me as being a modern miracle.

Mitchell said she was moved by the fact that so many people managed to get along. "For a herd of people that large to cooperate so well, it was pretty remarkable and there was tremendous optimism. So I wrote the song 'Woodstock' out of these feelings, and the first three times I performed it in public I burst into tears because it brought back the intensity of the experience and was so moving." One of those first three performances was at the Big Sur celebration, and although you can't see tears streaming down her face, the emotion in her voice is palpable as she hits the final, haunting notes.

THE PEAK EXPERIENCE

The feelings Mitchell describes in the creation of the song "Woodstock" could be interpreted as proof of what psychologist Abraham Maslow described as "the peak experience," where the ego disappears and one transcends self: "There is a fusion with the reality being observed, and a oneness where there was a twoness, an integration of some sort of the self with the non-self. There is universally reported a seeing of formerly hidden truth, a revelation in the strict sense, a stripping away of veils, and finally almost always the whole experience is experienced as bliss, ecstasy, rapture, exaltation."[10]

Peak experience creations are usually so steeped in universal truth, they resonate beyond the artist herself and ring for the masses. Mitchell's "Woodstock" captured the zeitgeist of the Summer of Love so completely that even Crosby—a highly accomplished and altogether prolific songwriter—admitted he tried to write his own song about the occasion after returning from Bethel, but there was no way he could match Mitchell's visual precision or emotional accuracy—which is kind of strange, given that he was actually there, in the primordial mud, and Mitchell was holed up with an antsy Geffen in urban Manhattan.

Whether it was loving homage or merely great marketing instincts, Crosby and his newly formed band recorded Mitchell's "Woodstock" shortly afterward on their debut album *Déjà Vu*. It was the only track on the LP that the entire band recorded together (the other tracks had each band member recording his own part in a separate session), and it reached number eleven on *Billboard*'s pop singles chart in 1970. The CSNY cover is considered the more "radio-friendly" version, but there are some who find it altogether unlistenable, including Iggy Pop: "I hated 'Woodstock.' Still hate it," he's quoted as saying in Neil Young's biography. "It's the worst. Crosby, Stills, Nash. Just so loathsome. Not music," said Pop, earning his "naughty little doggie" moniker.

The song went on to be recorded by others, including Matthews Southern Comfort (whose version hit number one on the U.K. album charts the same year), as well as Led Zeppelin, who incorporated fragments of the song into their live versions of "Dazed and Confused" (including a rather inspired take at a Vancouver show in March 1975 at the Pacific Coliseum that can be found on rare bootlegs).

Although Zeppelin's version of the tune is currently the subject of copyright litigation,[11] hearing Robert Plant howl, "We are stardust, we are golden, and we've got got yes we've got got to people yeah ooooh yeah ooooh yeah ooooh get back to the garden, back to the mamamama garden, back to the garden, garden, garden," as Jimmy Page caresses the strings of his electric guitar with a bow is beautiful, kick-ass proof of just how deeply Mitchell's portrait of the event sank into the popular consciousness.

Seminal Yippie and self-appointed generational spokesman Abbie Hoffman may have coined the term "Woodstock Nation," and god knows how many hundreds of thousands have created their own fantasies about attending the event, but there can be no question that over the course of one week-end watching TV, Joni Mitchell wrote the words that would signify an entire generation's ethos.

"Getting back to the garden" was more than a reference to rediscovering the lost innocence of Adam and Eve, who were tossed from the Garden of Eden for Eve's pursuit of knowledge. For countless souls—Mitchell foremost among them—it represented the genuine potential of humankind.

Condensing the thoughts of the Woodstock poster pil-grim, who appears in Mike Wadleigh's Woodstock movie as he marches down the clogged roads of the Catskills with his girlfriend, Mitchell captured the emotional and existential reality of the moment in her lyrics:

> I feel myself a cog in somethin' turning.
> And maybe it's the time of year,
> Yes and maybe it's the time of man.
> And I don't know who I am,
> But life is for learning.

It's brilliant poetry, but it's also cunning reportage, because the unidentified pilgrim addressed the same thoughts when he was approached by a man with a movie camera. He talked about what brought him to White Lake at that moment in time: "My father was asking whether I was in a Communist training camp or something... and I could understand where he's coming from. Because he's an immi-grant... he came over here to better himself and... make it better for me... He can't understand why [the things that have value to him] have [no] value to me. But then again, he does have the wisdom to allow me to be who I am. I will, by doing what I'm doing, learn for myself how to live. And that's what he wants me to do."[12]

Even the "billion year old carbon" reference is of the moment. Human beings were becoming aware of their place in the universe as a result of space exploration. The first moon landing happened on July 20, 1969, just weeks before Richie Havens took to the Woodstock stage and spontaneously composed his "Freedom" chant in the waning hours of that fateful Friday afternoon of August 15, 1969.

For a fantastic and all-too-brief moment, anything seemed possible. The sins of man—at this time symbolized by the "unjust and undeclared" and much-protested war in Vietnam—appeared to be cleansable as masses of young people converged on a single locale without destroying property or killing each other.

Even as esteemed broadcaster Walter Cronkite, the "most trusted man in America," mused in I Can Hear It Now/The Sixties, his radio salute to the decade: "The festival was declared a disaster area, and if there had been a riot, the commission that would have investigated it would have blamed negligent planning by the promoters... Yet there was no violence, relatively little illness for a population of this size. Three people died, two were born and in a rare happening, even the police got rave notices."[13]

More than forty years later, people are still a little dazzled at the idea that half-a-million young people could gather in a single location without violence. While I was writing this book, nineteen people died in Germany at the Love Parade, where anywhere between 100,000 and 1.4 million (the reports are that disparate, with network of record Deutsche Welle going for somewhere in between, at 500,000) were gathered to let DJs spin them into a substance-induced hypnosis. Also, my hometown of Vancouver erupted into a riot after our hockey team lost the last game of the Stanley Cup playoffs. The thousands who had gathered downtown for the party were all too eager to light Molotov cocktails and torch cop cars. Half a century hence, peace and love isn't part of the public agenda—unless you can cross-pollinate it with branded merchandise.

Back when musicians played real instruments on real stages, in three real dimensions, security was a real concern. And for then-governor Nelson Rockefeller, it was looking scary enough in Bethel to call in the National Guard to clear out the longhairs at gunpoint. But for some unfathomable reason—given the polarization between the older and younger generation—he ceded to the judgement of the twentysomething, independently wealthy promoters, who accepted full responsibility for what would happen over the next three days. In so many ways, everything that happened at Woodstock seems destined, as though the world was crying out for an emblematic moment of beauty and transcendence that proved humanity could be redeemed and we really could go "back to the garden."

WEEDING TRUTH AND FICTION

The only notable commentator of the era who saw Woodstock as an event but did not ascribe to it its own mythology was anthropologist Margaret Mead. In a 1970 issue of *Redbook* magazine, she writes: "I do not think the Woodstock festival was a 'miracle'—something that can happen only once. Nor do I think that those who took part in it established a tradition overnight—a way of doing things that sets the pattern of future events. It was confirmation that this generation has, and realizes it has, its own identity."[14]

This is an important observation because it adds the dimension of personal identity to myth: by following certain mythological strands, we can arrive at our own cave of meaning. Mead continues with a reference to, of all things, Jesus's Sermon on the Mount: "No one can say what the outcome will be; it is too new," she writes. "Responding to their gentleness, I think of the words 'Consider the lilies of the field...' and hope that we—and they themselves—can continue to trust the community of feeling that made so many of us say of those three days, 'It was beautiful.'"

Given what we know now, Mead's reluctance to anoint Woodstock's pilgrims as "messiahs en masse" seems rather astute. That doesn't mean Woodstock and its ethos didn't give us a lasting legacy of goodness. They did. The modern environmental movement can trace its thickening roots back to Bethel, especially in light of the fact that the first Earth Day took place just a few months later, in April 1970, as did the formation of Greenpeace—which launched itself with a fundraiser called Amchitka, hosted by none other than Joni Mitchell and then-lover James Taylor.

Somewhat ironically, but not altogether unexpectedly, one of the biggest critics of the Woodstock generation has been Mitchell herself. In a 2008 interview for *Mojo* magazine with former *Los Angeles Times* music critic and editor Robert Hilburn, Mitchell called her peers "the greediest generation in the history of America" and railed against the apathy and arrogance of those who swore to fix the system before they acquired the reins to power.

> In their youth, my generation was ready to change the world, but when the baton was passed to them in the seventies, they fell into a mass depression because all revolutionaries are quick to demolish and slow to fix... they kind of degenerated into the greediest generation in the history

of America. The hippie, yippie, yuppie transition from the sixties to the seventies to the greedy eighties and Ronald Reagan—my generation dropped the baton and spawned this totally lacklustre [next] generation... Machiavelli said, 'People don't know what to do with peace. It always degenerates into fashion and fornication'... and that's what we have. We are not building the kind of strong people in this third generation that we are going to need for the catastrophes that lie ahead. They aren't getting any ethical instruction. I'm reluctant to say 'moral' because... things that are done in the name of morality are completely diabolical."[15]

five

BUSINESS AND BULLSHIT

> "Businessmen drink my blood, like the kids in art
> school said they would."
> ARCADE FIRE, "Ready to Start," *The Suburbs*

RECONCILING THE NEEDS of art and commerce is probably the single biggest problem facing any artist—even the fire-hardened Joni Mitchell. Despite having her hands on the joystick of her career, Mitchell found herself in crisis several times as she faced the dissociating demons of fame, the vampires of the music business, and the media Minotaur. Fortunately, she found a coping mechanism early: she established distance from destructive doubt, intellectually, spiritually, and geographically.

Mitchell has reportedly cancelled more shows than she ever gave, and she's retired from the business so frequently not even she can keep count of her departures from the poker table. Yet, for every hand she decided to play, she finessed a win—maybe not on the commercial side of the spiritual spreadsheet but definitely on the creative one. Joni Mitchell never sold out to satisfy business interests, or her own ego. So while the Rolling Stones sold out to Microsoft, Bob Dylan sold out to the bank, and Leonard Cohen would be happy to sell a "Hallelujah" to just about anyone, Mitchell's music has yet to stump product. This creative stubbornness, which boils down to trusting one's inner self, is the most important creative lesson of all—but one we often silence because we're told money and financial success are more important. But greed, as Mitchell sings in "All I Want," "is the unraveling" that robs us of "all the joy that could be."

THE BIZ BOYS: ROBERTS AND GEFFEN

Before Joni Mitchell made it to Carnegie Hall and *The Dick Cavett Show* in 1969, she'd been playing in coffee houses for the better part of seven years—ever since her first professional gig at Saskatoon's Louis Riel café on Halloween Night 1962. By the time she left Chuck Mitchell and headed to New York City in 1966, she was already pretty self-sufficient. She was booking her own shows and had saved up a few hundred bucks in the bank. She's said she'd never felt more in control of her own destiny. Moreover, she was having fun playing the circuit—probably because she didn't have a huge ego stake in the performance side. "I was ready to retire from the beginning," she explained in 2000 on the CBC TV program *SpeakEasy*. "Because I got waylaid into music, you know. [But] I decided that I did enjoy playing in coffee houses and realized that it was much more lucrative than working in women's wear—which was the only other thing I knew how to do. I decided to look for a manager."[1]

The first person she looked to was Albert Grossman, Dylan's manager. He took her out for sushi, but the two didn't have a great rapport: he told Mitchell she was too "domestic" for the biz. Mitchell continued on her own until a demo tape of her music ended up in the hands of Buffy Sainte-Marie, who had a management deal with Chartoff-Winkler, where a young pothead named Elliot Roberts (née Rabinowitz) was working. "I'd been carrying a tape of Joni's with me and I asked Elliot to listen to it. He did, then he went to see her show [at the Village's Cafe au Go Go]," said Sainte-Marie. "That's how Elliot and Joni met—through me, I guess."[2]

Once Roberts caught a glimpse of Mitchell, he was entranced. "I stay for two sets and after that I go back to Joan and say, 'You kill me. I think I'm in love with you. I'd do anything to manage you," Roberts told Jimmy McDonough. The smitten Roberts made an insane business offer: to tag along unpaid, without any percentage obligations, just to see if they were copasetic. Turns out the two were closet reefer fans and shared an oblique sense of humour. They hit it off. "I grinned so wide [onstage] that my upper lip stuck to my gums. My mouth was dry from pot," said Mitchell. "Elliot was the first one to pick up on it. He started doing shtick in the audience and made me laugh all the more. So I said—Okay—I'll cut ya in. Just for the jokes, y'know. I was his first racehorse."[3]

Mitchell and Roberts would be business buddies for the better part of twenty years, and it's largely thanks to Roberts that Mitchell's career arc is so bold and unbroken, because he helped her secure the dollar side of the creative balance sheet. Shortly after Mitchell's songs were being recorded and pulling in coin for her publishing company (Siquomb—standing for She Is Queen Undisputedly Of Mind Beauty, no joke), Mitchell was getting offers from other labels, such as the folk pinnacle Vanguard. "Slave labour,"[4] is how Mitchell described the deal, so when she hooked up with Roberts, she asked him to separate her publishing rights from Chuck—essentially finalizing the terms of their divorce. She also empowered Roberts to negotiate that monumental deal with Warner's Reprise label, the boutique branch founded by Frank Sinatra. "Joan managed me for the first year. I didn't know about management—I never thought of negotiating," Roberts relates in McDonough's book. "Joni was very gracious—I made a ton of mistakes, but it was fine with her. She didn't give a shit. In my career, Joni was my big influence. Joni taught me how you build a legend—that singer-songwriters were gonna happen, that you didn't need singles. Joni taught me everything."[5]

Roberts was a close friend of another self-created legend who would be the commercial yin to Mitchell's creative yang: David Geffen. If Roberts did indeed learn everything he knew from Mitchell, then Geffen and Mitchell could have opened a boutique for forged brass testes. After reading about their stormy partnership, it's hard to tell which of the two former business pals was tougher.

Geffen's career started, somewhat infamously, in the mailroom of the William Morris Agency. He had falsified his resumé to get the job, claiming he'd received a degree in theatre arts from UCLA. After hearing that another mailroom slave had been fired for lying, he steamed open everyone's mail, every morning, looking for the letter that would have exposed him. He opened it, got his brother to forge a believable affirmation of attendance, and voila! Problem solved. From the beginning, David Geffen discovered that dishonesty was the secret to success in show business. Another important skill was sucking up to people and making them feel important and valued. He was good at both.

Eventually he and Roberts built up a talent roster and went into the management business together. Geffen would spin it off into a record label, Asylum, which signed the likes of his protege Laura Nyro, as well as Neil Young, the Eagles, and Jackson Browne.

The son of a girdle saleswoman who called him "King David," Geffen was just as ambitious as Mitchell, and the two were so simpatico they even lived together in the same Bel Air house once owned by Julie Andrews and Blake Edwards.

They shared this creative nest until the relationship blew up. In his Geffen biography, *The Operator*, Tom King writes that "Mitchell's affection for Geffen had been seriously diminished from the moment Bob Dylan had come into Geffen's life. She had grown jealous of and angry at the attention Geffen lavished on his newest signing. A year earlier, Geffen had told people that Mitchell was the best concert performer in America. But now, as she was out on tour promoting *Court and Spark*, the album that contained [the David Geffen–inspired] 'Free Man in Paris,' she stewed as Geffen seemed to care only about Dylan's live performances."[6]

Geffen's relationship with Dylan didn't last long either, but he can take credit for the 1974 reunion tour with Dylan and the Band. It was also Geffen who had a crying fit after the tour wrapped in L.A., and instead of thanking Geffen for all his hard work in orchestrating such a complex collection of egos and logistics, Dylan thanked "the legendary guy who put this whole tour together… Bill Graham."

Mitchell accused Geffen of non-payment on royalties shortly after he'd created his own label, Geffen Records. Geffen's relationship with Elliot Roberts exploded around the same time, when Geffen decided to sue Neil Young for making "uncharacteristic records" in the wake of the jewel-case coffin called *Trans* (1982), Young's first foray into electronics. The L.A. mogul didn't seem to care about alienating his former "friends," and the last thing he's quoted as saying about Mitchell is: "If I didn't talk to her for the rest of my life, I wouldn't miss her for a minute."[7]

FAME AND FORTUNE

Joni Mitchell isn't full of kind words for the business, or its moguls. "They're not looking for talent," she told James Reginato at W magazine in 2002. "They're looking for a look and a willingness to cooperate... And I've never had a willingness to cooperate."[8]

Indeed, Mitchell has been called "difficult" several times and seems to revel in her intransigence. I think this is the crucial misperception in the Mitchell story: her insistence on creative purity has made her appear standoffish and bitchy; she is the stereotypical "difficult artist" whose "stubbornness" appears self-indulgent.

"I don't know if the axiom about geniuses being the toughest artists to work with has ever been proven or not, but I can gladly attest that Joni Mitchell's overwhelming artistic genius is not surpassed by anyone in our time," said Howie Klein, then-president of Reprise Records, when he presented Mitchell with her 2002 Grammy Award for lifetime achievement. He continued:

> This Lifetime Achievement Award isn't the result of a popularity contest and may in some ways be more significant than the various individual Grammys she has been awarded for specific work over the years. This recognition of Joni Mitchell aims to celebrate the achievements of a rare person whose creative gifts have profoundly impacted and enriched the collective consciousness of humanity. She is thoroughly original and her work—as a sophisticated poet,

a pioneering musician, a powerful and unique vocal stylist, and a brilliant renaissance woman—continues to inspire countless artists around the world.[9]

It's not often you see a record industry executive credit an artist with enriching "the collective consciousness of humanity," unless he/she is trying to sign an act by blowing smoke up its pants and the promise of hookers and coke didn't already work. But there was Klein, acknowledging her as a genius and contributor to the music community and the world at large.

Mitchell is widely recognized for her unflagging integrity in an age of fizzy-pop Britneys and Mileys, and her name will no doubt live on for centuries because it's based in genuine accomplishment, not sex, scandal, or overproduced pop singles. More to the point, Mitchell moved forward in the music industry without being obsessed with fame. If anything, she resisted the tug of celebrity because it interfered with the creative impulse.

"I never liked the big stage. I liked the coffee houses. I never liked the idea of separating myself from people, or being elevated. Maybe it's Canadian! You know, stick your head above the crowd and we'll be glad to lop it off!" she told Jana Lynne White of *SpeakEasy*. "But something in me made me not like the separation. As the stages got higher and higher, the fickleness of the crowds, suddenly this was being taken seriously and there were critics sitting out there," she said. "I disliked the formalization of it as it went to the big stage and this need for perfection. In the coffee houses it was so experimental, so casual, so friendly. I could jump off the stage and sit down with them, stay at people's houses, go out to dinner. There was no inequity. I remember the first night when I heard someone suck in their breath when I went by. And I ran! It filled me so full of adrenaline that I ran for about six blocks in the opposite direction. 'That's Joni Mitchell (gasp!)' Boom! I was outta there!"[10]

In the face of fame, Mitchell's fight-or-flight survival mechanism usually resulted in flight. "I like to retire a lot," she told Malka Marom in a 1974 feature interview for *Maclean's*.[11] Mitchell first retired from show business at twenty-seven—an age with mythological significance in the world of rock 'n' roll. The "27 Club" was formed when Brian Jones, Jimi Hendrix, Janis Joplin, and Jim Morrison died at that age—all within the span of two years (1969–71), around the very time Mitchell stepped away from performance. Synchronistically, but sadly not surprisingly, Amy Winehouse joined the 27 Club during the writing of this book.

Mitchell says she's always been more excited by the creative burst of light than the suffocating darkness. She says she's never been a follower of the "suicide-chic" school of rock and that self-destruction isn't cool—or as she notes in the lyrics to "Blue," "everybody's saying that hell's the hippest way to go, well I don't think so."

As she once told the *New York Times*: "I cleared out the psychology and religious departments of several bookstores, searching for some explanation for what I was going through."[12]

In her *Maclean's* interview, Mitchell told Malka (as the performer/interviewer preferred to be called) she had "difficulty at one point accepting my affluence, and my success and even the expression of it seemed to me distasteful at one time, like to suddenly be driving a fancy car."

Success created a split in Mitchell's creative soul: "I had a lot of soul-searching to do as I felt somehow or other that living in elegance and luxury canceled creativity. I still had that stereotyped idea that success would deter creativity, would stop the gift, luxury would make you too comfortable and complacent and that the gift would suffer from it. But I found the only way that I could reconcile with myself and my art was to say this is what I'm going through now, my life is changing and I am too."

Mitchell understood the importance of creative evolution, which is why she's always standing next to her own self-portrait, ready to touch up the flaws or make them more obvious—depending on what makes for a better picture. Mitchell is complicit in the pop idol process. As she told Vic Garbarini, she was a willing storyteller. "First of all, the pop star is very self promotional. You know, 'I'm DA GREATEST LOVER, BAYBEEEEE!' The nature of the beast is to present yourself in the early years as some kind of teen idol," she said. "Initially I wrote those extremely personal songs like 'Marcie' as a response to the big roars from the audience. I would stand up there receiving all this massed adulation and affection and think, 'What are you all doing, you don't even know me.'"[13]

Mitchell's words echo last chapter's opening quote from Keith Richards, who felt fame made things absurd and removed the frame of individual meaning. It just wasn't real.

"Affection like that usually doesn't come without some kind of intimacy, like in a one-on-one relationship. So I thought, you better know who you're grinning at up here," said Mitchell. "And I began to unveil more and more of my inner conflicts and feelings. Then, after about four years... I guess it's just the nature of the press, having built you up, they feel it's time to tear you down," she continued. "So I began to receive a lot of unfavorable attention. At the same time it became harder and harder to sing these intimate songs at rock festivals. The bigger the audience I drew, the more honest I wanted to be," she added with a laugh.

Even while that was happening, Mitchell articulated the desire to ditch the iconographic imagery, telling *Rolling Stone's* Larry LeBlanc in 1971 that she was "isolated, starting to feel like a bird in a gilded cage. [Fame] has its rewards but I don't know what the balance is—how much good and how much damage there is in my position." The conflict between outward politesse and inner truth is something Mitchell feels instantly. "Inside, I'm thinking: 'You're being phony. You're smiling phony. You're being a star," she said, equating celebrity with artifice.[14]

"But if you're watching yourself over your own shoulder all of the time," she continued, "and if you're too critical of what you're doing; you can make yourself so unhappy. As a human, you're always messing up, always hurting people's feelings quite innocently... There are a lot of people you want to talk to all at once. I get confused and maybe I'll turn away and leave someone standing and I'll think, 'Oh dear,'" she said, proving her good Canadian manners had remained intact. All the same, "I've changed a lot," she said. "I'm getting very defensive, I'm afraid."

Complicating her relationship with fame were the diehard fans who devoted themselves to following her every move. Some of them were beyond ardent: they mistook the music, the persona, and the image of Joni Mitchell as pure truth. One fan camped outside her house for years, believing she had sent him a personal message about his dead sister in the song "This Flight Tonight." It all took a toll on the woman who grew up beneath an open sky.

Many of her observations about fame and its spiritual cost came out in the music, in songs such as "For Free" and "For the Roses," both of which address the dangers of public adoration to the creative soul. In "For Free" Mitchell writes about a clarinet player on the street who can play "real good" but is ignored because he's not famous. Meanwhile, she's living it up in limos because she's been on TV:

> I've got a black limousine
> And two gentlemen
> Escorting me to the halls...
> But the one man band
> By the quick lunch stand
> He was playing real good for free
>
> Nobody stopped to hear him
> Though he played so sweet and high
> They knew he had never
> Been on their TV
> So they passed his music by

Mitchell echoes the same sentiments to *Sounds* magazine's Penny Valentine in a description of seeing a "good friend" skyrocket to success (either Jackson Browne or James Taylor, most likely). "I was watching his career and thinking that as his woman at that time I should be able to support him. And yet it seemed to me that I could see the change in his future would remove things from his life. I felt like having come through, having had a small taste of success, and having seen the consequences of what it gives you and what it takes away in terms of what you *think* it's going to give you—well, I just felt I was in no position to help," she says. "But everything I saw him going through I thought was ludicrous, because I'd thought it was ludicrous when I'd done it," she recalls. "Like, go after it, but remember the days when you sat and made up tunes for yourself and played in small clubs where there was still some contact and when people came up and said they loved a song, you were really glad they loved it. After a while, when people come up, it begins to sound hollow," she concludes.[15]

When Mitchell was just a teenager, she almost seemed to prophesy the effects that fame would have on her. For a school assignment she wrote a poem about the celebrity couple of her day, Bobby Darin and Sandra Dee, called "The Fishbowl." She recited some lines of it for biographer Timothy White: "The fishbowl is a world diverse / where fishermen with hooks that dangle / from the bottom reel up their catch / on gilded bait without a fight. / Pike, pickerel, bass, the common fish / ogle through distorting glass / see only glitter, glamour, gaiety / and weep for fortune lost. / Envy the goldfish? Why? / His bubbles are breaking 'round the rim / while silly fishes faint for him."[16]

Mitchell says she always felt highly aware of the compromises fame necessitates, which is why she still finds it odd that she became a public performer in the first place. "It's very peculiar that I ended up in this game because I knew that I was more of a private person," she told White. "Maybe I don't handle adrenaline very well, but even the applause was hard. I know I have adrenal problems now, and I'm hypoglycemic—but back then I didn't. So my animal sense was to run offstage! Many a night I would be out onstage, and the intimacy of the songs against the raucousness of this huge beast that is an audience felt very weird," she said. "I was not David to that Goliath... I had to adjust to the din of that much attention."[17]

Mitchell writes about the din and the lingering, hollow emptiness that goes along with it in the song that really gets to the nub of the fame dilemma, "For the Roses": "Off to the airport / Your name's in the news / Everything's first class," she writes. "The lights go down / And it's just you up there / Getting them to feel like that." As in "For Free," she contrasts the fame with the original artistic impulse: "Remember the days when you used to sit / And make up your tunes for love / And pour your simple sorrow / To the soundhole and your knee / And now you're seen / On giant screens / And at parties for the press / And for people who have slices of you / From the company." The contradiction of loathing her own celebrity is not lost on Mitchell: "I guess I seem ungrateful / With my teeth sunk in the hand / That brings me things / I really can't give up just yet."

The imagery in the lyrics tells the whole story of where Mitchell was at, and pretty much remains, with the fame game: she sees it as a sort of martyrdom, where you're hammered to the cross and thrown up in public view for others to adore, or criticize, or maybe just gawk at. She sees the whole picture, where the artist becomes the centrepiece for a fancy party and a nice bauble for business folk to flaunt, but all the music industry really cares about is money.

Bitching about the music business is nothing new, but what makes Mitchell's poetic whining remarkable is how much responsibility she assumes for her own unhappiness. She even told Timothy White: "I started this thing, all this star machinery 'that brings me the things I really can't give up yet.' That was the dilemma. And I threatened to quit all the time, but it's, hey, you're in show business until you're in the poor house! [laughs] You either stay up there, or you begin your decline and the vultures come and pick the last little bit as you go down. As your money diminishes, so does your ability to buy good lawyers to fight the monsters."[18] Mitchell recognizes she's been a willing partner in this particular devil's bargain, but she's also eager to deconstruct the dimensions of her iconography and destroy the god she's become. She does this through creative discipline, through her words—and, most of all, through her sense of humour.

When she was selected as one of *Rolling Stone*'s clutch of "Guitar Gods" in 1999, she laughed at the honour but asserted her one true talent. "I never emulated anybody. I'm driven to innovate," she wrote. "Am I a god? I'm a godette."[19]

This ability to tear herself down to a human scale is evident throughout her career. She says she wanted to use a drawing of a horse's ass as the cover of *For the Roses*—a nod to the so-called "winner's circle" at the track, where the winning pony is draped in roses. Clearly, at that time, Mitchell felt more like a horse's ass than a winning thoroughbred because she was having such a hard time reconciling the two sides of herself: her creative need for truth and her ego need for fame. "The title itself was facetious," she said. And although she never used the ass image as cover art, she did use it as a billboard ad in Los Angeles. "It was my joke on the Sunset Strip, the huge drawing of a horse with cars and glamour girls, and it had a balloon coming out of the horse's mouth which said, 'For the Roses.' But nobody got the message."

Mitchell frequently mourns the fact that few listeners, if any, really understand the point she's trying to make with her work. Many of her more creative expeditions have been greeted with arched eyebrows of dismay by the label executives, who really just have one goal in mind as they swivel in their corporate chairs: selling units. Writes James Reginato in *W*: "She accuses Reprise executives of ignorance. Since they have never heard of, for example, Edgar Allan Poe or Job, they don't get the references in her lyrics. 'And they think if they don't, nobody else will,' she says."[20] "It was the same frustration Van Gogh ... felt," she says. "Misunderstood."[21]

Yet, for all the challenges, Mitchell continued to create music, despite the "soul-selling" and "whorish" aspect of it all. She learned to survive creatively because she kept her inner kid alive. "You wonder about people who made a fortune, and you always think they drank it up or they stuck it up their nose," she told White. "That's not usually what brings on the decline. It's usually the battle to keep your creative child alive while keeping your business shark alive. You have to develop cunning, and shrewdness, and other things which are not well suited to the arts."[22]

INK STAINS

"Flee, my friend, into your solitude: I see you stung by poisonous flies. Flee to where the raw, rough breeze blows!

Flee into your solitude! You have lived too near the small and pitiable men. Flee from their hidden vengeance! Towards you they are nothing but vengeance.

No longer lift your arm against them! They are innumerable and it is not your fate to be a flyswat."

FRIEDRICH NIETZSCHE, "Of the Flies in the Marketplace," *Thus Spoke Zarathustra*

If there's a front line on the battle for fame and success, it's the media. The Fourth Estate and its myriad products provide the sponsor-paid bridge between the rich and famous and the great unwashed. Mitchell has always had an uneasy relationship with reporters and credits her first of many retirements, in part, to media burnout. In 1970, she decided to stop doing interviews because they seemed pointless and shallow. "All people seemed interested in was the music and the gossip. I felt then that the music spoke for itself and the gossip was unimportant," she told Valentine.[23] In fact, something happened to Mitchell in 1970 that forever changed her relationship with the media, but before we get there, let's begin this examination with a single incident.

In the summer of 2010, *Rolling Stone* editor Jann Wenner took to Twitter. One of his first tweets was: "I don't know who this Ke$ha girl is, but she reminds me of a young Joni Mitchell." Clearly, a long-standing feud between Mitchell and Wenner wasn't over—because comparing Mitchell to pop queen Ke$ha, who brushes "her teef wif a bottle of Jack" on the catchy and hugely successful but only marginally poetic "Tik Tok," seems like the prison version of homage: a shiv between the shoulder blades. Not only does Ke$ha use a crass dollar sign in her name, she can't even sing. Every tune featuring her vocals has been digitally pitch corrected, and you can hear it—the voice tracks frequently sound like they're emanating from the ass of R2-D2. Wenner was no doubt going for ironic and droll sarcasm, given how opposite Joni and Ke$ha are from a musical perspective, but he was probably also giving Mitchell a middle finger salute, because for the past forty years the two have been playing a fun game of "f-you, too!"

Before Wenner issued the last salvo over the Internet—at a time when Wenner, by the way, had all of twenty-something followers—Mitchell was the one who had the last slap—almost literally. According to Mitchell, she threw a drink in Wenner's face at some awards show and told him to "Kiss my ass!" According to unattributed accounts, Mitchell was struggling through a knot of fans without help from the security people, and Wenner smirked as she was getting pawed and prodded. Hard to imagine the editor of *Rolling Stone* as a fratboy brand of smartass, but the event is dramatized in one of the few feedback-laden tracks Mitchell's ever recorded, "Lead Balloon" (from *Taming the Tiger*, 1998). Although the title may suggest a strange nod to Led Zeppelin, it's not. The song is more of a meditation on the music business and how Mitchell believes her record sales were hurt by her war of words with the pulp bible of rock 'n' roll: "'Kiss my ass!' I said and I threw my drink / It came a-trickling down his business suit / Must be the Irish blood / Fight before you think... An angry man is just an angry man / But an angry woman / Bitch!" Mitchell laments needing "to ask him for a helping hand / It came with the heart / Of a Bonaparte / Of a frozen fish / It's his town / And that went down / Like a lead balloon."

It's a catchy tune with a kick-ass message, but no one outside her loyal fan base has probably even heard it. Mitchell hasn't had what they call "heavy rotation" since *Court and Spark* in the mid-1970s. She's been acutely aware of her absence on the airwaves. She's even been known to complain about it in public, and on the record, on those rare occasions when she actually does interviews. "Artists like Madonna spend a lot of money to get themselves on the radio," Mitchell told the *Globe and Mail*'s Christopher Guly in 1996. "It's sickening." She added: "I've been undervalued for a long time, and it leaves a bad taste in your mouth, you know. How would you like it if you've been doing your job—an excellent job, if I may be so bold—and no one plays you on the radio and no one plays your videos? I'm still in the game, but all the doors have been closed."[24]

Mitchell blames some of those closed doors on her "bad experiences" with the press. One former manager, Steve Macklam, said it's a matter of broken trust. "Joni's had her problems with the press. She's been saying that for years," he said. "She has trusted certain people, then they just go and betray that trust."[25] But not doing press is a huge liability in a world where visibility and ink generally translate into a thick black bottom line. When Mitchell entered the business in the 1960s, traditional media such as newspapers, magazines, radio, and TV were the only games in town. Mitchell's early press glowed. *Rolling Stone* called her the "Queen of Rock & Roll," and the male-dominated sphere of rock writers couldn't help but notice her long blond hair, her soft features, and her full lips. It was a communal crush, even without décolletage or a leather bustier—which now seem *de rigueur* for any young ingenue looking to make it in the business.

Then, in February 1971, things between Mitchell and the media took a turn for the worse when *Rolling Stone* named Mitchell "Old Lady of the Year" and listed a number of her supposed flames, including David Crosby and Graham Nash. They also, apparently, named her the "Queen of El-Lay."

According to the "Joni Myth," created over the decades through mountains of press clippings and magnetic tape, Mitchell's hate-on for *Rolling Stone* started with the "Old Lady of the Year" comment, which, she was told, also featured a dynamic flow chart of her rumoured sexual conquests. Since then, people have referred to the "love chart" for half a century. It's now such an inherent part of the Joni narrative that some writers, looking to rephrase the whole thing in an original way, have changed the meaning of the slight— with one reporter saying she'd been called a "groupie" by Wenner's minions.[26] Given the differing reports of the infamous slag and its historic significance in the Joni story, I went a-lookin' for that graph with its alleged flowers, hearts, and dotted lines. I bought the complete *Rolling Stone* database on CD-ROM, which features every page of the magazine in its original layout. After arduously flipping the virtual pages for days, I finally found the "Old Lady of the Year" reference, which appeared in the New Year's edition of what was then still a newsprint tabloid. The writers of the magazine handed out awards to music personalities they felt merited a bit of backhanded ink. Given that the "Man of the Year" in 1971 was

Charles Manson, you'd think this gave Mitchell a much better ground for griping than did some brief and boring rundown of her sex life.

In truth, there is only a photograph of Mitchell with a cut-line next to it: "Old Lady of the Year: Joni Mitchell (for her friendships with David Crosby, Steve Stills, Graham Nash, Neil Young, James Taylor, et al.)"[27] This appears under a small photo of Mitchell in profile, surrounded by Grace Slick for "Immaculate Conception of the Year" (she was pregnant), as well as the tombstone covers for the recently deceased Janis Joplin and Jimi Hendrix.

Months later, I finally found the "love chart" with the hearts and arrows. On February 3, 1972, *Rolling Stone* published "Hollywood's Hot 100," featuring a chart of incestuous connections among the power hitters. The chart featured everyone from Herb Alpert to Rita Coolidge and chronicled the degrees of separation between the members of the music elite. Mitchell does appear on this graph—as a set of lips, surrounded by the words "kiss kiss."

The fact that she got so much media attention could have been seen as a feather in her cap, but she immediately felt defensive—even though she never actually saw the offending article with her own eyes. The information had been presented to her through friends, and she felt the editors of the youth mag were making a moral judgement—and in some ways, they were. Essentially, they were calling her a "slut" without actually saying it. In the seventies, you were a man-hating feminist who stood up for herself, a prude who wouldn't put out, or the alleged "Queen of El-Lay."

By the time Mitchell spoke to the *Toronto Star* in 1974, she was wary of anyone holding a steno pad and pencil: "Joni Mitchell has just been told there's a journalist in the hallway and she is not exactly enthusiastic about journalists," writes

Marci McDonald. "Now, Joni Mitchell extends a limp and wary wrist and makes it quite clear she doesn't do interviews anymore: 'I've had some bad experiences,' [Mitchell will] admit much later that night. 'And besides, I just don't find these things very interesting reading.'"[28]

Nearly a decade later, the "Joni hates the media" story was well established—as witnessed by her interview in 1983 with Vic Garbarini.[29] Garbarini prefaces his piece with a bit of background about trying to land an interview with the woman who was also called "the queen of hippie chic" and "the great Earth mother."

"Hi, got your letter!" says Mitchell. Garbarini asks why it took Mitchell two years to respond. "Oh, I liked your natural loose approach and the questions you raised about the creative process and inner growth," she says. "Sounded like we might have a decent conversation. I also like what you didn't want to ask me about." The reporter ventures to ask what they shouldn't talk about. "My romances!" she responds.

Mitchell probably didn't realize the media only cares about who you're fucking when you're young. TMZ doesn't obsess over middle-aged cougars. It only has time for the young and nubile, because as mythology tells us, the gods were all beautiful and immortal. Not even Madonna's sex life is all that sexy anymore now that she's perimenopausal. Garbarini focuses all of his attentions on Mitchell's art, calling her "an ace storyteller out of the Homeric tradition... conjuring up visionary landscapes of cinematic power that take the listener vicariously through the event. You emerge from the other side with the feeling that you've lived the event yourself and learned whatever lessons it inherently had to offer. Very exhilarating and a little spooky," he writes. "But then, artists have a predilection for that kind of thing." It's interesting to note how the balance of adjectives is now reserved for her creative gifts instead of her physical ones. She's being given the courtesy of growing old gracefully in the public eye.

In 1997, after another prolonged absence from the spotlight, in an interview with *Vanity Fair*, she circles back to the original slight. But Bill Flanagan assigns her a whole new role—one that has nothing to do with her looks, or her sex life: she is now the social observer, the gossipy matron at the great ball called show business. Mitchell uses colourful language to describe her feud with the paid interrogators in the press: "I love making records and I hate talking to the press. It's how Chairman Mao brainwashed China: it's Oriental torture. You're supposed to be this icon that transcends everything. 'Well, you should rise above that!' Nobody can rise above that! The cumulative psychological effect of being interrogated seven hours a day is how they break down hardened soldiers! Have dental work done at the same time and you're a prisoner of war."[30]

Later, she outlines the feud with *Rolling Stone* as one of the reasons why her entry into the Rock and Roll Hall of Fame came four years after she became eligible, prompting Flanagan to borrow a comment once reserved for Van Morrison: "Mitchell's capacity for holding a grudge is Serbian." When Flanagan mentions Wenner's name, Mitchell recoils and says that if Wenner had had anything to do with the selection process, she wouldn't have been inducted—even if she did make the cover of *Time* magazine in 1974. "*Rolling Stone* used to call me 'The Queen of Rock 'n' Roll.' Of course, there weren't that many of us. Me, Janis Joplin, one or two others passed the crown back and forth."

Flanagan describes Mitchell's commentary as "hilarious" and compares her to Dorothy Parker but then depicts a penitence of spirit. "The trouble is that, in print, her wisecracks can hurt others which makes Mitchell feel guilty later. So she is trying to curb her tongue," says Flanagan, concluding with Mitchell's own words of pop wisdom: "I don't want to be known as the Truman Capote of my generation."

PROTECTING THE CREATIVE SOUL—THE CAVE

Greta Garbo always felt she was misquoted on her famous "I want to be alone" line. She actually said "I want to be left alone"—and as far as she was concerned, there was a big difference. Garbo had no desire to move through life solo; she simply needed space from the public crush. Fame is exhausting, which is why most modern celebrities create a remote aerie where they can rest and regain a connection with their private, inner self. The sanest creators do this early. Robert Redford purchased his sprawling Sundance resort property in Utah after cashing in with Butch Cassidy, Celine Dion bought an island off Florida, and George Lucas built the Skywalker Ranch. Joni Mitchell did the same thing, because she has an almost reflexive drive for creative self-preservation. Instead of seeking numbness through drugs or other addictions (although she says she's tried everything—except heroin, "What's the point?"—and wrote "Song for Sharon" on coke), she fled into solitude and protected herself in a creative cocoon. Each time, she emerged from the chrysalis a new Joni with a new vision, a new sound, and a new purpose. This continual cycle of recreation is perhaps the greatest testament to her success as a creator because, unlike artists who become trapped in the velvet coffin of success, she resisted repetition and clichés—even the ones she gave birth to.

As she famously noted in impromptu stage banter that preceded her rendition of "The Circle Game" on the live album *Miles of Aisles* (1974):

That's one thing that's always been a major difference between, like, the performing arts to me, and being a painter, you know? Like a painter does a painting, and he does a painting. That's it, you know? He's had the joy of creating it, and he hangs it on some wall, and somebody buys it, and somebody buys it again, or maybe nobody buys it and it sits up in a loft somewhere until he dies—but nobody ever says to him, like nobody ever said to Van Gogh "Paint a *Starry Night*, again, man." You know, he painted it. That was it.

It's hard to turn your back on popularity, applause, financial reward, and sycophantic ego-stroking, because it all feels so good. It's candy for the immature soul but it's unhealthy and rots the creative root. Mitchell, somewhat miraculously given our culture's current insistence on empty fame and untalented nobodies, recognized this creative roach motel. It was the dark force of fame and reflected ego that pushed her to find the light of truth and molt, leaving her former selves behind like so much dead snakeskin. No wonder she says of her life's work: "I don't really think of this as a career, it's more like a journey."[31]

THE GREEK ODYSSEY

Every journey needs a destination, as well as a safe harbour, and Joni Mitchell found both after one of her first retirements, in 1970 (there's a *Rolling Stone* report of her retiring as early as 1969). She bought a chunk of real estate on British Columbia's rugged and romantically scenic Sunshine Coast. But before she set to work building her new, and decidedly ascetic, Canadian nest, Mitchell decided to take a year off and fly. She spent a large chunk of 1970 seeing places she'd long imagined to be magical. One place that had tremendous allure was Greece—in particular, a small Cretan village called Matala. The subject of a *Life* magazine article in 1968, Matala had become a destination for lost youth. You could live on $5 a day, sleep in a cave for nothing, and spend your time exchanging free love, singing songs around a campfire, and gawking with disgust at the raw meat in the local market. Mitchell decided to make the romantic trek to the land of Homer with a friend, a rather aptly named poet from Ottawa we know only as Penelope (the same name as the wife of Odysseus).

"Matala was full of kids from all over the world who were seeking the same kind of thing I was but they couldn't get away from... ummm," Mitchell told Penny Valentine in 1972. "I mean they may as well have been in an apartment in Berkeley as in a cave there because the lifestyle continued the same wherever they were. And the odd thing to me was that after my initial plans to be accepted into the home of a Greek family fell apart, we came to this very scene—the very scene we were trying to escape from—and it seemed very attractive to us."

Mitchell hoped to escape the demon of her fame and celebrity, which had just been cemented with a Grammy win for best folk performance or recording for *Clouds* as well as her first gold record with *Ladies of the Canyon*. She was tired and disconnected, and had just cancelled two pretty big concert dates: Carnegie Hall in New York City and Constitution Hall in D.C. She needed to rekindle her creative fire, and the very birthplace of western civilization seemed like a good place to start.

The plan was noble enough, but the angel of inspiration came to her in the form a "red red rogue" and a "bright red devil" who kept her in the increasingly touristy town. Cary Raditz was an American bon vivant who had done a variety of odd jobs, including art gallery dealer in Chapel Hill, before landing with the hippie hordes in Matala. He was the big man in town because he had the best hash. He also cooked in the local café and proved rather rude to Mitchell and her pal when they first arrived. The bad attitude won Mitchell's interest—perhaps because she was looking for anyone who wouldn't kiss her ass.

"He's got sort of a flaming red personality, and flaming red hair and a flaming red appetite for red wine and he fancied himself to be a gourmet cook," Mitchell says. "He announced to my girlfriend and I the day that we met him that he was the best cook in the area, and he actually was working at the time I met him—he was working at this place called the Delphini restaurant [AKA the Mermaid Café]—until it exploded, singed half of the hair off of his beard and his legs, and scorched his turban, melted down his golden earrings."[32]

With a new designer handbag laden with sketching supplies and a gorgeous new instrument, a dulcimer handcrafted by L.A.-based luthier Joellen Lapidus, Mitchell soon shacked up with the twenty-four-year-old former ad copywriter from North Carolina for a creatively enriched six weeks of cave dwelling and hash-smoking in one of the sandstone hollows along the shores. He was the inspiration for her song "Carey."

In Matala, Mitchell also met another oddball named Yogi Joe, who later lectured Mitchell on the importance of friendship when he crashed the Isle of Wight Festival—and became one of the more interesting parts of the documentary film about the pop party that went wrong. Mitchell was thirsty for eccentrics, and Matala was a freak parade of rich material. "Variety is the spice of life," says Mitchell, ever the explorer of emotion. "I prefer fun, all in all. But the light without the dark, and even negative situations, are not as valuable. And great beauty can come out of the negative. If you go through a bad

space in your life and you're able to turn it into something—
that's a wonderful thrill. You've turned it around in the yin
yang of it all; you've made the best of a bad situation."[33]

CREATIVE ITHACA

The trip to Greece was therapeutic to Mitchell's creative soul
and paved the way for what is arguably the best album of all
time: Blue speaks to the artistic soul in everyone because
it comes from an undeniably true place. Proving that great
art and suffering often go hand in hand, the rawness of the
record came at a price: Mitchell had just blown up her life.
She thought she could be happy with the safe and supportive
Graham Nash. But she needed her freedom. Nash wanted to
marry her, but she couldn't be "crown-and-anchored." By the
time Mitchell got back to North America, she'd already sent
him a formal goodbye note via telegram that read: "If you
hold sand too tightly in your hand it will run through your
fingers." She also had an album's worth of new material. Blue
begins on a decidedly Odyssean note: "I am on a lonely road
and traveling, traveling, traveling, looking for something.
What can it be?"

Mitchell says one of the things she learned on her Euro-
pean journey was the importance of the moment and
revelling in the experiences as they unfold because the rest
is simply beyond one's control. The destination doesn't really
matter. And, in most cases, it's a disappointment.

As she told Penny Valentine upon her return to the public
eye in 1972:

> I think that there's a new thing to discover in the devel-
> opment of fulfillment. I don't think it necessarily means
> trading the search, which is more exciting than the actual ful-
> fillment... drifting through lives quickly and cities quickly

you know, you never really get to understand a person or a
place very deeply... you can be in a place until you feel completely familiar with it, or stay with a person until you may
feel very bored. Then all of a sudden, if you're there long
enough, it'll just open up and flash you all over again. But
so many people who are searching and travelling come to
that point where it's stealing out on them and they just can't
handle that and have to move on.[34]

Conjuring a line from Kris Kristofferson's "Me and Bobby
McGee," she said, "freedom is deceptive... just another [word]
for nothing left to lose," and added that it implies "a lot of
loneliness."

Fittingly, Kristofferson was one of the first people who
heard the finished recording of Blue, and it blew him away. It
wasn't the music that had the Rhodes Scholar's jaw on the
floor but the clarity of the whole record. "I remember when
Blue was first recorded... It was like, nothing left to lose, let's
spit it out. And when it was finished, I went over to a friend's
house and Kris Kristofferson was there," Mitchell told Bill
Flanagan for Musician magazine in 1985. "I played it. He said,
'Joni, save something for yourself.' It was hard for him to look
at it. There was an odd sense of respect. Like it was a Diane
Arbus photo book or something. I've heard some of the writing called that, and yet I find it hard to relate to those images.
These are not strange people in the basement of apartment
buildings. These are all of us."[35]

She's right. Blue is the classic it is because it was so truthful
that it nailed the universal. Mitchell acknowledges Blue was
probably her most naked record, but she had to go there—she
needed to get naked and crucify her own celebrity so people
could see her humanity. It worked, but it involved suffering.
"I'll just tell you, though, about what you have to go through

to get an album like that," she said. "That album is probably the purest emotional record that I will ever make in my life. In order to get that clean..." she paused, pondering,

> You wouldn't want to go around like that. To survive in the world you've got to have defenses... but they are in them-selves a kind of pretension. And at that time in my life, mine just went... Actually, it was a great spiritual oppor-tunity, but nobody around me knew what was happening. All I knew was that everything became kind of transpar-ent. I could see through myself so clearly. And I saw others so clearly that I couldn't be around people. I heard every bit of artifice in a voice. Maybe it was brought on by ner-vous exhaustion. Whatever brought it on, it was a different, undrug-induced, consciousness.

Mitchell was a little surprised by the awareness, because it made her realize her writing up to that point wasn't entirely honest. "The music that I was making was very different from the music I loved," she told biographer Michelle Mercer. Mitchell was also more emotional than she was used to. As she recalled the moment with Bill Flanagan, she said: "When the guy from the union came to the studio to take his dues I couldn't look at him. I'd burst into tears. I was so thin-skinned. Just all nerve endings. As a result, there was no capability to fake. The things that people love now—attitude and artifice and posturing—there was no ability to do those things. I'll never be that way again and I'll never make an album like that again."[36]

ARTISTIC ORTHOTIC

Mitchell never made an album like *Blue* again, although *Shine*, the last record in her catalogue (she's formally retired now, but she's done that so many times, it's hard to know for sure), comes awfully close to personal, as well as political, catharsis. After her year of travel, and after her artistic exhaustion on *Blue*, Mitchell needed to recharge her creative solar cell and figured she could "lead a 'Heidi'-like existence, you know, with goats and an orchard."[37] She looked for the alpine feel on Canada's west coast, near a coastal hamlet called Pender Harbour. Located just north of Vancouver, the Sunshine Coast is home to rich retirees, pot growers, back-to-the-landers, and all brands of social misfits who can't live within the city limits. (And, yes, there are many "normal" people who live on the coast, too.) Geographically, the Sunshine Coast is part of the mainland, but thanks to the rugged Coast Mountain range that cleaves it from the Interior, and the endless indents of fjords and inlets, it's only accessible by float plane or ferry. This separation from the rest of the province lends it a feeling of remoteness and isolation—all of which helped the fragmenting folk icon reintegrate.

"The land has a rich melancholy about it," she told Valentine. "Not in the summer because it's usually very clear, but in the spring and winter it's very brooding and it's conducive to a certain kind of thinking." This "certain kind of thinking" is the creative space, the amorphous and indescribable inner landscape that nourishes and inspires the artistic soul with its chaos, grace, and immutable beauty.

Mitchell says she experienced a different type of recreation on the rugged Sunshine Coast: she rebuilt herself from the ground up, and at the same time, she built her artistic orthotic of a home that peers into the Pacific. "[The house is] almost like a monastery," she said of the original seventies-era structure, which has since been renovated. "All stone and hardwood floors and hardwood benches, everything that would be corrective. No mirrors. Fighting for all that good virtue in myself," she said. "When I left my house in Laurel Canyon I looked around and it seemed too soft, too comfortable, too dimly lit, too much red upholstery," she said. "It was really ridiculous. [So] I just made this place really uncomfortable, like a corrective shoe."[38]

Building the house wasn't just a physical act that gave her a sense of belonging and safety; it was the symbolic rebirth of her identity: she literally built her own house and lived in it.

Her new sense of wholeness came across when she talked to Marci McDonald after her return to public life in 1974: "An artist needs a certain amount of turmoil and confusion and I've created out of that—even severe depression. But I had a lot of questions about myself, the way I was conducting my lives... life," she said, betraying her self-diagnosed multiphrenia. "Most of it was moral confusion."

The cover of her next album, *For the Roses*, features a photograph of Mitchell on the Sunshine Coast property. She's hanging out fully clothed on a rock, but on the inside gatefold, she's completely naked. (She originally wanted to have the nude on the front, but Elliot Roberts cautioned her against it, saying: "Joan, how are you going to like it when you see '$2.98' plastered across your ass?"). She told radio host Pete Fornatale: "I withdrew—I went into my hermitage there. I retreated to a piece of property that was infinitely interesting. The light was different on the water every day. There was a lot of wildlife. I got myself back to the garden," she said, picking up her own lyric. "I thought, you know, I took my own advice... with the optimism of living off the land. Well, I am too urban as it turns out and in a year or so I was back in the cities again. But it was a good—it was a good period of retreat."[39]

In Timothy White's interview, she described her time in retreat as "a solitary period; a melancholy exile—there was a sense of failure to it."[40] According to most creativity experts, a sense of failure makes for very bad creative kindling: it's too damp, too green, and too absorbed in self to make a crackling blaze in the brain. The fresh cuttings need to dry out for a bit in the sun before they can be useful, and Mitchell gave herself the time to heal. Most people don't have the privilege of taking a year off to think about their creative potential, but thanks to her previous successes, Mitchell did just that, and successfully bellowed the burning embers into a bonfire. That year may have been the most important moment in Mitchell's creative life because it took her from a place of perceived failure—over her love life, her conflicting feelings about the business, and her abandoned maternity—to a place of creative liberation.

CREATIVE RECONSTRUCTION

In her book *Tending the Fire*, psychologist Ellen Levine writes that art therapy is particularly useful for treating depression because it gives a shape and form to experience. "This shaping of experience into an artistic form provides the container," whether it is a painting, a dance, a poem, a song, or a piece of theatre. The creative products "hold the internal world of the artist" in "external form." However, the process must begin in formlessness. "Before the dance can emerge, there is play and experimentation with different possibilities." In other words, there are going to be many drafts, many misses, before the perfect piece of prose hits the page. But these "failures" are a crucial part of the process. "To really play at this stage means to give up any sense of a fixed idea of what will happen or of knowing anything beforehand. This attitude of letting go must be practiced and cultivated," Levine says. "It comes more easily to some than to others. Entering the chaos of formlessness and letting go can be frightening. Order, structure or form for experience thus needs to emerge organically out of playful experimentation."[41]

Mitchell's time on the B.C. coast was playful and profoundly life-altering. She learned to let go and discovered she was just fine exactly the way she was. "One day about a year after I started my retreat in Canada, I went out swimming. I jumped off a rock into this dark emerald green water with yellow kelp in it and purple starfish at the bottom. It was very beautiful," she says. "And as I broke up to the surface of the water, which was black and reflective, I started laughing. Joy had just suddenly come over me, you know? And I remember that as a turning point. First feeling like a loony because I was out there laughing all by myself in this beautiful environment. And then, right on top of it, was the realization that whatever my social burdens were, my inner happiness was still intact."[42] This epiphany blasted a ray of light into every corner of Mitchell's existence. She recovered her ability to play in the chaos and release her true creative spirit.

"With writing," she told Jenny Boyd, "you have to plumb into the subconscious, and there's a lot of scary things down there, like a bad dream sometimes. If you can extricate yourself from it and face up to it, you come back with a lot of self-knowledge, which then gives you greater human knowledge... To know yourself is to know the world; everything, good, bad, and indifferent is in each one of us to varying degrees... So in that way, the writing process is fantastic psychotherapy—if you can survive."

six

GODS AND MONSTERS

"He is three…
Which one do you think he'd want the world to see
Well world opinion's not a lot of help
When a man's only trying to find out
How to feel about himself
In the plan oh
The cock-eyed plan
God must be a boogie man!"

JONI MITCHELL, "God Must Be a Boogie Man," *Mingus*

THE FIRST HALF of this book probed the primary creative question of identity: "Who Am I?" The second half will endeavour to take it one step further, because we can't truly understand ourselves as creators without questioning our relationship to creation and the great Creator—or the concept we commonly refer to as God.

From the moment we are born, we're exposed to the fundamental dynamic of creator and creation: God-human, parent-child, state-citizen. The lines of power are clearly drawn within this dynamic, and it's familiar and comforting to feel like the perpetual child who will be cared for, nurtured, and loved for simply obeying the rules. This is one of the reasons why religious texts have proven so successful for the past millennia: they create crisp boundaries around the concept of creator and creation, ensuring we understand our place in the universe as small, corporeal creatures with a limited ability to grasp truth. In return for our unquestioning belief, we're promised salvation, a joyous family reunion in the afterlife, and a sense of connection to the throbbing mystery of the galaxy.

Religious texts do not encourage us to be creators. That divine act is reserved for the ultimate and omnipotent Creator. However, when we allow ourselves to become the artist, what was once a one-sided, fixed equation becomes dynamic. As an artist, the human being can be both creation and creator—thawing the fluid life force of the creative impulse and giving us a new sense of personal control through free will.

The creative act can lift us into a new understanding of the god-state. Jenny Boyd describes such a moment in her introduction to *Musicians in Tune*, as she relates the story of her "spiritual awakening":

> The traditional Christian beliefs I had been taught as a child crumbled as I suddenly recognized that there was no God above or hell below. God was everywhere, inside each one of us, I saw everything as a circle: life, death and rebirth, or reincarnation," she says. "The circle represented the spiraling journey of the spirit, reaching toward a state of union with God. It was as if a veil had been lifted to show me something I had somehow known all along. It was my first truly intuitive moment and would one day influence my creativity.[1]

One could describe Boyd's sensation as an epiphanic moment: she saw the world through a new set of lenses and it changed her feelings about herself. She gained a new sense of trust in her creative potential: she could feel God around her and within in her—not above or below her—but as a part of her. Quite simply, by becoming creative, we channel the creative spirit of the universe and, in so doing, feel "at one" with the spheres.

This link is achieved through the process we call "inspiration," a moment where we are so deeply moved, we feel a compulsion to create. The root of the word reminds us that this is very much a physical phenomenon: "inspiration" comes from *inspirare*, which is Latin for "breathe"—the basic autonomic function of being alive.

In *Minstrels of the Soul*, Paolo Knill, Helen Barba, and Margot Fuchs outline what happens at the moment of inspiration: "An aesthetic response... a distinct response, with a bodily origin, to an occurrence in the imagination, to an artistic act, or to the perception of an art work. When the response is profound and soul-stirring, we describe it as 'moving,' or 'breath-taking' (in German *Atem beraubend*)... revealing itself in the quick in-breath—or 'inspiration'—we might experience in the presence of beauty."[2]

Negotiating the metaphysical significance of inspiration takes us to the biggest question of all: "Why Am I Here?" Joni Mitchell asked herself this question over the course of her creative life. Dancing on both sides of the creator-creation equation, she found the power to recreate herself without losing faith in the larger mystery. In the process, she bumped up against many god-related questions. As she told Barney Hoskyns in a 1994 interview for the forthcoming *Turbulent Indigo*: "In a lifetime, I think everyone sinks to the pits, and without that you don't really have powers of empathy. You may have powers of sympathy, but if you've been to the bottom you have an opportunity to be a more compassionate person. I have had a difficult life ... no more difficult than anyone else's but peculiarly difficult all the same. A life of very good luck and very bad luck, with a lot of health problems," she said. "But I don't think I've ever become faithless; I've never been an atheist, although I can't say what orthodoxy I belong to."[3]

Before Mitchell could use her creative power to reconcile her place in the universe, she needed the "inspiration" of others. So let's take a deep, collective breath, and look at the sources of Mitchell's creative expression. She told *Rolling Stone's* David Wild in 1991 that "most of my heroes are monsters, unfortunately, and they are men."[4] She didn't list them off in that interview, but in reading the vast Mitchell archive, three names emerge more prominently than any others: Leonard Cohen, Bob Dylan, and Friedrich Nietzsche. Of the former two, she said: "The only poets who influenced me were Leonard Cohen and Bob Dylan," adding they were both "points of departure." Of the latter she said: "Nietzsche was a hero, especially with *Thus Spoke Zarathustra*. He gets a bad rap; he's very misunderstood. He's a maker of individuals, and he was a teacher of teachers."[5]

There's no question Cohen, Dylan, and Nietzsche make for a rather odd triumvirate of spiritual and creative power— especially given the inherent religious connections to each, with Cohen being a good Jew (at least in the beginning), Dylan being a lapsed Jew who turned to Christianity (at least in the beginning), and Nietzsche having been connected with the rise of fascism and the Third Reich. And yet, as we shall soon see, the former polio victim who beat the iron lung found a way to inhale all three as inspirations and express them in her own unique breath.

THE LADY KILLER: LEONARD COHEN

"And the poets lie too much."

FRIEDRICH NIETZSCHE, "On the Blissful Islands,"
Thus Spoke Zarathustra

Joni Mitchell says Leonard Cohen "owns the words 'naked body,'" and she believes he may be incapable of inspiring his own priapic brand of poetry without dipping into his deep well of past loves. She should know. She was one of the many—many, many, many. The fact that Leonard Cohen and Joni Mitchell had a brief encounter is not only a handsome part of Canadian lore, but the connection seems destined: they were two Canadians with poetry and sex appeal pumping through their veins, circulating through the smoky folk circuit at the same time. They were opposites, but together they found a creative dynamic tension: one a lanky blond WASP from the prairies who could sing prettier than a songbird, the other an urban Jew poet with the croak of a crow who wore sex on his black sleeves. Their meeting had every reason to be transformative, and for Mitchell—at least—it was. She said Cohen was a "mirror to my work," who showed her "how to plumb the depths of my own experience."[6] Mitchell's use of the term "mirror" is key to understanding the process of inspiration, because it's about seeing who you are and feeling the urge to recreate yourself.

"Chuck Mitchell had had a degree in literature and I had flunked grade 12," Mitchell told Michelle Mercer. "So he had the pride of the educated, and he basically thought I was stupid. I came out of the marriage with a chip on my shoulder. Shortly after that, I met Leonard and I said to him, 'I'm illiterate, basically. I haven't read anything, give me a reading list.'"[7]

Cohen complied and offered a get-literate-quick series of titles that included works by Lorca, Camus, and the I Ching.

But recent years have seen a diminishing of her reverence for the man who was almost broke until "Hallelujah" saved his Jewish bacon. She told Mercer she now finds him superficial and reductive: "I used to give Leonard and Dylan credit for growing up the pop song. After I read Camus and Lorca, I started to realize that Leonard had stolen a lot of their lines—I mean, he handed me the source of his plagiarism in the reading list that he gave me. That was very disappointing to me," said Mitchell. "'Walk me to the corner, our steps…' That's a direct lift out of Camus."

The comment may seem like one of those fabulous Joni paradoxes, given Mitchell has also borrowed large swaths of prose from the likes of Yeats and Kipling. Yet, where Cohen—and, as we've already noted, Dylan—incorporated others' stanzas into their own work without specific attribution for the material, Mitchell credits all her sources in the liner notes. She's consistently untainted when it comes to creation, which gives her good reason to be a little self-righteous, and just a tad disappointed by the creative posturing of her peers.

In the beginning, though, Joni Mitchell was downright adoring. The love story began at the 1967 Newport Folk Festival, two years after Dylan first plugged in and sent an electrified shiver down the collective spine of the folk movement. Mitchell had yet to record an album, but her songs were gaining attention—thanks to people like Dave Van Ronk, one of the fixtures on the New York music scene who not only covered the recent divorcee's tunes but also introduced her to the community. It was through Van Ronk that Mitchell met Steve Katz and Roy Blumenfeld, two members of a

band called the Blues Project—shortly after her departure
from the matrimonial nest, Mitchell woke up to a Chelsea
morning and dated both of them.

Blumenfeld told Sheila Weller that Mitchell was like "a
Canadian Dorothy from the Wizard of Oz," and he was happy
to have nabbed the "perfect shiksa... [with] the high cheekbones, the sculpted face"[8] until his fiery French girlfriend,
Marie, returned from the land of Gauloises and forced him to
fold his manly poker hand. Mitchell was dumped like a cold
latke. To ease her pain, she headed to a bar—the Tin Angel
(which would earn its own song)—and hung out with Blues
Project keyboardist Al Kooper, a kid who found fame at fourteen when he penned "Short Shorts" and later formed the
band Blood, Sweat & Tears.

Kooper is also credited with the opening Hammond organ
swirl on Dylan's "Like a Rolling Stone," and he was onstage for
that infamous 1965 Newport set when Bob Dylan decided to
amp up (incurring the wrath of Pete Seeger, who said if he'd
had an ax, he would have cut the cables).[9] On this particular
night, Kooper would earn his rock 'n' roll chevrons for pall-
ing around with the moping Joni and heading back to her
apartment to hear her sing. It hardly seems like a noble calling—more like a booty calling—but Kooper was so impressed
by Mitchell's songs, he called up his friend Judy Collins in the
middle of the night.

Collins didn't hang up. She needed material to round out
her album *Wildflowers*, which already contained two Cohen-
penned tunes: "Hey, That's No Way to Say Goodbye" and
"Sisters of Mercy." She told Kooper she could pick up Mitchell on her way to Newport, where she was booked to play and
lead a workshop the following day. Collins was taken by a
tune called "Both Sides Now" and wanted to hear the rest of
Mitchell's repertoire.

Bubbling with enthusiasm, Mitchell packed her bags and waited for Collins to show up at her apartment door—but she never did. She completely bailed on the young ingenue, leaving Mitchell's ego a little bruised after she waited at the curb for a car that never came. It was only after Collins arrived at the folk festival and heard someone butcher one of Mitchell's tunes that she sent a car for the singer and made good on the promise.

The only thing standing in the way of Mitchell and a Newport audience now was Joan Baez's mother, Joan Bridge Baez, who apparently had little time for the fair-haired—and striking—Mitchell, lest she steal the limelight from her own girls, Joan Jr. and Mimi Farina. Mama Joan tried to stop Mitchell from taking the stage in what would prove to be the first of several showdowns—she is a recurring character in the annals of Mitchell's backstage life, and a rather comic one at that.

Born in Scotland, "Joan Senior," or "Big Joan," as she was frequently called, kept a close eye on her daughters, but Joan in particular. Maybe her penchant for keeping a very, very close eye on her progeny came from her husband, Albert Baez, a Mexican-born physicist credited with co-inventing the X-ray microscope (he also wrote one of the bibles of university physics, *The New College Physics: A Spiral Approach*). Either way, Big Joan's stage-mother instincts went rabid whenever Mitchell was around. Even Baby Joan Baez remarked on it years later, when she and Mitchell were sharing a stage once more on the Rolling Thunder Revue, a gypsy caravan of a rock tour initiated by Dylan in 1975, with the likes of Ronee Blakley, Roger McGuinn, Ramblin' Jack Elliott, and Kinky Friedman. Baby Joan pulled journalist Larry "Ratso" Sloman aside backstage during Mitchell's set and said: "My mother will be showing high signs of disinterest at this point 'cause I'm her daughter."[10]

Mitchell was aware of the dislike and felt it was shared by both Joan generations, saying Baby Joan Baez "would have broken my leg if she could."[11] But in keeping with her creativity-matters-more-than-ego pattern, she never let either of the Joans get under her skin, and she has never slagged the earnest protest singer's talent. But back in 1967, Mitchell wasn't so confident about her place in the limelight. She needed backup, and she got it from Judy Collins—who threatened Big Joan with a public scene if Mitchell didn't get her chance at the mike. If Mitchell didn't go onstage, nor would Collins or Cohen. Big Mama Joan relented, allowing Cohen to make his performance debut and Mitchell to embrace a big audience of new fans.

The adrenaline rush of Newport seemed to fuse the two Canadian souls together in an arc welder's·flash as the opposites connected for the first time. Already a published and well-regarded poet and prose stylist, the young man did nothing to change Joni's taste for non-Gentile males, as well as educated ones.

After Newport, the two hooked up and travelled to other music festivals, including Mariposa. By the time Mitchell moved to California and bought her home in Laurel Canyon, the signs of Cohen were still evident—even though she was now in love with Graham Nash. A 1969 interview in the Globe and Mail describes a grandfather clock that was given to her by Cohen, as well as a much-quoted line on the shared Canadian sensibility: "We Canadians are a bit more nose-gay, more old-fashioned bouquet than Americans," Mitchell said. "We're poets because we're such [a] reminiscent kind of people. I love Leonard's sentiments, so I've been strongly influenced by him. My poetry is urbanized and Americanized, but my music is influenced by the Prairies. When I was a kid, my mother used to take me out to the fields to teach me bird calls."[12]

Mitchell credits Cohen with her penchant for character sketch songs, such as "Marcie" and "Nathan La Franeer." In return, magazines like *Rolling Stone* have described Mitchell as the embodiment of Cohen's Suzanne, who "shows you where to look among the garbage and the flowers."

The affair barely lasted four months but it left a lasting impression on both artists. Cohen's great song of redemption, "Hallelujah," has been called an ode to Mitchell's "musical onomatopoeia"[13]—the chordal movement follows the lyrical prompts: "The fourth, the fifth / the minor fall, the major lift." In turn, Mitchell's time with Cohen inspired many acts of creation. She says she abandoned her box of paints when she got into music, but after being with Cohen and spending time in Amsterdam's Van Gogh Museum, she was inspired to paint a portrait of Montreal's brooding poet. And it was Cohen's friend Mort Rosenthal, a noted sculptor, who gave her one of the most valuable lessons she ever received in art practice. Mitchell says that Rosenthal "gave me a very simple exercise which freed my drawing—[and] gave it boldness and energy. He gave me my originality."[14]

It's a fitting tribute to Cohen's creative stoking and poking of Mitchell's furnace that her first painting after several years was what she called a "really bad" portrait of Cohen in the style of Van Gogh. She gave it to a friend. Shortly thereafter, the friend's house burned down—taking the Cohen portrait with it.

Fortunately, there are more lasting artifacts of the brief affair to be found in Mitchell's catalogue. She would write several songs inspired by and about Cohen, from "That Song About the Midway"—in which the young poet "stood out like a ruby in a black man's ear" and was "playing like a devil wearing wings"—to "A Case of You." This classic, probably my favourite Mitchell song of all time, refers to her former lover as in her "blood like holy wine" and pouring out of her in "these lines from time to time."

Although Mitchell doesn't like narrowing the context of her material down to specifics, preferring that her vast catalogue speak to the universals of experience rather than a gossip-rag obsession with sexual trysts, even Cohen believes "A Case of You" to be about him. In December 1975, eight years after their first meeting at Newport, the two reunited in Montreal when Bob Dylan and his band of merrymakers pulled into town in a cloud of coke dust for the Rolling Thunder show. Cohen had been invited to participate in the crazy rock 'n' roll circus. He declined, but he did take in the show—which had recently enlisted the talents of Joni Mitchell.

Larry Sloman records what happened next in *On the Road with Bob Dylan*.[15] Arriving just as Mitchell was strumming the last chords to her set, the grand seducer greets her with the patronizing line: "Joni, my little Joni." Mitchell seems unfazed by the diminishing term and asks Cohen why he won't get up onstage and sing. "No, no, it's too obvious," he says, proving the famed ladies' man was probably just a little obsessed with appearing cool. The next night, Mitchell, McGuinn, and Sloman head over to Cohen's house for dinner.

Mitchell talks about how the tour has helped her gain a better understanding of both her personal and performer's ego: "It's really interesting... cause people are always testing each other all the time, you know, misreading you," she says. "Coming from a position where I need always to be sincere and to be understood, I, like, allowed myself to float through situations... It's so exciting to me. It's not giving a shit. It really is an interesting thing because it's a traveling commune," she continues, reaffirming the creative liberation involved in simply letting go of ego.

Inherent in this conversation is Mitchell's perception of Cohen as a kindred spirit: she's been aching to share her deeper, philosophical observations of the tour with someone she knows will understand. As a result, the degree of candour in Sloman's vérité reportage is unprecedented. Sloman was on the tour, and recorded everything on tape, the transcript of which forms the core of his book.

Mitchell goes on to address the issue of identity and its role in the creative process: "I've come to deal with my multiphrenia: They're all realities. There are so many ways to look at [yourself], you know that as a writer, cutting through the layers of personality to get to the one who is the most honest."

Cohen responds with an equally candid remark: "I don't know how honest I am… I'm unstable." Mitchell counters with a competitive "Maybe I'm more unstable than you… You have a more consistent character than you play out," she says, foreshadowing the "superficial" remark that would come years later. Cohen replies with an acknowledgement of the funniest lyric in "A Case of You." "Oh yeah," he says, "I'm as constant as the North Star," referring to the passage: "Just before our love got lost you said / 'I am as constant as a northern star' / And I said, 'Constantly in the darkness / Where's that at? / If you want me I'll be in the bar.'"

"A Case of You" reveals a relationship unlike any other in Mitchell's life because the mutual respect and shared creative zeal did not involve any sense of being threatened. She could "drink a case" of Cohen and still be on her feet. The line is a great metaphor for the intoxicating quality of love, but moreover, it's an inside Canadian joke about liquor content. Our beer is stronger—usually a percentage point or two above American beer—frequently leaving plenty of American bands drunk before they even play their first set. When Canadians go to the States, we can drink a case of Miller—and still be on our feet. This shared Canadian identity plays out beneath the entire song as she talks about drawing a map of Canada with "your face sketched on it twice."

These mutual cultural roots place both Cohen and Mitchell outside fame's fishbowl. Canadians are natural observers. It's this ability to pull back that gives the poetry of Cohen and Mitchell as much power as it has. Even Larry Sloman, who would prove to be a thorn in Mitchell's side during the Rolling Thunder tour, conceded that Cohen and Mitchell probably have more in common than any of the other songwriters on the bus. "I'd say out of all those people, you probably have the most affinity with Leonard, but I don't know if that's a cultural thing," he tells Mitchell, who had just finished writing the songs for The Hissing of Summer Lawns. "Up to a certain point," she replies. "Except my work now is much…"

Mitchell never did finish that sentence, but over the course of 1975, everything in Mitchell's creative valise was re-evaluated. She was desperate to stay original and resisted the idea of painting more Starry Nights—she embraced more challenging musical forms, such as jazz and syncopated African beats, and incorporated literary inspirations. The Rolling Thunder experience had a fundamental role in that recalibration as it spawned tracks for Summer Lawns as well as Hejira—two of Mitchell's most original works. She sang an early version of "Coyote" (which would appear on Hejira) in the Rolling Thunder dressing room. The song is about another brief lover, Sam Shepard, who joined the Rolling Thunder bandwagon along with Allen Ginsberg to write scenes for the accompanying movie, Renaldo and Clara. The movie also featured appearances from Mitchell and Roger McGuinn, but for all its rock cred, it was critically panned. The only markets where the four-hour surrealist reel had any legs were Minneapolis, Kansas, and Vancouver, Canada. But I won't hazard a guess as to why.

Mitchell's switch in songwriting was partly the result of her confrontation with the egos on the tour and partly just plain growing up: "Like three times I had this ego battle and it was emotional immaturity, knowing that it really didn't make a difference in that my longevity as an artist is not affected in any way by what position I'm in this thing or whether they say Joni Mitchell was ineffective or whether they don't even mention my name... but from time to time... I begin to say, 'Like wait a minute. I'm a sophisticated musician in a naïve kind of way. I'm a sophisticated observer.'"[16]

These comments, recorded by Sloman, illustrate a creative distance and an understanding of the bigger picture, as well as her place in it. She's giving herself some credit because she's not the twentysomething naïf she was at Newport in '67. She's a self-created thirty-two-year-old whose fame is quickly eclipsing those of her peers. Notably, she sees this through Cohen—her self-described creative "mirror."

Her 1975 encounter with Cohen during Rolling Thunder marked the high point of her appreciation for the winking Lothario. In the taxi back from that dinner at Cohen's home, she told her cabmates, "I'm a stone Cohenite. Dylan," she added with a flap of her wrist, "ehhhhh..."[17]

BOB DYLAN: "THE MALE JONI MITCHELL"

Mitchell's limp attitude to Dylan had been gestating for a long time. The two had been circling each other on the folk circuit for years and were frequently cited in the same breath as folk poets and musical innovators—with Mitchell often called the "female Bob Dylan." The term drove her crazy—she loathes it even more than "confessional songwriter"—but she accepted the dynamic. She recognized she and Dylan "were good pace-runners" because they pushed each other forward in a spirit of friendly competition. There was grudging respect between them but also a sense of cool playfulness that lasted until the last salvo, when Mitchell famously called Dylan a plagiarist and a fake.

What was all that about? To really understand the Joni-Bobby relationship, it behooves us to look back on the rich history of David Geffen's couch. No, we're not going to talk about his infamous heavy petting with Cher—thank god. We're going to look at a famous listening party he held in his Copley Drive home in Bel Air.

Geffen had just leveraged his next career move as the head of the newly merged Elektra/Asylum, and he was about to embark on the most successful phase of his life—when he would earn a reputation as the man with the "golden touch" for releasing the three top albums on the *Billboard* chart: Bob Dylan's *Planet Waves*, Joni Mitchell's *Court and Spark*, and Carly Simon's *Hotcakes*.

The listening party was for the former two, who were easily David Geffen's prize ponies. Mitchell was living at Geffen's mansion while she recorded *Court and Spark*. But Dylan was Geffen's big "get," the cornerstone of his recently expanded roster on the Warner-owned subsidiary—a new company that gave him a $1-million-a-year salary (in 1973), as well as the coveted chairman's title. He'd recently wooed Dylan away from his long-time home at Columbia and was bragging about it to anyone who would listen. Geffen was intensely focussed on the sessions for *Planet Waves*.

Mitchell remembers the evening as she hung out with Geffen, Dylan, and members of the Band. "There was all this fussing over Bobby's project, 'cause he was new to the label, and *Court and Spark*, which was a big breakthrough for me, was being entirely and almost rudely dismissed," she told

Cameron Crowe. "Geffen's excuse was, since I was living in a room in his house at the time, that he had heard it through all of its stages and it was no longer any surprise to him. Dylan played his album and everybody went, 'Oh, wow!'"[18] Mitchell says the sycophantic reaction to Dylan was constant, and she found it entirely off-putting. She recognized it was part of a widespread deification, but she saw through the myth and she saw through Bob, especially when he started sawing logs.

You see, right in the middle of the joint listening party, as the strains of *Court and Spark* vibrated through David Geffen's swanky sofa, Dylan drifted off into snoresville. "I played (my songs), and everybody talked ... and Bobby fell asleep."

Mitchell had the last laugh. Sales for *Planet Waves* dried up, though its failure doesn't seem so tragic when you consider it was recorded in all of three days. But *Court and Spark* is considered one of Mitchell's finest—if not *the* finest, depending on who you're talking to. (A monograph by Sean Nelson refers to the album as "her most accessible work" and a pop record that contains "multitudes.") As she told Crowe, Mitchell had enough creative confidence to know the work was good: "I said, 'Wait a minute, you guys, this is some different kind of music for me, check it out.' I knew it was good. I think Bobby was just being cute."

Whether they like it or not, Bob Dylan and Joni Mitchell are seen as the torchbearers of the whole singer-songwriter movement and its supposed desire to recreate the world. They are constantly compared to each other and, in many cases, ranked in order of their respective skills and lyrical genius. Although it's quite certain neither party would be happy about it, they operate as a binary system, with Mitchell representing the edgy and chaotic side of creation, and Dylan representing a slightly sunnier and more commercial side. To truly understand the dynamic between her and

Dylan, and how initial idolatry morphed into a sense of sibling rivalry and, finally, an old couple's petty bickering about who did what better and who did what first, we'll go back to square one.

In the beginning, only Bob was tooling around the nascent folk Eden. Then known as Robert Zimmerman, Bob dropped out of college in 1960, and in January of 1961 made his pilgrimage from the American Midwest to New York City in search of folk fame and some face time with his hero, Woody Guthrie, who was languishing in a hospital with the symptoms of a neurodegenerative disorder called Huntington's disease. Dylan officially became Dylan in 1962 and released his debut album on Columbia the same year. The subsequent year saw the release of *The Freewheelin' Bob Dylan*, featuring Dylan on a snow-covered New York City street with an attractive woman on his arm. I mention the artwork because it shares some elements with the cover of Mitchell's debut album, *Song to a Seagull*, which featured Mitchell on a New York City street in equally bad weather.

The two wouldn't meet until 1969, after they were both firmly established as solo artists at the crest of the breaking folk wave. "What unites Bob and Joni, the royalty of songwriting, is their common starting point," writes Michelle Mercer. "They both came of age in folk music's pop heyday (and) broke away from the folk tradition with as much inevitability as the so-called confessional poets broke away from modernist dicta in the 1950s."[19] Mitchell herself has cited Dylan as her earliest influence as a songwriter because he wrote in a bracingly personal way that made a deep impression on the young art student. "What always bugged me about poetry in school was the artifice of it," she says. "When Dylan wrote, 'You've got a lot of nerve to say you are my friend,' as an opening line [in the song "Positively 4th Street"], the language was direct and undeniable. As for Plath and Sexton, I'm sorry, but I smell a rat. There was a lot of guile in the work, a lot of posturing. It didn't really get down to the nitty-gritty of the human condition. And there was the suicide-chic aspect."[20]

"Positively 4th Street" was recorded in 1965 and was met with critical and commercial success, even though it was just a single—and wouldn't hit an album groove until Dylan's first greatest hits collection. At this time, Mitchell was getting over the surrender of her baby and doing her best to make her way in the folk clubs of Toronto's Yorkville. When she wasn't playing other people's songs, she was waiting tables or modelling clothes, or hanging out with like-minded souls such as Neil Young, her fellow convalescent. Mitchell had yet to find her creative voice, but it wouldn't take long.

By 1969, Mitchell had two studio albums to her credit, *Song to a Seagull* and *Clouds*. Dylan, meanwhile, had released a whopping nine albums in just seven years, including *The Times They Are a-Changin'*, *Highway 61 Revisited*, and *Blonde on Blonde*.

They finally met on the premiere of *The Johnny Cash Show* on June 7, 1969. They were joined as opening night guests by Cajun fiddle player Doug Kershaw. The *Detroit News* carried a small item on the premiere, describing Mitchell as a "current happening on the national scene," thanks to her song "Both Sides Now," which had recently been covered by Collins as well as Frank Sinatra. Mitchell's former hometown paper, the *Saskatoon Star-Phoenix*, also carried a tidbit glorifying the fact that Saskatoon was mentioned on U.S. network TV. "Not often do U.S. produced television shows give recognition to Canadian entertainers and their home towns." Good golly. It was exciting! And sadly, we Canadians still explode out of our socks whenever our bands, artists, and bergs are given Yankee ink.

Mitchell and Dylan didn't have a whole lot to say to each other at the studio or even when they ended up at Cash's home afterward. Mitchell told Cameron Crowe that she "always had an affection for [Dylan]," but "over the years there were a series of brief encounters. Tests. Little art games." Mitchell went on to relate a story about Dylan asking her about paint and the rules of colour mixing, then she says her next meeting with Dylan was on the *Queen Mary*, when they were both guests at a Paul McCartney party: "Everybody left the table and Bobby and I were sitting there. After a long silence he said, 'If you were gonna paint this room, what would you paint?' I said, 'Well, let me think. I'd paint the mirrored ball spinning, I'd paint the women in the washroom, the band...' Later all the stuff came back to me as part of a dream that became the song 'Paprika Plains.' I said, 'What would you paint?' He said, 'I'd paint this coffee cup.' Later, he wrote 'One More Cup of Coffee.'"

Dylan would offer his inimitable Bobby charms on a continuing basis—and Mitchell would take them as a grain of salty homage. Throughout her career, and in several interviews, she's been known to imitate Dylan's rasping nasal voice and poetic grandiosity with astonishing accuracy. This usually happens when she's trying to point out the effect ego has on one's life as a performer—as she did when she told Vic Garbarini about her two-year withdrawal from the public eye between 1970 and 1972: "I became a hermit. I felt extremely maladjusted about...the contrasts that were heaped on me. It was just too much input...it was as if (sings like Dylan) 'People just got UGLIER and I had no sense of TIME!' (laughs)."[21]

The teasing goes both ways. When Mitchell hooked up with Dylan's Rolling Thunder Revue in 1975, Larry Sloman described an ambivalent reaction from Dylan: "Joni? Which Joni?... I don't know. Is she on the tour? I don't know if she is or not. I don't know, she just showed up in the last town," he said with a yawn, "and got on the bill."

Mitchell's presence on Rolling Thunder was unplanned. She says she'd been in Toronto and Vancouver to see friends and her parents. "It was like a cycle, I had my ticket and everything, then I got sucked into [the tour] and the magic happened for me at Niagara Falls... I couldn't get off it."[22]

There are a few elements in this quote from Sloman's book that I'd like to note before moving on. The first is the notion of surrender to something "magical"—as though she recognized a creative force greater than her own will was at play. The other is this "cyclical" dynamic; she still feels like a "cog in something turning" and sees Dylan as an inherent part of that spinning dynamo—as peer, competitor, and teasing older brother. Mitchell and Dylan, as opposites, pushed each other creatively.

The enthusiasm from both parties permeated the raw-silk tapestries of the backstage dressing rooms like so much incense, because the alternately happy-irate vibe just keeps crackling. When the caravan pulled into Montreal, Mitchell talked to her old high school friend Ruthie at her swanky home atop Mount Royal and confessed her conflict about not being more prominent on the bill. Sloman recorded the conversation, in which Mitchell says, "I'm in the position in the show of being an opening act and I'm receiving that kind of press attention, whereas in fact, I have attained a much higher..." Mitchell doesn't finish her sentence, because her friend Ruthie interrupts with a query—with a wee barb attached: "Why is Joni not number one?" Joni has an answer for that one: "I'll tell you why: It's experimental. I'm having a good time. It's like a rolling party... I have nothing to lose by it. To me, this is the most interesting thing: I've felt highly productive, that's another reason why I've stayed. In the slot I have, like if I was to go out and do the most popular material the effect would be different. It's much more interesting, like, winging it."[23]

She was experimenting with every aspect of her professional persona, from the music she wrote to the character she assumed onstage. Mitchell's feelings about the tour were mixed, as were her feelings for Dylan. One minute she was laughing with him backstage, the next she was telling her friend Ruthie that her one-time idol "has a mean streak. He gets mean."[24] This was a reference to an argument Mitchell and Dylan had earlier in the tour, while shooting a scene for *Renaldo and Clara*. As Mitchell later recalled in a conversation with Leonard Cohen: "I quoted from pure Nietzsche and Bob wouldn't let me give him credit. I said, C'mon Bobby, I got to say like *Thus Spake Zarathustra*, and I can't be like an intellectual quoting from Nietzsche, with no originality, give me a break. With Dylan, he just like strikes you out of a scene or puts you in the scene where he wants you to manifest different parts of yourself, it's different. He's got the power, he's got the hammer."

Using more tool metaphors, she added that Dylan "just keeps whittling away at you until he finds the place of you which you're the most afraid of and then, whew, he just like presses on 'til he gets you, then says, 'No Fear.' It's an excellent exercise." Mitchell was turned on by the creative challenge her peer was putting out there. But she was also pushed into examining what she did for a living and her ego stake on the stage.

She also saw hypocrisy in Rolling Thunder's two main goals: to publicize the plight of jailed boxer Rubin "Hurricane" Carter, who was serving a life sentence for a crime he said he didn't commit, and to recreate the rules of rock 'n' roll touring by making it a group effort, instead of a hierarchical ceremony based on mass popularity. Mitchell thought it was all a sham. She called Carter a "phony" who comes on "like a spiritually enlightened cat and he's not... bullshit. I think he's really an egomaniac... Let him use some of his karmic pseudo-spirituality to cool the audience out if he's so powerful. He's not; he's a fake." She had the same bracing message for Dylan's supposedly raceless, classless, genderless revue: "Billing? Do you know how much politicking there was? Do you know how many times when I started to get too hot in my spot, how, like, I let people cut my power off?"[25]

The importance of ego and personal recognition can never be undervalued, but in the music industry, the strokes are meted out according to sales—and for a time, Dylan and Mitchell were neck and neck at the record stores.

The changes taking place in the music business during the time of Dylan and Mitchell's rise to fame provided the context that made them unwitting siblings in the same commercial pod. The record industry was transitioning from the hit-parade culture of the 1950s, when bands produced singles that were powered by AM radio airplay, to the era of album sales. Labels realized they stood to make a lot more money with an album sale than a single (as much as four to ten times more per sale), given the unit cost of each recording. The technological change that brought forth the long-playing (LP) record pushed record companies to fill the extra grooves with material people wanted, and as the singer-songwriter movement evolved, so did the notion of the "concept album"—a record you would play from start to finish to hear a larger narrative. People like David Geffen realized you needed compelling storytellers to sell an album, which would be the key to sales for the next decade, and he had landed the two biggest singer-songwriters of his day—possibly the biggest two who ever were, or ever will be.

Mitchell was smart enough to recognize bits and pieces of herself in Dylan, and it explains her bipolar approach to her pop culture sibling. "He's gutless a lot of times," Mitchell tells Sloman, referring to a lyric change Dylan decided to make at the last minute onstage so as not to offend his audience. But when Sloman says the Quebec City audience "hated him," Mitchell leaps to his defence. "They didn't hate him … it's a provincial town. What did you expect?"[26]

The teeter-totter of affection was in constant motion, and it reframed Mitchell's view of her own performer's identity. At one point in the tour she took three days off and hung out in New York, the site of her creative birth after leaving Chuck Mitchell. She says she did it to "re-examine my attitudes in different spaces of consciousness, away from people consciousness, hyper consciousness, lampshade consciousness."[27]

Years later, Mitchell talked with Cameron Crowe about her Rolling Thunder experience. She said she stayed on the tour "for mystical reasons" and that she started as a "foot soldier": "I made up songs onstage. I sang in French, badly," she said. "I did a lot of things to prevent myself from getting in the way. What was in it for me hadn't anything to do with applause or the performing aspect. It was simply to be allowed to remain an observer and a witness to an incredible spectacle."[28]

Mitchell says it was her desire to remain a spectator that finally resulted in her removal from *Renaldo and Clara*. Although she was featured in several scenes, she refused to grant Shepard and Dylan permission to use her performance. After investing as much time and money in the film as Dylan had, it must have been frustrating to have Mitchell hijack great swaths of the negative. The resulting film is largely considered unintelligible—and extremely long at 292 minutes. *Variety* refers to it as one of "the worst excesses of the period" and a grand testament to ego.

Mitchell knew there were circus elephants in the room: "I studied ego, that's all I did on Rolling Thunder," she told Michelle Mercer. "I watched these malformed egos as they interacted with my own and ended up delving into my own malformed ego."

Perhaps one of the problems was the rampant use of cocaine on the tour. Mitchell says she had never been a serious coke user until she signed on. *Reader's Digest* quoted her as saying: "They asked me how I wanted to be paid, and [it was like] I ran away to join the circus: Clowns used to get paid in wine—pay me in cocaine because everybody was strung out on cocaine."[29]

As fate—or her will—would have it, her brief addiction to coke and the big E—Ego—came with its own remedy: Allen Ginsberg, friend of the late Jack Kerouac, was also on Rolling Thunder and would often bring up the name of a Buddhist master by the name of Chögyam Trungpa. When Mitchell finally wrapped up her stint with Dylan, she went home but headed out on the road almost immediately afterward. A friend of hers was travelling to Maine to assertively settle a custody issue, and Mitchell was a prisoner of the white lines once more. Along the way, just before Easter, she was cajoled into seeing Trungpa. He asked her if she believed in God, and as she told Michelle Mercer: "I said 'Yes'—and then—this was such an asshole comment—I produce this bag of coke and say, 'This is my God and this is my prayer.' He didn't flinch, but his nose started to flare. And then I thought: Does he want some [coke]? That's when he started breathing, and...I didn't notice I was being zapped." For three days, Mitchell says in Mercer's biography, she was back in the metaphysical garden. "My mind was back in Eden, the mind before the fall. With the 'I' gone, you no longer have a divisional mind that goes 'good, bad, right, wrong.'" She says what brought her out of it was an awareness of self: her first "I" thought. The three days felt "simple-minded, blessedly simple-minded. And then the 'I' came back, and the first thought I had was, Oh, my god. He enlightened me. Boom. Back to normal—or what we call normal but they call insanity."[30]

The Mitchell-Dylan dynamic produced more golden moments. The two reunited onstage in 1976 for The Last Waltz, Martin Scorsese's concert film about the Band's "final show" at the Winterland Ballroom in San Francisco. Band member Levon Helm said, "The film was more or less shoved down our throats... do it, puke, get out."[31] Dylan, who at Geffen's urging had been on tour with Robbie Robertson and company just two years earlier, was supposed to show up for rehearsals and never did. Mitchell, however, was a keener. She rehearsed with the Band, but no one could figure out her tunings. The show, as the movie proves, was a collection of so-so musical performances but now-legendary rock 'n' roll moments—particularly the grand finale, which features the entire ensemble singing "I Shall Be Released." You can see Mitchell in a Neil sandwich (between Neil Young—with a giant chunk of coke famously dangling from his nose—and Neil Diamond), looking uninterested as Dylan hurls his voice into the microphone.

At least they were standing far apart. When they shared a microphone in Nara, Japan, for the 1994 Great Music Experience concert, Mitchell complained about Bobby's halitosis to a Mojo reporter: "Oh, he's such a little brat, you know. He really is," she said of Dylan. "He's never been very complimentary to my face—most of the boys haven't. But he loved 'Sex Kills,' and was very effusive about it. Anyway, we played three concerts, and they kept shifting my position on the mikes and which verses of the songs I was going to sing," she said. "On the third night they stuck Bob at the mike with me, and that's the one that went out on tape. And if you look closely at it, you can see the little brat, he's up in my face—and he never brushes his teeth, so his breath was like ... right in my face—and he's mouthing the words at me like a prompter, and he's pushing me off the mike. It's like he's basically dipping my pigtail in ink. The press picked up on it and said, 'Bobby Smiles!' Yeah sure, because he was having a go at me out there."[32]

What goes around comes around. Mitchell, Dylan, and Van Morrison shared a bill in 1998 at the Gorge in Washington State—probably the most beautiful venue in the world, thanks to its natural slope amphitheatre with expansive views of the Columbia River valley. Mitchell decided it was time for some payback—and cajoled Van Morrison into crashing Dylan's final set. They both jumped onstage for his encore, "I Shall Be Released."

"Bob got a big kick out of it," Mitchell told Jody Denberg of the *Austin Chronicle*. "It was really rough and I blew the words on it and blew the rhyme and had to make one up. And Bobby was looking at me grinning, 'What is she going to rhyme with it,' because I got the first rhyming line wrong."[33] The correct lyrics are: "Yet I swear I see my own reflection / Some place so high above this wall / I see my light come shining / From the west unto the east / any day now, any day now / I shall be released." Mitchell's impromptu appearance resulted in a spontaneous rewrite, which, according to a spectator, went like this: "I see my own reflection / Right above the mighty beast." The accidental recreation couldn't be more telling, because it encapsulates the Mitchell/Dylan dynamic. In Dylan, Mitchell saw her reflection as an artist, but she also saw the mighty beast of ego and the burden of being a "folk icon"—two anti-creative forces from which she would eventually "be released."

HAS ANYONE SEEN MY NIETZSCHE?

Sometime around the summer of 1997, Joni Mitchell lost one of her favourite cats: a little, yellow-eyed "part ocelot," part Abyssinian mix. His name was Nietzsche, but she also called him "Man from Mars" because "he's a little lavender lion who looks like an alien and walks on his hind legs as an expression of affection for me."[34] The two had a ritual that involved petting, exchanging "deep long looks," gentle hair chewing, and climbing the stairs in tandem. "We stop at the top, he stands on his hind legs, I swoop down, he takes my fingers in his mouth and he chews on them," Mitchell told KCSN radio's Rene Ingle in 1999. "Then we skip the next three steps, and he stands on his hind legs on the third [step]. Then we skip the next two [steps] and he stands up again and sometimes he stands up twice on each stair if he really loves me a lot that day."[35]

The kitty was "wild" and known to pee on furniture, but Mitchell was unfazed by most of it until "he got mad at me about something, and he got up on this chair and he peed right close to my ear." She told the story to Elvis Costello in their 2004 marathon chat for *Vanity Fair*, which yielded fifty thousand words of transcript:[36]

> He jumped off from there and ran with his belly to the floor. He knew he did wrong. I caught up to him and I took him by the tip of his tail and the scruff of the neck and I held him at arm's length so he couldn't scratch me, because he's really strong. I said, "O.K. If you're going to act like an animal, you can live like an animal." I put him outside for the night, which I would never do [normally, because of the coyotes]. Well, he's very sensitive, you know. I hurt his feelings. And he didn't come back the first night. He didn't come back the second night.

Mitchell soon realized how much she missed the cat: "With him absent, the stairs became a painful place. I mean every time I went down them, there was hole in me."

Intent on finding the missing feline now roaming the arid hills of affluent Los Angeles, she decided to issue a public notice to her neighbours. First, she needed to find a picture of the cat but discovered the only snap of the MIA mewler had been taken when he was a kitten. Moreover, it used the wrong type of film—daylight balanced, not tung-sten—resulting in lilac-tinted fur. "It didn't look like him. I thought, I'll never get him back from this. So I painted him," she told Costello. "I had to make him grow into an adult from the picture, the source material I had." Mitchell found the right colours for the pelt on her palette, and a day and a half later, she had a finished canvas of the lost cat. She photo-graphed it and took it to a printer. She got it back "in laminate form on the fifth day, and hand-delivered it into everybody's mailbox in a three-mile radius. On the back it said, 'Have you seen my Nietzsche?' and gave the phone number to call."

Mitchell says Nietzsche was gone for eighteen days, and like a "method actor I took the pain of his absence and wrote the song 'Man from Mars.' Even in the mix [of the recording] you can hear it. I had been out there listening for him and my ear was hearing three miles away. It is the deepest mix that I ever did, with little sounds going way, way, way back into the mix," she says. "So I finished the song. It took me seven days... He stayed away just long enough for me to write [it]." In the song's poignant lyrics, "Since I lost you / I can't get through the day / Without at least one big boo-hoo / The pain won't go away... There is no center to my life now / No grace in my heart." The deep listening Mitchell described to Costello is also present in the lyrics: "I call and call / The silence is so full of sounds / You're in them all / I hear you in the water / And the wiring in the walls."

The story has a happy ending. Not only did Mitchell find a way to cope with the loss of the cat through an act of artistic creation, but she was also reunited with the rogue tinkler. "A gardener called up and said, 'He's in our yard.' So I went down and [Nietzsche] yelled at me. He was so skinny and had such a hurt look. And he yelled and he yelled and he yelled. And I yelled back and I noticed that he wanted to duck and belly up but then he changed his mind. No, he still had more madness to get out," she says. "So he yelled at me some more, but I softened my tone, you know, into a pleading tone, and finally he bellied up and I took him home with me. So that painting actually saved him from the wild because he was too proud to come home. I hurt his feelings so bad."[37]

Joni Mitchell has owned many cats over the years, but none has been given as much ink in the annals as Nietzsche, nor has she talked about them in such detail. She and Nietzsche clearly had a special bond. It's been sewn into the rich quilt of Mitchell iconography because she put a self-portrait featuring the prodigal kitty on the cover of the 1998 release *Taming the Tiger*, her first collection of new material since 1994's double-Grammy winner, *Turbulent Indigo*.

"Have you seen my Nietzsche?" is a question I'd like to answer myself, because I have seen Joni's Nietzsche, and what a furry beast it is. Mitchell's Nietzsche is everywhere—even if he is one of the "monsters" she mentions as an inspiration. The man who gave her feline Martian his name, Friedrich Wilhelm Nietzsche (1844–1900), was a noted German philosopher who infamously offed God. In his legendary tome *Thus Spoke Zarathustra* Nietzsche sounds a bit like a Monty Python sketch when he asserts: "This old god no longer lives... He is quite dead."[38]

Killing God in print, and in theory, was probably the most revolutionary and scandalous act of the nineteenth century, but Nietzsche felt a compulsion to recreate the paradigm of the human condition because he thought man was in a state of moral and creative stagnation. He believed we were denying the very essence of our divine nature by worshipping a creator larger and more important than ourselves. By removing God from the human equation, Nietzsche believed, we wouldn't just be removing the wire cage of religious limitations and dogma; we'd be forced to take full responsibility for our own actions: "No longer to bury the head in the sand of heavenly things, but to carry it freely, an earthly head that creates meaning for the earth!"[39]

In short, killing God allows us to redefine the fundamental relationship between the creator and the creation. If we become the creators, we become the masters of our own destiny. It's not easy cutting your own path in the tangled garden of spirituality or creating your own identity in a cacophony of consumerism. It takes the courage of a lion to counter the old laws. But "the will is a creator," says Nietzsche. One must learn to "unharness the will from its own folly" as well as the "spirit of revenge and all teeth-gnashing" in order to free it and, in so doing, "become the redeemer and bringer of joy." This is what Nietzsche called "the will that is the will to power." And it got him in a lot of trouble. Fortunately, he was dead for most of it.

Thus Spoke Zarathustra has been called the work of a heretic, a Satanist, and the Antichrist—the latter designation was self-dubbed, because Nietzsche wasn't without a sense of humour, or drama. What really stains his reputation is his association with Adolf Hitler, a man he never met and most certainly would not have liked. Nietzsche was long dead before the Nazi rise to power, but thanks in part to his nutty supremacist sister, who had control over his creative output, "the will to power" was a tagline the Nazis glommed onto—giving rise to Leni Riefenstahl's creepy-but-beautiful *Triumph of the Will* and other warped interpretations of Nietzsche's call to creative arms. For this reason, not to mention the God thing, Nietzsche is considered "a monster" or "the bad guy."[40] Most benevolently, we can look at *Thus Spoke Zarathustra* as Nietzsche's "how-to" book for spiritual recreation—or "chicken soup for the godless soul." It urges the reader to ask, "What are we?" and "Why are we here?" without looking up to the heavens for answers but into the mirror, where we must find our own.

Nietzsche had a huge effect on Mitchell. She mentions *Thus Spoke Zarathustra* throughout her career, saying she's "a fan" of the book and that it became a personal "bible." "Nietzsche was a hero, especially with *Thus Spoke Zarathustra*," she told Jody Denberg in 1998. "I discovered Nietzsche, who's the bible for the godless, really... but you have to really kind of sink into the pits to understand Nietzsche because he looks at more truth than most people could. Even Carl Jung opened up his writings, slammed it shut, and said, 'Whew! He'll have no friends.'"[41]

Yet Mitchell identifies with Nietzsche. She sees a reflection of herself in his struggle for health, as well as his insomnia. "I believe convalescence in bed develops a strong inner life in a young child. I think it solidified me as an independent thinker," she told Bill Flanagan in *Vanity Fair*, "Nietzsche was a convalescent." And, like Zarathustra, Mitchell calls herself an insomniac: "I'm trained to go to bed at 7 in the morning, which is ten o'clock on the East Coast. I'm nocturnal, and after midnight the phones stop ringing and I contemplate, whatever." Zarathustra, in a metaphorical take on creative awakening, says "stay awake in order to sleep well."[42]

Given the stigma surrounding Nietzsche's work, it's rather surprising that Mitchell would have regarded the supposed madman as a mentor. But as we've seen, Mitchell defied expectation—a trait she credits to none other than Nietzsche. So let's take a look at how this creative relationship came to be—and how a flaxen-haired prairie girl found herself knee-deep in the philosophy of a syphilitic nihilist.

THE BEGINNING OF THE BLOOD TRAIL

According to Mitchell, her first brush with Nietzsche was at Queen Elizabeth Public School, circa 1954. She had just moved from the hamlet of North Battleford to the big city of Saskatoon, where she'd already established an identity as the school artist. "I was hanging up pictures for a parent/teacher day in the hallway," she told the BBC's Mary Black in 1999, "when a good-looking Australian came up to me and said, 'You like to paint?' I said, 'Yes.' He said to me, 'If you can paint with a brush, you can paint with words. I'll see you next year.'"[43]

The Aussie with the athletic build was Arthur Kratzman, a former track star with a picaresque gold tooth. He had moved to Canada without the right teaching credentials, for which Mitchell says they tried to punish him by sending him to teach on First Nations reserves. But that turned out to be a great joy for Kratzman, who happened to be reading Nietzsche over the course of his exile. "You know... to send a teacher to the Indian reservations in Saskatchewan was like being banished to Siberia. But he took to it with a relish and he was a very, very soulful man. He'd been a racing partner to the great gold-medal-winning racer Johnny somebody-or-other,[44] so he was a really good runner. And he was a teacher-maker and a writer-maker and an athlete-maker," said Mitchell, picking up the same phraseology she's used to describe Nietzsche. "He said, you know, 'I'm not going to teach it to you. I'm going to cram you in the last two weeks. You'll all pass with flying colors. I'm going to teach you what I know.'"

When it came time to hand in her first poetry assignment to Mr. Kratzman, she was desperate to impress her new hero. She tried to assume a more sophisticated persona and decided to lift a few words from the family's stack of *Reader's Digest* magazines for her poem about stallions. She really thought she'd outdone herself with the line: "equine statues bathed in silver light." But when she got her paper back, it was drenched in red ink. "For an eleven-year-old . . . it was quite a precocious poem," says Mitchell. "He circled it all over 'cliché, cliché,' you know, 'good adjective,' you know, 'you've used this adjective,' 'cliché,' and he marked me harder than I think American college professors mark at this point—at [the age of] eleven," she says. "He said to me, 'How many times did you see *Black Beauty*?' I said, 'Once.' 'What do you know about horses?' I said, 'Well, I go riding at [the stockyard] on the weekends, you know, whenever I can. I like horses.' And he said, 'Well, the things that you've told me that you've done on other weekends are more interesting than this . . . 'Write in your own blood,' he told me. 'Write in your own blood,' which is Nietzsche, I found out later."

It is Nietzsche, and it's from *Thus Spoke Zarathustra*, Mitchell's "bible": "Of all writings I love only that which is written in blood. Write with blood: and you will discover that blood is spirit."[45]

The sanguine criticism pierced Mitchell's creative skin to the bone, because she not only thanks Mr. Kratzman on the liner notes of her debut album *Song to a Seagull*—"This album is dedicated to Mr. Kratzman who taught me to love words"— but she also tells this anecdote more than any other, pulling it from her pocket whenever an interviewer asks about her insistence on originality.

Chronologically, the next reference to *Zarathustra* comes just after she met David Crosby in Coconut Grove. We already know she and the ex-Byrd nested sexually for a brief stint, but in order to consummate his love for Mitchell, Crosby felt the noble need to ditch his then-squeeze, Christine Hinton.

Hinton was entirely dedicated to Crosby. She not only rolled his joints; she took him back after his affair with Mitchell hit the skids. Tragically, they would not be together for long because Hinton died in a car accident shortly after the reunion. According to Sheila Weller in *Girls Like Us*, Hinton was taking a sick cat to the vet with a friend on September 30, 1969—the same day the debut album *Crosby, Stills & Nash* went gold. The friend in the passenger seat, Barbara Langer, had the cat wrapped in a blanket, but just as they entered the freeway, the cat got loose and jumped on Hinton, and she swerved into the oncoming lane. She was killed instantly. Her friend survived.

Distraught over the loss, Crosby took his closest friends—including Mitchell and her new beau, Graham Nash—on his yacht, the *Mayan*, for an extended trip to scatter Hinton's ashes at sea. According to Ronee Blakley, who was on the boat with her husband, Bobby Ingram (who introduced Crosby to Mitchell that fateful day at the Gaslight South), she and Mitchell would cover themselves with tanning oil and slide around on the top deck in the choppy seas. They would also listen to music, such as Billie Holiday and Edith Piaf, as well as read together:

"We both found Nietzsche inspiring and would comb through *Thus Spoke Zarathustra* for signifying phrases," relates Blakley. "Joni was struck by 'Anything worth writing is worth writing in blood,' which had been her writing teacher Arthur Kratzman's motto, and she was jolted by the passage where Nietzsche was 'scathing,' as she put it, towards the poets—calling them vain—but then talked about a new breed of poet, 'the penitent of spirit,' which was what Joni wanted to be."[46]

The image of Blakley and Mitchell sliding into the rails like greased eels is a pretty good one, and their choice of reading material speaks nicely to the particular moment. Mitchell was beginning to gain widespread fame in the wake of her debut album and the covers of her songs that were getting huge airplay. She was feeling the burden of popular expectation, and Nietzsche seemed to be offering the young artist a torch-lit path through the dark jungle of creativity.

She sought the Nietzschean glow once more, while on the road with Dylan, as evidenced by her desire to quote *Zarathustra* in the ill-fated movie *Renaldo and Clara*.

Interestingly, the next reference to Mitchell's affection for the tome subtitled *A Book for Everyone and No One* comes up when she talks about Jaco Pastorius, the genius jazz bassist who translated Mitchell's need for spontaneous rhythms through his inspired, thumping fretwork. Pastorius and Mitchell clearly heard the same beat, because their work together on *Hejira* feels effortless. She told Bill Flanagan, "He was one of the few other people I ever met who thought Nietzsche was funny. We used to laugh about *Thus Spoke Zarathustra*. Jaco was a good friend. I enjoyed his company."[47]

But the relationship heightened Mitchell's awareness of the fame precipice. "As he got on the scene, he kind of went too far over the other way. He used to push his bass up in the mix. Everybody thought it was because he was my new boyfriend!"[48] Pastorius died of head injuries suffered in a scuffle with a Florida bouncer in 1987 at the age of 35, but he gave Mitchell the anchor for her new jazz sound on *Hejira*, *Don Juan's Reckless Daughter*, and the live album *Shadows and Light*. His problems with substance abuse, mental illness, and the ego-surge of fame led to his downfall, but they also reaffirmed Mitchell's need to distance herself from the music industry she loathed so much by continuing her experimentation, surrendering her ego to the creative force, and fashioning art with a nod to Nietzsche—sometimes literally.

ZARATHUSTRA IN A NUTSHELL

Because *Thus Spoke Zarathustra* was a significant influence on Joni Mitchell, I believe a brief recap is in order—just so we can see the chalk-mark outline of the journey, and spot the parallels when they appear.

The book opens with Zarathustra emerging from his mountain cave after a ten-year absence from society. You see, he grew weary of the world at thirty and decided to become a hermit. He had lost his faith but eventually realized this loss was actually a great gift because he was now truly free. He could laugh. He could dance. He could do all the things his spirit told him to, without guilt. He wanted others to feel the same happiness, so he decided to leave the cave he shared with his two pets—an eagle (the proudest animal) and a snake (the wisest animal)—and spread his gospel.

He picks his way down the mountainside and soon meets an old saint, who sings to the old god. The saint doesn't have much respect for humankind. "Give them nothing,"[49] he cautions Zarathustra, who laughs, because he wants to give them the greatest gift of all: freedom to think for oneself. The saint wanders away clueless, while Zarathustra carries on into the village called the Motley Cow.

Zarathustra is empowered, but when he arrives at the village, the people are not ready for his version of godless freedom and ridicule everything he says. "And now they look at me and laugh. And laughing they still hate me. There is ice in their laughter. Perhaps I have lived too long in the

mountains," says Zarathustra, who decides to laugh it off.[50]
Original thinkers are always the enemy. He knows this, but
soon the crowd's attention is diverted to a tightrope walker,
who promptly falls to his death—"a vortex of legs and arms."[51]
The dying man blames the Devil for his fall, but Zarathustra tells him, "All you have spoken does not exist: there is no
Devil and no Hell." Confused, the broken acrobat thinks his
life has been meaningless, but Zarathustra comforts him,
saying, "Not so. You have made danger your calling, there
is nothing in that to despise."[52] Before the tightrope walker
expires, he thanks Zarathustra for his understanding and the
promise of a proper burial.

Shaken by the events of the day, Zarathustra realizes
he needs friends—"living ones, not dead companions and
corpses...the creator seeks fellow-creators."[53] It's not easy to
find kindred souls, and the beaten path won't lead you in the
right direction, but Zarathustra finds inspiration watching
his animal companions. He sees the eagle and the serpent flying together—the snake curled gently around the eagle's neck
in friendly harmony—suggesting wisdom and pride can live
side by side.

As Zarathustra's voyage continues, he meets several more
characters, all of whom elicit a particular message: a dwarf, a
shadow self, the Ugliest Man (who killed God), and the kings
and "higher men" who seek enlightenment because their
grand egos demand a higher spiritual station than the great
unwashed below.

There are times when the journey is too much for Zarathustra and the persistent pain of being misunderstood forces
him back to his cave, where he "waits like a sower who has
scattered his seed."[54] He's waiting for his theories to find root
in the public imagination, but it's no use. "My enemies have

grown powerful and have distorted the meaning of my doctrine, so that my dearest ones are ashamed of the gifts I have given."[55] Realizing first-hand communication is the only way to sell the freedom of a godless state, he returns to the people and continues teaching by example.

At the end of the book, the so-called "wise men" end up back at Zarathustra's cave, where they eat a feast, get drunk, and make an ass dance. They've been awakened by Zarathustra's words and are giddy about their new creative freedom, but they make the mistake of worshipping him for his service—which Zarathustra finds distasteful. After all, he spent all that time tearing down the walls of worship; the last thing he wants to become is a god in others' eyes. It would be the ultimate folly.

He reaffirms his original thought: man must save himself, and the only way he can do so is to question every truth he takes for granted—to challenge and chastise his own gods out of love. If he's courageous enough to face the abyss of a godless universe, he has a chance at transcendence, where he can reconcile life and death—being and not being—without resting on the crutch of denial, the afterlife, or all the pretty angels and demons we've learned to defer to when it comes time for ultimate judgement.

Transcendence takes work. Zarathustra identifies three distinct stages of enlightenment on the way to the ultimate state of the "Superman" or "Overman." The first is the camel, the beast of burden that renounces and is irreverent but dutifully shoulders the weight of humankind and our petty needs. The second is the lion, who overcomes the traditions with his roar of courage. The lion destroys old values because he is strong and fierce, but he cannot recreate the world. For that, you need the third manifestation of man: the one with the eyes of a child who can rediscover innocence in all that is new and recreate the world without raging against it or carrying the burdensome baggage of the old ways.

THE DEVIL IS IN THE DETAILS

The content of Nietzsche's work is woven into Mitchell's oeuvre—from the diction of the lyrics to the use of imagery and metaphor. In fact, once you start combing through Mitchell's work looking for Nietzschean nits to pick, they are everywhere. The god-killer lurks in every corner and crevice of Mitchell's creative odyssey because, like Zarathustra, she learned to chastise her own god—and her own rise to pop goddess status.

We can start with a song that Mitchell herself has discussed at length: "The Three Great Stimulants," which is a direct reference to Nietzsche's *The Birth of Tragedy*. As Mitchell told Elvis Costello in *Vanity Fair*, she wrote the song for the next generation struggling to deal with an increasingly vapid value structure. She says she had already gone through the dislocating effects of being worshipped and idolized, of being simultaneously famous and misunderstood, and figured she could look back on the phenomenon to squeeze meaning from it.

"The three great stimulants of the exhausted ones are artifice, brutality, and innocence," she explains. "The more decadent a culture gets, the more they have a need for what they don't have at all, which is innocence, so you end up with kiddie porn and a perverse obsession with youth." Costello seems to agree but points out the obvious: "You can point at them in the length of a song, but even with all your skill, you run the risk of people pointing the finger at you." Mitchell accepts the responsibility: "But you have to. It's just too serious."[56]

Except for the ever-earnest Bono, "too serious" is a sentence fragment you don't hear from the mouths of most pop idols. But as a true creator, Mitchell feels the responsibility of her calling, where critical and financial success is second to seeking truth. These are the themes Nietzsche addressed at the age of twenty-seven in *The Birth of Tragedy* as he attempted to issue the wake-up call to the enlightened, who recognize the need for something deeper—but often end up lost in the candy store of pleasant intellectual distraction: "One is chained by the Socratic love of knowledge and the delusion of being able thereby to heal the eternal wound of existence," he says. "Another is ensnared by art's seductive veil of beauty fluttering before his eyes. Still another by the metaphysical comfort that beneath the whirl of phenomena eternal life flows on indestructibly."[57] These three stages of illusion, Nietzsche concludes, stall growth.

Mitchell translated these elements into "artifice, brutality and innocence." "The Three Great Stimulants" confused a lot of people when it came out in 1985 on *Dog Eat Dog*, but Mitchell was unfazed. As she tells the *Vancouver Sun*'s John Mackie in January 2010, in one of her last interviews:

People go "we don't know what she's talking about and we don't care." Especially "The Three Great Stimulants," which was never understood... well that's Nietzsche the philosopher talking about Germany rotting. Well, we're rotting just like Germany. So I borrowed that concept. What do you do when you're in a state of moral and ethical decay? You call to the three great stimulants of the exhausted ones. Artifice, you escape through entertainment. Brutality, our generation produced the most sadistic art in the history of film, anyway. And comedy, everything lost its heart and became brutal. And innocence of course should be corruption of innocence, that's why all this pedophilism and sexual tourism is on the increase, because what do rotten decadent pigs like best but to pervert innocence.[58]

In the same breath as Mitchell attempted to decrypt "The Three Great Stimulants" for interviewers, she often found herself explaining another tune with Nietzschean threads: "The Reoccurring Dream" from 1988's *Chalk Mark in a Rain Storm*. Nietzsche wrote about "eternal recurrence" as the essential fact of existence because life is a cycle, a great big circle game of being and not being. He made Zarathustra its central icon. "I, Zarathustra, the advocate of life, the advocate of suffering, the advocate of the circle—I call you," Zarathustra says in the chapter "The Convalescent." "I hear you! My abyss speaks, I have turned my ultimate depth into the light!" Merging the beginning with the end is an act of recreation because it redefines all notions of time and space: it can make the night day, and day night. The image Nietzsche associates with this dynamic process of constant rebirth is the Ouroboros—a snake biting its own tail. "Everything goes, everything returns; the wheel of existence rolls for ever," he says. "Everything departs, everything meets again; the ring of existence is true to itself for ever."[59]

Mitchell's "Reoccurring Dream" highlights our shallow quest for pleasurable repetition and distraction—"This is the reoccurring dream / Born in the dreary gap between / What we have now / And what we wish we could have"—and condemns its commercial exploitation: "Glamorous picture people rise / Radiant! / Gleaming down from screens and pages / Ooh glamour before your very eyes!... If you had this / If you had that / Wouldn't it be fabulous... Order your youth secrets of the stars / Call now just $9.99."

Yet again, no one understood the arrow Mitchell launched from her bow, even though it landed in the blood-red bull's eye and nailed our consumerist culture as the culprit that is forever pulling us away from our core selves and the creative essence. As she told Costello: "So nobody understood 'The Reoccurring Dream,' but after September 11, when we were coerced to do a national duty and go out and shop, surely people could begin to see what I was getting at."

Mitchell poked at the same pompous posers in *Dog Eat Dog*'s "Fiction"—a song that points out various levels of communal denial:

Fiction of the moralist
Fiction of the nihilist
Fiction of the innovator and the stylist
Fiction of the killjoy
Fiction of the charmer
Fiction of the clay feet and the shining armour
Fiction of the declaimers
Fiction of the rebukers
Fiction of the pro and the no nukers
Fiction of the gizmo
Fiction of the data
Fiction of the this is this and that is that ahh!

The song contains some tantalizing Nietzschean content, from "the nihilist"—a term synonymous with Nietzsche—to the running theme of fact vs. fiction, what is and what could be—and the very notion of absolutes, which Nietzsche perceived as a sign of intellectual decrepitude. Unfortunately for us, the state has enshrined these notions of good and evil and sold us the lie of creative realization through consumption—as Nietzsche's Zarathustra observes, "The state is the coldest of all cold monsters. This lie creeps from its mouth: 'I, the state, am the people.' It is a lie!" he protests. "It was creators who created peoples and hung a faith and a love over them: thus they served life. It is destroyers who set snares for many and call it the state."[60]

Nietzsche's words weren't understood in their day, and Mitchell's "Fiction" met a similar fate. Few understood the song that contained a cameo from Rod Steiger as a holy roller and the electronically rendered "voice of truth" that sounded like it was coming from a bullhorn. "Fiction" and "The Reoccurring Dream" were frequently cited as examples of Mitchell losing her way. She expresses her frustration about these misperceptions to Costello with an anecdote about how one radio host listed a variety of Joni clones (from Rickie Lee Jones and Suzanne Vega to Tracy Chapman and Sarah McLachlan), only to conclude the imitators were better than the original. "The commentator said, 'There are all these young women coming up and they have all listened to Joni Mitchell. You can even tell what records that they are listening to,'" Mitchell explains. "And they played this song with the first three chords you learn on the guitar, insipid lyrics, no depth, no clarity, no metaphor, nothing. Then at the end of the show they said. 'All of these girls are beating Joni at her own game. Look how she's lost perspective,'" Mitchell laments. "And they played 'The Reoccurring Dream.'"

In several interviews, Mitchell defends the song and tries to explain why it's misunderstood. "['The Reoccurring Dream'] is a beautiful piece of music, but melody is not the point of it. It's textural and there are snippets of melody," she told Jody Denberg. "One of the hardest things for me to bear is to be told again and again that I have no melodic sense or that there's no melody here. My argument is… does Marvin Gaye have melody? I try to sing the words and give them their proper inflection. Every time I sing it, I sing it different."[61]

The red circles Mr. Kratzman drew on her school-assignment poems must have danced in Mitchell's head, because she resisted cliché at every turn, even at the cost of her commercial success. She sings things differently every time. This immersion in Nietzschean philosophy bubbles up on just about every album, sometimes directly. *Dog Eat Dog* contains the lines: "Money is the road to justice / and power walks it on crooked legs / Prime Time Crime/ Holy hope in the hands of / Snakebite evangelists and racketeers / and big wig financiers." The skepticism about organized religion and hate-peddlers is Nietzschean in feeling, but the actual words "power walks… on crooked legs" are taken directly from Nietzsche's "Of the Chairs of Virtue" in *Thus Spoke Zarathustra*: "Honour and obedience to the authorities, and even to the crooked authorities! Thus good sleep will have it. How can I help it that power likes to walk on crooked legs?"[62]

There's more. Mitchell's lyrics frequently allude to lions and dragons, which have Nietzschean resonance: the lion is the beast with enough courage to rise up and growl in the face of the status quo; the dragon is the fire-breathing dogma of the old god. The song "Trouble Child" describes a "dragon shining with all values known / dazzling you—keeping you from your own / where is the lion in you to defy him?" and "Slouching Towards Bethlehem" includes the lines, "Shaped like a lion / It has the head of a man / With a gaze as blank / And pitiless as the sun / And it's moving its slow thighs / Across the desert sands."

"Slouching Towards Bethlehem" is a reference to W.B. Yeats's poem, "The Second Coming," written after the First World War. As Mitchell writes in an explanatory note for *The*

Fiddle and the Drum, the Alberta Ballet production inspired by her music, "I've included two new songs in the ballet but most of the material comes from an album called *Dog Eat Dog*, which was poorly received in the '80s, and was almost immediately repressed for more than 20 years. The set also includes two poems, which I set to music but did not write. One is Rudyard Kipling's 'If,' and the other a song I call 'Slouching Towards Bethlehem,' which was adapted from Yeats's poem 'The Second Coming.'"

Yeats was a huge fan of Nietzsche—a fact well chronicled in academic circles and in his bookcase, which contained a copy of *Thus Spoke Zarathustra*, given to him in 1902 by the American lawyer John Quinn.[63] "But in the loneliest desert the second metamorphosis occurs: The spirit becomes a lion; it wants to capture freedom and be lord in its own desert. It will be an enemy to its ultimate God, it will struggle for victory with the great dragon," writes Nietzsche. "The great dragon is called 'Thou shalt.' But the spirit of the lion says 'I Will!'" Joni Mitchell was fluent in all these different philosophical stances because she dramatizes the metaphysical struggle in songs such as "Slouching Towards Bethlehem," "The Sire of Sorrow," and "The Priest." More importantly, she questions fundamental Judeo-Christian concepts. "Slouching Towards Bethlehem," for instance, probes our relationship to the god concept and the so-called "ultimate creator" above us: "Surely some revelation is at hand / Surely it's the second coming / And the wrath has finally taken form / For what is this rough beast / Its hour come at last / Slouching toward Bethlehem to be born... Raging and raging / It rises from the deep / Opening its eyes / After twenty centuries / Vexed to a nightmare / Out of a stony sleep / By a rocking cradle / By the Sea of Galilee."

This raging beast, rising from the deep, is the repressed spirit of man—the one with the power to recreate the world through the gift of creation. Weak faith won't heal and release us. Only creation can. In a 1997 interview with music theorist Daniel Levitin in *Grammy* magazine, Mitchell discusses how the creative experience realigns the creator-creation dynamic by making it internal and self-exploratory. Levitin says, "You said 'great singing is between the singer and God.' Are you actually singing to God?" Mitchell replies, "I don't really call in spirits or deities, or anything. I just quietly centre myself; I sober myself… I hardly ever use the word 'God.' As a matter of fact I asked Dylan one time: 'What do you mean by God, 'cause if you read the Bible, I can't tell God from the devil half the time! They seem to me to act very similarly.' And Dylan said, 'Well, it's just a word that people use.' I said, 'yeah, but when you use it, what do you mean?' And he never answered me."[64]

But later, when Dylan went through his Christian phase, Mitchell says, "He came up to me and said, 'remember that time you asked me about God and the devil? Well I'll tell you now.' And he launched into this fundamentalist crap, and I said 'Bobby, be careful. All of that was written by poets like us; but this interpretation of yours seems a little brainwashed.' 'Poets like us…' he said. He kind of snickered at that. But there certainly is a creative spark whether or not it has gender or personification."

Mitchell's isolation of the "creative spark" proves her awareness of something pulsing in the spheres—she just refuses to call it god. She'd prefer to take responsibility for the creative power within her. She says she could call some of what happens "divine inspiration," but she'd rather not. She sees herself as a secular humanist—and that can be a risky place to occupy in the increasingly dogmatic dogpatch of the U.S. "If you're a fundamental Baptist or a Catholic, these are really dangerous thoughts," she tells Levitin. "I am forbidden literature on a lot of church lists because I raise doubt, and because I'm opposed to blind faith. I know the power of blind faith and it's a beautiful power. Don Juan in the Castaneda books has a beautiful, unifying line: I believe, not because I care, but because I must."

Levitin eventually circles back to Dylan to close the discussion of the divine, but I'm going to push forward into the white blindness of faith to draw a closer bead on where Mitchell really stands in the face of the Almighty and organized religion.

At the age of seven, Mitchell says, she broke from the church because it demanded empty-headed, mechanical worship, a concept that little Joan Anderson found repugnant to her wide-open prairie sensibilities. Two years later, she contracted polio and was told she might never walk again. She decided to pray. But she didn't know whose name to summon for help. "The Bible stories were full of loopholes. I liked the stories, but they didn't like my questions," she says.[65]

Joni Mitchell questions all theology. It's one of the reasons why you should never, ever, call her a "confessional songwriter." "It's as close as someone could come to calling me a nigger," she says.[66] Mitchell hates the term because it has religious connotations, namely the patriarchal brand of Christianity that spawned places like the Magdalene laundries—the home of horrors for unwed mothers she describes in her song of the same name, where the "bloodless brides of Jesus... leech the light out of a room."

As she told Mojo's Robert Hilburn: "To be called a 'confessional writer' is repugnant to me... The term makes what I do seem cheap and gimmicky. 'Confession' to me is having a gun stuck to your head or going, 'Forgive me Father for I have sinned.' That's not what I do. If someone calls me a confessional writer, it is ignorant and insulting."[67]

During her in-depth interview with Mitchell in 2007, Michelle Mercer brought up the topic of St. Augustine of Hippo.[68] Considered the father of autobiography for his thirteen-tome collection *Confessions*, written in the fourth century, St. Augustine hoped that in writing about himself, and attaining safe creative distance, he would know himself better. "I have become an enigma to myself," he wrote.

Mitchell calls St. Augustine a "champion bullshitter," who cut out huge chunks of what would later become the Bible—including the chapter on Lilith, Adam's sister and the inspiration behind Sarah McLachlan's femme-centric rock tour, Lilith Fair. Mitchell also accuses St. Augustine of phoniness, because he claimed to look at himself in the mirror but actually lied about what he saw so he could prop up a false god. Mitchell accuses him of replacing the creator's impulse, the very lifeblood of the universe, with dogma, a leech that sucks passion, originality, and sex from our existence.

Everything that was magic about the human condition—namely our ability to create through intellect and through flesh—was flattened through Augustine's prudish, guilt-laden lens. "Through a synchronistic event... he opened up [the Book of Romans] and came across this passage that was really hostile to lust," she says. "This synchronicity was something that people valued back then. Of course, it's still alive and well today in the arts community." Sadly, Augustine misinterpreted the pulse of the spheres and, in turn, warped the very foundation of the Judeo-Christian approach to creation. "He formed this crazy interpretation of Genesis," says Mitchell.

The artist in Mitchell clearly didn't like the way the fourth-century thinker put the body in a cage of dogma, and she didn't like the way he translated the great relationship between god and earth, between the creator and the creation, into one of good and evil, of blind righteousness and punishment.

It's partly this religious baggage that makes the "confessional" label so repulsive to Mitchell. She says the only real confession she's ever made in a song was when she admitted in "Man to Man" (on the 1982 album *Wild Things Run Fast*) that when she's scared she gets "phony" and "stoney."

That Mitchell is in touch with her "phony" moments is important, because it suggests she's aware of where her truth lies—an awareness she achieved by questioning herself, her creative power, and the great Creator. This act of questioning is the first step towards self-creation; according to Zarathustra, "What is the greatest thing you can experience? It is the hour of great contempt. The hour in which even your happiness grows loathsome to you, and your reason and your virtue also. The hour when you say: What good is my pity? Is not pity the cross upon which he who loves man is nailed? But my pity is no crucifixion!"[69]

Mitchell experienced this great hour of contempt in the wake of achieving celebrity and fame. She attracted the attention of the masses, who identified with her, cried with her, loved with her, and worshipped her. The more blood she poured onto the page, the more acolytes she pulled to her heaving chest. But eventually the cycle grew repulsive and she had to destroy her own god-like image. She didn't enjoy her role in the propagation of adoration because she found the texts hypocritical, a point she makes in the under-discussed song "The Priest" from *Ladies of the Canyon*:

> Then he took his contradictions out
> And he splashed them on my brow
> So which words was I then to doubt

When choosing what to vow
Should I choose them all—should I make them mine
The sermons the hymns and the valentines
And he asked for truth and he asked for time
And he asked for only now

Inexplicably, this song about a priest has been tagged to Mitchell's relationship with Leonard Cohen because it describes a "holy man," the same phrase contained in "Rainy Night House" ("You are a holy man on the FM radio"), which has also been called a song about Leonard Cohen. Mitchell dismisses as erroneous all lyrical nods to Cohen, save the lines in "That Song About the Midway." The more likely inspiration for "The Priest" is Nietzsche, especially in light of the fragment: "Come let's run from this ring we're in / Where the Christians clap and the Germans grin." *Zarathustra* has a whole chapter, "Of the Priests,"[70] dedicated to men of the cloth. Nietzsche writes about the spiritual emptiness of the churches where "false values and false scriptures" collect dust in "counterfeit light" and "musty air." Only when the roofs have blown off to reveal the blue sky and the limitless truth of man would Zarathustra be able to see the priestly mission as spiritually correct: "Only when the clear sky again looks through broken roofs and down upon grass and red poppies on broken walls... will I turn my heart again towards the places of God." Nietzsche's thoughts are translated into Mitchell's lyrics, in which the old saint trashes the open sky of free thinking, while at the same time acknowledging the emptiness of his cathedral: "He said you wouldn't like it here / It's no place you should share / The roof is ripped with hurricanes / and the room is always bare."

These hollow images reinforce the idea of an absentee creator, or a god who listens to the cries of his creations without compassion. Either way, man has been abandoned—and if there's one story that gets to the very nub of faith, spiritual ambivalence, and the mystery of creation, it's the story of Job—the man who had everything until God decided to take it away as a test of faith at the Devil's urging. Job is considered the greatest literary work in the Bible. It's also the basis for *King Lear* and the reason why we have the expression "in the pits"—because that's where Job ends up, sitting in an ash pit surrounded by the ruins of his former life. Job will always resonate because people always ask God: "Why me?"

This was Job's chorus, and it's one Mitchell takes to heart in her song "The Sire of Sorrow." "Let me speak let me spit out my bitterness / Born of grief and nights without sleep and festering flesh," Job says in the song. "Once I was blessed; I was awaited like the rain / Like eyes for the blind, like feet for the lame / Kings heard my words, and they sought out my company / But now the janitors of Shadowland flick their brooms at me." He cries out to his god: "Oh you tireless watcher! What have I done to you? / That you make everything I dread and everything I fear come true?"

When Job asks God, "Tell me why do you starve the faithful? / Why do you crucify the saints? / And you let the wicked prosper / You let their children frisk like deer / And my loves are dead or dying, or they don't come near," he is answered by "the antagonists," as they're labelled on the lyric sheet: "We don't despise your chastening / God is correcting you."

On recordings of the song, the antagonists are played by an all-male chorus with stern voices. They could be seen as Job's jeering friends who've now turned against him because he's no longer popular. Or they could be read as the hostile voice of God, because they certainly offer no answer—just as God offered Job no easy answer. "Where were you when I laid the foundations of the universe?" is what God asks Job. In essence, I am the greatest creator you could ever know, so how could you possibly decipher my meaning? I am mysterious, and divine, so shut up and take it.

Job has fascinated many, including Nietzsche, who wrote a whole chapter in *Zarathustra* called "The Sorcerer"—Job's story,[71] told through a post-God lens. "What do you want, waylayer, from me? You God veiled in lightning! Unknown one! Speak, What do you want, unknown—God?" When Zarathustra sees the old man whining to the heavens, he loses his patience because it's such a weak pose: what loser keeps knocking on a door that no one answers? Zarathustra whops the whiner on the side of head with his cane and mocks his pathetic display. "In whom was I supposed to believe when you wailed in such a fashion?" he says. The miserable man answers back: "The penitent of the spirit … it was he I played: you yourself once invented this expression—the poet and sorcerer who at last turns his spirit against himself, the transformed man who freezes through his bad knowledge and bad conscience."

Mitchell told *Mojo* writer Barney Hoskyns that "The Sire of Sorrow" came out of a difficult time—she was being sued by her housekeeper for an alleged kick to the shin and had been suffering through two years of dental surgery—when she was asking, "Why me?" The sandpaper of self-pity left a few scars, but it also scraped the surface clean. The song was cathartic. As she says, it was a way for her to "cleanse" herself; she didn't want to carry the darkness forward. She didn't want her loved ones to feel "burdened by [her] bitterness."[72]

There is a healing penitence in her creative spirit, and this brings up the other most-used phrase in the Mitchell-Nietzsche search parameter: "The new breed of poet" who is "the penitent of spirit." Zarathustra talks about the poets at length because they are the verbal creators with endless capacity to speak truth. As a result, they are on the front line of change. The tragedy for Zarathustra is that too few poets really plumb the depths: "I have grown weary of the poets, the old and the new," he says in "Of Poets." "They all seem to me superficial and shallow seas. They have not thought deeply enough... They are not clean enough for me either: They all disturb their waters so they may seem deep. And in that way would like to show themselves reconcilers, but to me they remain mediators and meddlers, and mediocre and unclean men!"[73]

Mitchell often refers to this passage. In a 1985 interview with *Musician* magazine's Bill Flanagan,[74] she talks about her seminal Nietzschean encounter with Mr. Kratzman, then goes on to talk about her desire to live the life of the penitent poet—getting awfully close to the exact wording from *Zarathustra*, proving she's pretty much committed it to memory (as Nietzsche would have hoped—he said people who write in aphorisms don't want to be read, they want to be known by heart). "I had a great seventh grade English teacher who told me it was important to write in my own blood. And I had become a fan of *Thus Spoke Zarathustra*: 'The Poet is the vainest of the vain, even before the ugliest of water buffalo doth he fan his tail. I've looked amongst him for an honest man and all I've dredged up are old godheads,'" she quotes. "'He muddies his waters that he may appear deep.' And on and on, insulting the poet mentality."

Mitchell pauses on the poetic note and finishes her *Zarathustra* citation with a nod to the new breed of truth seeker: "'But I see a new breed. They are the penitents of spirit. They write in their own blood.'" Mitchell was transformed by the idea of the penitent poet who sees his art as part of his larger creative purpose, whether it's embraced by the masses or not.

"I thought, 'Yeah, that's the only way to do this with any kind of dignity,'" she says. "I don't think I even thought about the risk. I just thought this had to be done. But then you find out that when you get slammed, it's you that's getting slammed, not your act. Everything is that much more personal."

In urging Mitchell to dip her nib into a throbbing artery of personal experience, Mr. Kratzman started her on a lifetime voyage of deep personal discovery. He pushed her to be original at every turn, and for the first half of her career, this inspired legions of loyal fans to respond to her work in a deeply personal way. The second half of her professional life wasn't as charmed because her creations weren't always embraced. They were often too innovative.

Mitchell's first creative turn towards penitence was *The Hissing of Summer Lawns*. "No one understood that album," said Mitchell. Says Zarathustra: "They do not understand me, I am not the mouth for these ears." The very same words seem to spring from Mitchell's mouth over the course of her career: "I have in my time been very misunderstood," she told Penny Valentine, iterating a line she would repeat in almost every interview she's ever done.

Any time you try something new, you will be attacked for it—or "crucified" as Nietzsche says: "They crucify him who writes new values on the new law-tables, they sacrifice the future to themselves—they crucify the whole human future!"

Mitchell seems happy to let herself be slaughtered for stepping away from the fold, but that hasn't stopped her from speaking out against rigid thinking. When *Shine*, her last album, came out in 2007, she told Tim Murphy of *New York* magazine that she had remained silent for half a decade because she was too angry: "Angry at the American people. At Christians. At theology—the ignorance of it. And I didn't want to write about it. I removed myself from society and painted. It was a method of avoiding the anger, not addressing it." But she eventually confronted the rage through research and creation: "I confronted a lot of it and worked it out to a point. I read the Koran, I started Genesis, Augustine, did a lot of theological research." When Murphy asks if she's religious, she says the "God of the Old Testament is the depiction of evil" and she prefers a Buddhist view, which is more compatible with "original Gnostic Christianity. It's not theological. You have to work on yourself—you don't have a saviour. It's self-study."[75]

RIVER

When Mitchell tells us she has no saviour and she's self-studying spirituality, she's affirming the core Nietzschean idea of emancipation through creation: the old Creator is dead; long live the new creator. It's an empowering sense of purpose, but living in a world without God can be alienating. Mitchell articulates this sense of dislocation, as well as several Nietzschean metaphors, in the oft-covered song, "River," which begins:

> It's coming on Christmas
> They're cutting down trees
> They're putting up reindeer
> And singing songs of joy and peace
> Oh I wish I had a river I could skate away on

Just about everyone can agree that this is one of the saddest yule-time tunes ever written. Ask your friend why it's so sad, and she'll tell you it's because she's just broken up with her boyfriend—"the best baby she ever had." There's no doubt that's one level of the narrative, but the whole backdrop of the song refers to Christmas and the idea that people are putting up reindeer and singing songs of joy and peace. The narrator seems unable to relate to these actions, and so she pines for a long stretch of frozen water she can escape on—she wants a frozen river.

"River" can be a big word in philosophy, because it's often used as a metaphor for life itself. Ever since Heraclitus said you can't step into the same river twice, the image has been used to convey the notion of flux and change, the unknowable dimensions of existence. Nietzsche pushed the metaphysical metaphor into a trenchant question about God when he likened a frozen river to the icy, thin veneer of religious meaning. The river of life is always moving, but in a god-state we live with the illusion the world is fixed— that good and evil are absolutes and that we can pass from one side of river to the other without drowning. "Over the stream everything is firmly fixed, all values of things, the bridges, the concepts, all 'Good' and 'Evil:' all are firmly fixed!" writes Nietzsche in "Of Old and New Law Tables" from *Zarathustra*. "But when the hard winter comes, the animal-tamer of streams, then even the cleverest learn mistrust; and truly, not only the simpletons say then: 'Is everything meant to stand still?'—that is a proper winter doctrine, a fine thing for unfruitful seasons, a fine consolation for hibernators and stay-at-homes. 'Fundamentally, everything stands still'—the thawing wind, however preaches to the contrary!"[76]

This notion of "fundamental" ideals getting in the way of spiritual flow resonated for Mitchell when she wrote "River." She understood that a long, frozen stretch of water isn't just an icy river: it's a spiritual escape route. Nietzsche used the frozen river as a metaphor for what happens to the soul in a God-dominated deep-freeze, and Mitchell skates away with it on the tune that cranks up every Christmas. She wants a

God she can love and believe in on Christ's birthday, so she can belong to the same reality where kitschy Christmas decor feels good and she can fly away in distracted bliss. But she doesn't. She has no him. And she has no Him, which explains why "River" is such a melancholic Christmas song: it's not just mourning the end of a relationship; it's a dirge for the dead God.

seven

LOVE
The Big Production

"All I really really want our love to do
Is to bring out the best in me and in you too
I want to talk to you, I want to shampoo you
I want to renew you again and again
Applause, applause—life is our cause
When I think of your kisses my mind see-saws
Do you see—do you see—do you see how you hurt me baby
So I hurt you too
Then we both get so blue."

JONI MITCHELL, "All I Want," *Blue*

EVEN THE WORD was made flesh. So now is the time to strip
the meta off the physical and get down to the naked truth of
Joni Mitchell: she, like the rest of us, is an animated bag of
water subject to great emotional swells of feeling. The only
real difference between Mitchell and the masses is her ability
to channel those tidal movements of emotion into song—and
not just any songs, but music that will most likely last the ages
because it continues to resonate in the hearts and minds of so
many, particularly when it comes to matters of love.

Romantic love tears off the clothes of intellect and forces us to rub up against the Other and, in so doing, understand ourselves a little bit better. And that's just spiritually. Creatively speaking, we're "making" love—and experiencing the same immersion in the moment as artists describe when making a masterpiece. The sexual act offers proof of our fleshiness and in its explosion of fluids and hormonal secretions, reminds us we are physical and, as such, mortal. The pleasure and the pain, the fullness and the emptiness, all the dimensions of the human condition find immediate and accessible form through the hot pulse of romantic love. As a result, songs about this swollen feeling in our soul have a tendency to stick around and form the soundtrack of our lives.

Joni Mitchell's music is on the jukebox of a generation. Her songs of love and heartbreak form an emotional and sonic prairie of experience. The love song—seemingly trite when in bloom and cathartically pure in mourning—lets us surrender to the human condition through creative communion.

Mitchell's image as the wailing lover and mentor for mopes is a large part of the Joni mythology: it's the reason why she was labelled "confessional" despite her many protests. Yet the reality of Mitchell's love life is actually far more cryptic than her open-artery songs would lead you to believe. And her feelings about sex seem far more convoluted than any chart of hearts and arrows.

When Morrissey interviewed Mitchell for Rolling Stone in 1997, the black-trousered sex symbol asked her if she was ever promiscuous. "In terms of the times, I guess we all were. It was a hedonistic time, you know," she said. When he asked her if she was still promiscuous, she said: "No. I've always been a serial monogamist. But there was a time when you were traveling—a traveling woman, like a traveling man—and there were some brief encounters."[1]

There's just a hint of revisionism in this. Evidently, she was embarrassed by the indirect accusations she was a slut, but she herself sings: "I used to count lovers like railroad cars / I counted them on my side / Lately I don't count nothing / I just let things slide." The lyrics for "Just Like This Train" (off *Court and Spark*) continue: "The stationmaster's shuffling cards / Boxcars are banging in the yards / Jealous lovin' will make you crazy / If you can't find your goodness / 'Cause you lost your heart." The honesty of these lyrics is the core of Mitchell's mythical power as love's poetic oracle: she's honest enough to bare the ugliness of jealousy and the "sour grapes" of losing on the battlefield of love. Her reflective courage gives us permission to indulge and purge at the same time.

Mitchell draws so much content from her romantic connections, there are times when you have to wonder which need is serving which: is she making love to a variety of different men because she's eagerly seeking a lifelong mate? Or is she using the relationships to stoke the wood stove of creativity? The answer is both, because as much as Mitchell has been hurt by her love affairs, she's managed to transcend the heartbreak through creation. Moreover, she seems to assume an almost voyeuristic role in romance as a way of maintaining a safe distance, as well as critical perspective. Like many women, she's used sex as a tool—even a machete.

Mitchell blazed an impressive trail through the sexual moonscape of L.A.'s arid canyons and dry gulches. After conceiving with Brad McMath only to be abandoned with a baby in her belly, Mitchell appears to have made a decision to take charge of her own sexuality—and make it work for her, regardless of how many hearts got broken along the way. And she was a heartbreaker. David Crosby admits he fell into the so-called "cement mixer," and that Mitchell just isn't the "kind of person you have a relationship with." Another ex,

Dave Naylor, points out Mitchell's ability to create and re-create the thread of history using her own will: "If you're in Joan's life, you're going to get blamed," he explains in Sheila Weller's book. "Joan rewrites history really well, and once she tells a story once or twice in her head, it comes true to her—I call it her iron whim."[2]

THE NITTY GRITTY

We know Mitchell hates talking about her love life. She says the music speaks for itself and the gossip is unimportant, but it's part of the historical record thanks to the big names she bedded, so even if it's distasteful, we have to catalogue the highlight reel of her apparent conquests. There were more than are listed here, but this is a book about the creative experience, not a coffee klatsch about Mitchell's sex life. The focus of the sexual encounters will follow the arc of her creative evolution, because love begets creation, and no one found a way to make love work—emotionally and creatively—better than Joni Mitchell.

If we go back to Mitchell's descriptions of growing up on the Canadian flatlands, boys don't really figure into the mix. She was attached to cigarettes, her first uke, and dancing on the wrong side of the so-called tracks. She was also transported by Rachmaninoff's *Rhapsody on a Theme of Paganini* and confesses to having a hopelessly romantic side. The first real boyfriend of note was McMath, the art student who headed to California when he found out Joni was pregnant. He didn't last long as a lover, but his actions did indirectly inspire "Little Green." He also forced the young artist into a completely different life track, forever making her Joni Mitchell and setting her on a creative journey where love, and its fleshy expression, could always be seen as a potential liability.

Chuck Mitchell followed, and while the marriage did not last, it was a creative endeavour. They toured together, but when egos started to clash, the relationship disintegrated—but not before Mitchell was legally entitled to work in the U.S. While single and exploring her sexuality in New York City in 1967, she wrote the song that would lay the foundation for her career and cement her into the annals of popular culture: "Both Sides Now."

It's almost impossible to believe a love song as profoundly wise and tempered as "Both Sides Now" came from the brain of a twentysomething kid from Saskatchewan, but it did, and even Mitchell seems mystified by the process that led to a timeless look at the reality of love. "I was reading *Henderson the Rain King* on a plane," she says, "and early in the book Henderson… is also up in a plane. He's on his way to Africa and he looks down and sees these clouds. I put down the book, looked out the window and saw clouds too and I immediately started writing the song. I had no idea that the song would become as popular as it did."[3]

Mitchell says she started writing "Both Sides Now" while she was still married to Chuck Mitchell, which almost explains the world-weariness within the song—as well as its long view of life: "Something's lost, but something's gained in living every day." She sounds like an aging matron sitting with a granddaughter on her knee, darning socks: "Life happens, dearie." The song's timelessness resides not only in its lyrical acceptance of life's disappointments, both romantically and spiritually, but also in its obvious melodic appeal. "Both Sides Now" is a catchy tune—as witnessed by its *Billboard* ranking (number eight pop single) and Judy Collins's Grammy for best folk performance. A few years after Collins's single, Mitchell recorded her version and ditched the glossy production used by Collins in favour of a more stripped-down sound. Mitchell's vocal phrasing also feels more grounded, avoiding the grand gymnastic runs in the climax—as if to say: life is what it is, and we don't know shit.

"Cactus Tree," off her debut, was written after "Both Sides Now" but recorded earlier, and from the beginning, it establishes Mitchell's emotional distance as a thematic strand. "She will love them when she sees them / They will lose her if they follow / And she only means to please them / And her heart is full and hollow / Like a cactus tree." Mitchell told Penny Valentine that "Cactus Tree" was a song about a "modern woman" who saw the world was full of "lovely men" but found herself driven by "something else other than settling down to frau-duties." Mitchell said the song "has to do with [her] own experiences" because she, too, is a seeker—a woman on the move obsessed with freedom. She wants to find a way of living that allows her to extract all the wonders without sacrificing huge slices of herself.

The quality of "Both Sides Now" and "Cactus Tree" suggests there are great creative riches to be extracted from love that's not quite right, as well as romantic partnerships that sit like a burr under the saddle.

Mitchell carried this lesson forward, and by the time she met Leonard Cohen, it appears she was on the same page as he was when it came to romance. After all, Mitchell had already given birth, gotten married, and was now divorced. She had boyfriends. She went drinking alone. She was only in her early twenties, but she had a secure sexual ego. She was the "greatest lover." She played the fearless conqueror with an almost manly bravado. From the famous face of Leonard Cohen, she moved on to bona fide rock star David Crosby—whom she tossed into her cement mixer and emerged with concrete creative results: a record deal that guaranteed her creative autonomy, big buzz as the hottest new thing in folk music, and an association with Guinevere—the legendary beauty who made King Arthur a cuckold, as well as the song Crosby wrote around the time he met Mitchell in Coconut Grove.

If she had been writing a book on success in show business, Mitchell couldn't have scripted it better. "She was such an unusual, passionate and powerful woman," says Crosby. "I was writing things like 'Guinnevere'… things like that made me very attracted to her."[4] Mitchell's first impression of Crosby was nowhere near as glamorous, or as fawning, but it was affectionate: "I remember being introduced to him and thinking he reminded me of Yosemite Sam. I used to call him secretly Yosemite Sam in my mind… David was wonderful company and a great appreciator. When it comes to expressing infectious enthusiasm, he is probably the most capable person I know. His eyes were like star sapphires to me. When he laughed, they seemed to twinkle like no one else's."[5]

It was those twinkling eyes that seduced her into singing into a piano and forever established the "bell jar" soundscape that affirmed the Mitchell optics: chiselled, pure, and oddly fragile. We know now that was largely a creative fiction—Mitchell operated more like a piece of heavy machinery than a dainty floral specimen—but that's where the listener's imagination takes over and ascribes meanings to songs that may, or may not, be entirely accurate.

People have looked at the words and music for "The Dawntreader," for instance, and immediately associated it with Crosby because of its sailing references, but Mitchell is loath to pin any tune on a particular romantic donkey. She's far more eager to distill the universal so that the range of emotion is accessible to anyone. "I have felt that it was perhaps my role on occasion to pass on anything I learned that

was helpful to me in the route to fulfillment or a happy life…
including anything I've discovered about myself," she told
Jenny Boyd. "I feel that the best of me and the most illuminat-
ing things I discover should go into the work. I feel a social
responsibility to that. I think I know my role: I am a witness.
I'm to document my experience one way or another."[6]

This conviction in the larger purpose of the music is something Mitchell shared with another ex who proved a creative
inspiration as well as a compelling romantic partner. Graham
Nash met Mitchell in Ottawa, the quaint Canadian capital
city, in 1968. Nash had already been warned about Mitchell
by his new friend, and soon-to-be singing partner, Crosby.
"Watch out for this woman," Crosby said, according to Nash.
When the former singer for the Hollies laid eyes on her, he was
immediately smitten. "I saw this woman sitting by herself
with what looked like a Bible on her lap. She was something
to behold," says Nash in Sheila Weller's book. "So I walked
over and introduced myself and she invited me to her room in
the hotel, and I ended up spending the night with her, and…"
Nash drifts off into space. "I haven't been the same since."
Mitchell didn't use her physical presence to woo the English-
man, though it was clearly part of the love elixir brewing that
night. She pulled out her instrument and started strumming.
"She played fifteen songs, almost her entire first record, and a
couple of different ones too." Nash says, "By the time she got
through 'Michael from Mountains' and 'I Had a King,' I was
gone. I had never heard music like that."[7]

Mitchell and her new love eventually moved in together
and set up a common creative hive in Laurel Canyon. As in
previous love relationships, there would be a lot of creation
going on—and just enough conflict to keep things cooking.
"She was a little skittish about commitment," Nash told Sheila
Weller. "She didn't want to be like her grandmothers: They

had given up artistic careers to take care of husbands... [it] was always an unspoken thing between Joan and me."

The house at 8217 Lookout Mountain had pine panelling, stained-glass windows, and the grandfather clock that Leonard Cohen had given to Joni. It also had a piano—a Priestly piano, according to *Rolling Stone*—that Mitchell and Nash would race to every morning. "It was an intense time," Nash told Weller, "Who's going to fill up the space with their music first? We [were] two very creative writers living in the same space, and it was an interesting clash: 'I want to get as close to you as possible.' 'Let me alone to create!'"

This creative friction proved empowering to Mitchell, who was in the midst of recording *Clouds*. Having already experienced the creative-romantic conflict with Crosby in production, Mitchell asserted herself in the studio and became her own producer—a decision that shaped the rest of her career, until her next big love affair recalibrated the gears of autonomy. For now, though, Mitchell was giving herself the space to make mistakes but always with the ambition of finding her true voice as a creator. "I was working with a producer and we were pulling each other in opposite directions," she told the *New York Times*. "I was working within this framework of sound equipment, and the sound was fantastic, but I felt stifled. Now the sound isn't so good, but at least I know I'm doing what I want to do."[8]

Mitchell's second taste of domesticity turned out to be short-lived, but the music that came out of her failed relationship will last the ages. Neil Young wrote "Only Love Can Break Your Heart" after watching his buddy mourn his relationship with Mitchell. Nash wrote a song about their time together, the rather twee "Our House," with its sentimental rush of innocence and longing in every lyric: "I'll light the fire, you place the flowers / In the vase that you bought today

/ Staring at the fire for hours and hours / While I listen to you play your love songs / All night long for me, only for me." The tune is a showstopper every time the boys get together for a $125-a-ticket round of nostalgia. But Mitchell's oeuvre from the era does more than elicit endless applause or wide-eyed appreciation.

Now part of music history, Blue is widely considered the all-time classic of lover's laments. From the title track, which features Mitchell literally heaving vocal sobs in the final verses, to the romantic ambivalence of "All I Want" ("I hate you some, I love you some"), Blue is Mitchell's transparent testament to the acid strength of love. "[On Blue], there's hardly a dishonest note in the vocals," she told Cameron Crowe. "At that period of my life, I had no personal defenses. I felt like a cellophane wrapper on a pack of cigarettes. I felt like I had absolutely no secrets from the world, and I couldn't pretend in my life to be strong. Or to be happy. But the advantage of it in the music was that there were no defenses there either." Blue is the exposed emotional and musical nerve, and its undeniable accuracy has earned it a marquee placement in the annals of pop culture.

Whenever Mitchell's name bubbles to the slick surface of today's media sea, it's usually in this regard—as a shorthand reference for sensitive men and emotionally unlaced women. In Lisa Cholodenko's 2010 film *The Kids are All Right*, Mark Ruffalo's character is immediately considered emancipated because he owns a copy of Blue. The movie stars Annette Bening and Julianne Moore as a lesbian couple raising two children conceived through artificial insemination. They also love Joni Mitchell, and all this mutual Mitchell love eventually creates an unexpected love triangle—because if you love Joni, you share something profound. You believe in love. You believe in pain. But as Mitchell herself is only too well aware, love can be destructive instead of creative if it's applied incorrectly and without compassion.

Mitchell's readiness to accept responsibility for her own limitations in matters of the heart is a signal of her creative ability to transcend, and it reappears on the 1972 follow-up to Blue, For the Roses, which contains more great lyrical turns about love, such as "I get so damn timid / Not at all the spirit / That's inside me / Oh Baby I can't seem to make it / With you socially / There's this reef around me." She told Crowe she came to a significant turning point: "The terrible opportunity that people are given in their lives. The day that they discover to the tips of their toes that they're assholes," she said, solemn at first, then swelling with "a gale of laughter." Mitchell said she was in the midst of her "inquiry about life and direction and relationships" and she found something cold inside. "I perceived my inability to love at that point. And it horrified me some. It's still something that I . . . I hate to say I'm working on, because the idea of work implies effort, and effort implies you'll never get there. But it's something I'm noticing."[9]

Mitchell doesn't just "notice" things. When they come into her field of vision, she takes a microscope to her emotional petri dish of experience. On For the Roses, it shows through in a sense of scientific detachment. Her romantic revelations include her intermittent impulse to partner on "Let the Wind Carry Me": "Sometimes I get that feeling / And I want to settle / And raise a child with somebody / But it passes like the summer / And I'm a wild seed again," as well as her resignation regarding relationship failure on "See You Sometime" ("O.K. hang up the phone / It hurts / But something survives / Though it's undetermined / I'd still like to see you sometime").

At times, the emotion is bittersweet, but mostly it's determined and self-aware—or just plain matter-of-fact: "I'm not ready to / Change my name again." Mitchell is committed to her freedom and her evolving sense of self. But that didn't stop her from becoming involved with some fascinating bachelors when she got back to Los Angeles after an extended hiatus on the Sunshine Coast.

One of the more cryptic chapters in Mitchell's love life is her brief romance with Jackson Browne, one of David Geffen's discoveries. Geffen had thrown Browne into the opening slot for several Mitchell shows, spawning a mentor-student kind of love affair with Joni in the driver's seat. Mitchell was in her wheelhouse, but when Browne dumped her, she reportedly fell apart. The pretty boy who "makes friends easy, he's not like me" broke her heart when he tossed her for fashion model Phyllis Major. Browne had defended the fashionista in a bar fight, and Joni was bounced by the man she would later call a "phony" and a "seducer."

According to Sheila Weller's *Girls Like Us*, Mitchell took pills, cut herself, and threw herself against the wall as she waited for Browne to show up for what we can only assume to be a fiery rendezvous. Browne never did drive up her sloping street (resulting in the truly catchy tune "Car on a Hill"), and Mitchell ended up in therapy. According to this story, it was Geffen who patched Mitchell up, got her medical attention, and eventually convinced her to move in with him so he could monitor the effects of what was becoming a rather public depression.

In the end, it was Major who killed herself. But the story didn't end there. Mitchell and Browne hit the tabloids in 1997 after the writer of "The Pretender" publicly stated he thought "Not to Blame," on *Turbulent Indigo*, was about him. The song addresses issues of domestic violence, and Browne had just been accused of hitting his then-girlfriend Daryl Hannah. Browne has denied all the allegations, and a subsequent investigation by the Santa Monica police department resulted in no charges, but Mitchell's alleged suggestion Browne was violent prompted him to describe his former lover as "disturbed."[10]

The rough romantic road wasn't enough to deter Mitchell's libido. She added boxcars to her train, but her locomotion was creative and constant. She even revisited the theme a decade later on *Wild Things Run Fast*, in the song "Man to Man": "I've been moving / Man to man to man to man to man / Oh what am I looking for? / Man to man to man to man. / A lot of good guys gone through my door."

Mitchell says "Man to Man" is a personal song, but "it's also for all the women of my generation. Unlike generations before us, we have been with several men—or in some cases, many men. It raises the question, 'Why?'"[11]

It's a good question. And one every woman has to answer for herself. The easy answer, and one that seems most satisfying, is that the quest for love is an inherent part of identity building. In seeking the partner that will supposedly "complete us" and make us "whole," we can probe the parts of ourselves we feel are missing. And just like modern-day shopping, if we don't find what we want in one store, we can always check out the store next door. More importantly, we can be inspired by the search itself. And, more often than not, the more fruitless the search, the better the music.

In a 1974 interview with Malka, Mitchell says she writes about love because her central interest is human relationships and the exchange of feelings on a one-on-one basis. She's also attracted to romantic themes because of how love changes over the course of a relationship:

> Love is a peculiar feeling because it's subject to so much...
> change... I keep asking myself, "What is it?" It always
> seems like a commitment to me when you said it to
> someone, "I love you"... It meant that you were there for
> them, and that you could trust them. But knowing from
> myself that I have said that and then reneged on it in the
> supportive—in the physical—sense, that I was no longer
> there side by side with that person, so I say, "Well, does
> that cancel that feeling out? Did I really love? Or what is
> it?" I really believe that the maintenance of individual-
> ity is so necessary to what we would call a true or lasting
> love that people who say "I love you" and then do a Pygma-
> lion number on you are wrong. Love has to encompass all
> of the things that a person is. Love is a very hard feeling to
> keep alive. It's a very fragile plant.[12]

After tearing up the yard with Jackson Browne and shortly afterward with "Sweet Baby" James Taylor (whom she called her "best lover ever"), Mitchell started a new garden with plants that weren't quite so fragile. Steering clear of lead singers, she opted for members of the backup band—first drummer John Guerin, and later percussionist Don Alias.

Guerin, who headed the L.A. Express, was enlisted to bring a different rhythmic sensibility into the studio when Russ Kunkel said, "I think you're going to have to play with jazz musicians, because the subtleties you're asking for we can't really give you."[13] But Guerin got the beat, and as he and Mitchell stared at each other from opposite sides of the glass, a connection developed. "She was the whole orchestra in one guitar," he marvelled to Weller. "You didn't go whis-tling Joni's tunes... [they] didn't have the usual hook; she would form the music to her lyrical thought and sometimes go across bars and in different time signatures—she didn't care," he said. "But then it all made sense. It really did."¹⁴

Mitchell realized she wasn't the best gardener after she bolted from the hothouse of her steady relationship with Guerin and surrendered to the cocaine-fuelled sexuality of the Rolling Thunder Revue. Larry Sloman chronicles Mitchell's offstage antics, including her affair with Sam Shepard. "No regrets, Coyote," she sings of the brief encounter, "There's no comprehending / Just how close to the bone and the skin and the eyes / And the lips you can get / And still feel so alone." The flesh can only get you so far, and Mitchell's growing awareness of romantic love's limitations seems to hit home while on the road.

Sloman transcribed a conversation between Mitchell and Roger McGuinn about monogamy¹⁵ and whether it's a realistic expectation—a frequent topic for people who've been screwing around with one another in order to share the burden of guilt. When McGuinn says he opposes possessiveness and monogamy, Mitchell replies that she practised it for two years. McGuinn counters that he did it for five. "Really?" says Mitchell. "You didn't cheat on the road?" "Not once," answers McGuinn. "I sure broke down in a hurry," says Mitchell with a shake of her head.

When McGuinn says, "I'm not talking about this trip," Mitchell laughs. "Yeah," she says, "We all know about this trip. It's very difficult and it's very limiting and very indulgent at the same time, none of us are mature enough to be able to accept the fact that other people can love other people. We all want to be the conqueror, the one and only in every relationship we begin." After a pause, she explains that "there's a duality that I can't make out. I don't mean to be a victimizer but sometimes I find I am by my own spontaneous nature, you know, like gravitating to people who interest me in a room and neglecting the one who is like hurting by my interest in other people. "

Mitchell's recognition of "the duality" demonstrates her openness and eagerness to engage with others, but she's determined to remain free at a core level because she's naturally curious about others. "We love our lovin'," she sings. "But not like we love our freedom." In the wake of her hedonistic immersion in Rolling Thunder, Mitchell said, "It got to a point where I just wasn't willing to bleed for people in romantic love anymore."[16]

After she broke up with Guerin, she moved in with Neil Young for a stint and worked out the ghosts of romance on her road trip across the U.S. in 1976, the creative results of which would become *Hejira* (taken from the Islamic word for "exodus" or "odyssey"). Mitchell takes up the themes of self-isolation and her questionable ability to love again in the song "Amelia": "Maybe I've never really loved / I guess that is the truth / I've spent my whole life in clouds at icy altitude / And looking down on everything / I crashed into his arms / Amelia it was just a false alarm."

The verse is a thematic coda to "Both Sides Now" in its flight imagery, as well the idea of emotional aloofness. "Amelia" picks up these airborne ghosts and reasserts Mitchell's suspicion that she's spent her whole life at "icy altitudes," unable to truly ground herself in the terrestrial forces of domestic life.

Not that she doesn't keep trying: Mitchell hooked up with Don Alias in 1977, after they met on the sessions for *Don Juan's Reckless Daughter*. Alias told Weller they fell in love dancing at On the Rox, a private club above the Roxy: "I fell in love with her childlikeness, that wide-eyed childlike quality." Eventually, though, he grew tired of being awoken at all hours of the morning by a creatively frenetic girlfriend. "I got swallowed up in the Mr. Joni Mitchell syndrome," he told Weller. "At four, or five in the morning, she's like asking me, 'What do you think of this? What do you think of that?' I'm like, Jesus Christ, give me a break!"[17]

The relationship couldn't handle the creative tension, and this is true in many artist partnerships: each partner is competing against another love and another passionate obsession—the oeuvre itself. There's no denying the intertwining of art and the sexual urge, because they're both inherently creative.

Mitchell understands the primal connection we have to her art and the romantic impulse, but she's also aware of her own boundaries. "If some people had their way, they'd just want me to weep and suffer for them for the rest of my life, because people live vicariously through their artists. And I had that grand theme for a long time: Where is my mate? Where is my mate? Where is my mate? I got rid of that one," Mitchell told Rolling Stone's David Wild in 1991. "For a while it was assumed that I was writing women's songs. Then men began to notice that they saw themselves in the songs, too. A good piece of art would be androgynous."[18]

Mitchell reaffirms this idea in an earlier interview with Bill Flanagan, in which she talks about love's expanding horizons and how it reaches outward as one grows older, from the domestic and specific to the civic and universal: "In the natural order of things, your instinct as an animal is to find your mate. When you settle into your family, then you turn your attentions to the civic. You begin to expand. Love is taken care of. I'm a late bloomer—I didn't find my mate till I was almost forty."[19]

Mitchell's "mate" at this time (1988) was Larry Klein, a kid from the "deep suburbia" of California. A bassist who became disenchanted with "a real narrowness of the jazz world,"[20] Klein met Mitchell when he was enlisted to record sessions for Wild Things Run Fast in 1982. They bonded early, thanks to a shared passion for pinball and Nietzschean philosophy. Says Klein: "She was a whole other species for me... able to hold rambling discourses on everything from Beethoven to Nietzsche to politics to the environment." Klein found his years with Mitchell to be creatively enlightening: he'd never worked with anyone who strove so ceaselessly to get things right. She had "that incessant and unfailing way of seeking out how to get to the core of a song and really make something that was fresh and new and true."[21]

Creatively speaking, Mitchell felt very alive while recording Wild Things Run Fast. The love buzz was palpable. Even long-time engineer Henry Lewy noted the sessions felt substantially different. "She was very happy while she was making this album," he told Rolling Stone. "The records are always reflections of her mental attitude and she really found the groove for this record about halfway through, when she got a new boyfriend and everything in her life solidified."[22]

People have called Wild Things Run Fast the "I Love Larry Album," but it was Dog Eat Dog (1985) that proved the relationship solid: for the first time in years, Mitchell shared producer credits—not only with her new hubby and bass player Klein but also with engineer Mike Shipley and electro-pop's enfant-savant Thomas Dolby. When asked about the others by Iain Blair of the Chicago Tribune in 1985, Mitchell got prickly. "If I'd had my way, there'd be no producer listed at all," said the woman who once noted that neither Mozart nor Beethoven needed producers. "I'm basically unproduceable, and used to letting my albums take their own eccentric course for better or worse, making my own mistakes."[23]

Bringing in Thomas Dolby was the idea of Elliot Roberts, who felt Mitchell needed to reboot her career with some new programming. Dolby blinded everyone with his science: he was an expert at the then-cutting-edge Fairlight CMI (Computer Musical Instrument), a device that gave the eighties their mechanical-kazoo sonic edge and an instrument Klein was beginning to learn in the hope of broadening his musical horizons with new sounds and rhythms. He felt he'd been stagnating in his session work, so he took classes and put his knowledge to work in a new Fairlight-equipped studio that he and Mitchell built in their Malibu home and dubbed the Kiva.

Eventually, the idea of working with Thomas Dolby didn't seem like such a bad idea. Mitchell agreed to the collaboration with the synth-whiz, but the sessions soon spiralled. "Well, I'm very fond of him, but man!" she told Blair. "He was very quiet—and stubborn—and when we disagreed, we'd have these discussions and he'd say, 'Well, I'm not getting anything out of these adult talks, Joan,' and then I'd say, 'Well, then, neither am I,' and we'd be stalemated."[24]

Needless to say, things with Dolby didn't go down so well. He was forced into the "more menial" task of assistant while Mitchell essentially regained control of the final product—with Klein backing her up. Most of the tracks Dolby designed were never used. Said Mitchell: "I just can't work that way, and I couldn't give over that much territory. I felt very mixed up about it, I must confess. On one level, I thought perhaps I'm not being very cooperative about it, but on the other, I thought, 'No, this is composition, and if my structure is radically altered at the beginning, I don't want to be interior-decorated out of my own music.' I've always had the luxury of making my own mistakes, and that's something important to protect."[25]

Mitchell was following her instincts. She had surrendered to love with Larry, and she even relinquished controls in the studio, but she wasn't about to let an interloper like Dolby meddle with her music. For Mitchell to cede an inch creatively, you had to share the sheets—and even that was no guarantee. Mitchell never compromised her creative vision, but she did give Klein the keys to the machine, and the albums the couple made together feel different than the rest.

Dog Eat Dog enters fresh, politically charged lyrical terrain and features a variety of cameos, including Rod Steiger's holy roller (because long-time Mitchell buddy Jack Nicholson couldn't get past security at the studio). Other players include former lover James Taylor, as well as Eagle Don Henley and Doobie Brother Michael McDonald. Even the cigarette machine at the studio got a chance to play star on the track "Smokin' (Empty, Try Another)." It's a brave and wacky record that gave Mitchell a taste for casting roles in songs—while maintaining deed and title to her work. But of all her albums, it's one of the very few that feel dated—only as a result of the instrumentation, specifically that Fairlight CMI.

Dog Eat Dog wasn't well received by critics, and it was the beginning of the end of Mitchell's partnership with Elliot Roberts, but it proved Klein and Mitchell could weather a storm together. By the time they made *Chalk Mark in a Rainstorm* three years later, they were in synch—even if everyone around them was out of the loop. As Mitchell told Divina Infusino in 1988:

> People working with you need to know where you're going with an idea. But I don't have an intellectual plan. So there are times when people working with me think I'm lost. But part of my process is to get good and lost. I start to work

in random mode and try out crazy ideas. I put my critic to sleep during that process. But if I'm surrounded by minds with their critic wide awake, it's frustrating for me, for everyone. That's one of the reasons I like working with Larry, my husband. We've worked together on three albums now. He knows how I work. Recording together has also brought us closer in our marriage as well.[26]

Well, at least for a little while. As Mitchell herself is all too aware, romance can only last so long before it starts to wear: "Part of this is permanent / Part of this is passing," she writes on *Taming the Tiger*'s "Stay in Touch."

"Romance is like, 'Oh God, I'm so nervous, so excited, I hope he loves me,'" she told Robert Hilburn. "I had a pattern of going through very brief relationships where the romance never had a chance to develop into anything else. If you have set up a certain kind of promiscuousness, the buzz is eventually gone and you move on. That's the world of Don Juans and Don Juanettes and I was a part of it." She said her love with Larry was significantly different: "It's not built on insecurity, it's built on caring." To complete her point, Mitchell quoted Corinthians: "Love is kind. Love has no evil in mind, love gives without asking in return."[27]

The two creative souls found an artistic union through the work, but everything wasn't unfolding the way Mitchell thought it should. The production in the studio was creative but slightly off the Mitchell mark: "There is that period when all of a sudden everything was extraordinarily bright. I think it was all the cocaine or something. It was fingernails-on-the-blackboard bright," she told Costello of the production values on her work from the 1980s. "I didn't really like that. However, the drum machines did afford me the ability, right or wrong, to dictate the rhythm and where the major pushes were. Some of them are eccentric, I admit… but even in the use of programs, it was still really creative."[28]

Klein echoes the creative and romantic collision that marked their time together. "I started out just being the bass player on *Wild Things Run Fast*, but when Joni and I became involved romantically, she wanted my opinion as that project was being finished. We ended up working somewhat as a team. Making a record together is not much different than raising a child. You have to do your job really, really well or else it affects a lot of other parts of your life. On the positive side, it's incredibly gratifying to create something together and share the satisfaction of making something of beauty and putting it out in the world."[29]

When the relationship started to sputter a decade later, Klein says he and Mitchell never lost respect for each other, but it wasn't easy working together: "I'd be lying if I said it was an easy thing to collaborate since we've separated. The three records we've made together since then have been difficult records to make, but some pearls have come out of the difficulty."[30]

Mitchell cut the romantic cord with Larry in 1993, shortly before beginning work on what would be her finest record in a number of years: *Turbulent Indigo*. Mitchell said she had to let him go. "My main criterion is, am I good for this man? If at a certain point, I feel I'm causing him more problems than growth, then if he doesn't have the sense to get out, I have to kick him out!"[31] Mitchell kicked Klein from her life, and she was reawakened creatively, with *Turbulent Indigo* becoming the most decorated album of her career.

The two attended the Grammys together, each with a different date, and as Mitchell relates the story in *JazzTimes*, it was a bittersweet and surreal moment when they went up to accept the prize. "I hadn't slept in fifty-eight hours, so I was delirious when the thing hit. Klein grabbed me and swung me around and we went onto the stage and I was kind of in a dream state. I let him talk, and he went, 'Uh, uh, uh,' and in my delirium all I could think was 'Gee, this is why we got divorced: I always have to finish his sentences.'"[32]

Moments of great romantic crisis and disillusionment often add up to timeless love songs, and what this says about the dynamic between true love and creative output is a tad depressing, because it suggests pain is more prolific and far more successful with the masses than bliss. It suggests the most beautiful melodies are mournful—which we can almost sense intuitively to be true. However, there are a great many songs that have romantic value on both sides of the win-loss column, and most of the great songs known to humankind have been written about love. The investigation into the very fibers of romance is often what keeps an artist going, and Mitchell is no different.

In 2000, she released *Both Sides Now*—a compilation of her own material, as well as torch song classics such as "You're My Thrill," "Comes Love," and "You've Changed"—all recorded with a full orchestra. Mitchell says it was one of the high points of her career to hear her songs with a full symphony. She also says reinterpreting romantic standards helped her bring some magic back to love. Although one reviewer called it "pointless," in Mitchell's view *Both Sides Now* was "one of the most romantic albums... that was ever made."[33]

No critic likes too much earnestness, and Mitchell literally wore her heart on her sleeve: the album cover self-portrait features a heart painted into Mitchell's green sleeve. The original self-portrait had been painted years earlier, but Mitchell says she needed a cover and she just happened to see an old painting "lying around." Heartened by former lover Don Alias's fondness for the image, she repainted her face to age it (with a modest jowl job) and used the final product to package her symphonic ode to Cupid's joy. "I went, heart on the sleeve, that's romantic, that'll do!"[34] Mitchell wanted to share the pulsing spirit of love's beauty through classical means, and reunite the heart and mind. "Science has reduced romance to a trick of nature," Mitchell told her audience for the live show in Philadelphia. Her hope was to reclaim "love's mysteries" and to celebrate them.

The record does just that, with Mitchell's throaty alto pouring into the crevices of the classics and lifting them off the page anew. The cover track, which revisits her first taste of success as a songwriter, sounds like a completely different tune. The heavy strings and swooping winds bring it the gravitas it deserves, and Mitchell's voice, originally so high and pure, now has the texture of age and worldly wisdom. It feels like the song it was always supposed to be: slow, emotionally laden, yet joyful all at the same time. The tune brings Mitchell full circle musically, but the whole record nods to the beginning of her career, from her time with Leonard Cohen to her childhood memories listening to the radio.

And since we're going in circles, we can now come back to the ever-offending Rolling Stone love chart. It doesn't matter whether it was homage or slag; it made an impression on Mitchell regardless and affected the course of her personal and public life. She stopped giving interviews to Rolling Stone, felt abused by the sexist bent, and became defensive about her desire to explore humanity with a sexual appetite. To Mitchell, the chart was the stone hurled from the rabble—the big challenge to her creative nobility. No wonder it's a fixture in the Mitchell archive. She brings it up again in 2010 in an interview with Matt Diehl of the Los Angeles Times. When she attempts to explain her incredible creative courage, she says: "I never actually tried to be shocking... The madonna-whore thing was very prevalent, though, even in the 'Summer of Love.' Rolling Stone even called me 'Old Lady of the Year,' and made a graph of all these hearts I'd theoretically broken. Grace [Slick] and Janis Joplin were [sleeping with] their whole bands and falling down drunk, and nobody came after them!"[35]

Mitchell's quotes were lifted out of context by several outlets, which felt the girl-fight aspect of the story was sexy, again frustrating Mitchell's relationship with the media and pushing her further into the cave of self-exile. At least on the topic of sex and love, Mitchell did find some tangible lessons—and, in turn, used them to guide her creative progress. "In spite of all my yelling at my lovers in public (laughs), I've received a lot of affection in my time. People have been as good to me as they could, but... yeah, I guess it is all about compatible madnesses," she told Vic Garbarini. "There are pockets where people flat-out don't understand each other, they come to impasses. And they stubbornly hold to one side or another, conflicting points of view. So, yeah, those paradoxes are dramatized in love relationships. All along I guess I've been trying to figure out (sings) 'What is this thing called love... this crazy thing called love?'"[36]

Mitchell is still scratching her head on that one. She hasn't found her love for the ages, but in one of her last interviews, with Robert Hilburn in 2004, she said she was very happy: "So happy. So much in love with life, but romantic love is over for me. I'm very happy about this leg of my life."[37]

eight

I'M OKAY, YOU'RE O'KEEFFE

"Singing has always seemed to me the most perfect
means of expression. It is so spontaneous. And after
singing, I think the violin. Since I cannot sing, I
paint."

GEORGIA O'KEEFFE

WHEN THE NAME "Joni Mitchell" echoed through the red-
carpeted Shrine Auditorium in Los Angeles on February 28,
1996, there was an audible gasp in the press room. "What?"
said a woman from an unidentified publication. "That's total
bullshit! Why does everybody hate Mariah?" Joni Mitchell
had just won the Grammy for best pop album for *Turbulent
Indigo*, beating out the odds-on favourite Mariah Carey (*Daydream*), as well as the Eagles (*Hell Freezes Over*), Madonna
(*Bedtime Stories*), and Annie Lennox (*Medusa*). For Carey, who
was shut out completely for *Daydream*, it was the beginning
of a nightmare. For Mitchell, it was a fortuitous collision of
two creative worlds: she didn't just win the award for best pop
album, she also won the Grammy for best album art (with art

director Robbie Cavolina) for the cover design—a portrait of herself as Van Gogh.

A recreation of his post-ear-amputation portrait, the image shows Mitchell with a bandage wrapped around her head. It could be read as a funny nod to the injustice she felt at the hands of the record industry, which didn't recognize her genius and kept asking her to repeat successes of the past. But it could also be seen as a challenge to Mitchell's own view of herself as an artist—since, after all, that's exactly what the painting is: Joni Mitchell painting herself as a famed artist. The Dutch artist who hung out in Arles in 1888 and painted some of the most important works of the twentieth century famously cut his ear off after a fight with his patronizing buddy, Paul Gauguin. The act was proof of Van Gogh's deteriorating mental state and alienation. But it was also a testament to his commitment to being an artist: he argued with Gauguin about starting an artist colony to embrace the act of creation for creation's sake. His wound was symbolic of his desire to shut out the voices of the naysayers (and no doubt the deafening cicadas), so for Joni Mitchell—a singer and musician—to symbolically slice off an ear on canvas in faux martyrdom made for an even deeper subtext.

"Basically, I relate to his frustration," she said.[1] The painting meant a lot to her. She even brushed up her brush skills to execute the work as sentient homage. "I wanted to get my chops up to do that spoof on Van Gogh for the cover of *Turbulent Indigo*," she told *Vogue*'s Charles Gandee in 1995 (for a piece titled "Triumph of the Will"). "It's true, a lot of people don't know what a Van Gogh painting looks like, so they're not going to get a big guffaw out of it. I wanted to help them by having little tin ears fall out of the album, but it was too expensive."[2]

Van Gogh was a frequent source of inspiration. The only terrain Joni Mitchell has revisited on practically every outing is her own reflection. Her album covers offer a continuous chronicle of Mitchell's evolution as an artist, not just technically as a painter but as a self-aware creator who recognizes the role of self-perception. Her consciousness of the subject comes out in a conversation relayed by photographer Joel Bernstein, who quotes Mitchell on the subject of the double-exposures in her photographic work: "I'm the observer, it's putting the viewer in the viewed; it's just illustrating that those two things are happening at once, rather than simply, as usual, giving you the point of view out of the camera."[3]

Mitchell is comfortable with the idea of "two things happening at once" because her oeuvre has been unfolding in twin arcs of creation. Music was the public sacrifice, but painting was the private pleasure. Each time Joni Mitchell painted herself for the cover of an album, she let the two worlds bleed together. The result, as one critic noted, and not so nicely, was Mitchell's artwork is "a mini-autobiography without a shred of darkness; the kind of mementoes you find stuck to refrigerators."[4]

The satirical Van Gogh portrait seems to be a silent "screw you" to all that posturing, and it tells us exactly where Mitchell was at the moment of *Turbulent Indigo*'s creation: technically adept with her brush, artistically assured—given she paints herself as a modern master—and capable of seeing herself in a context where commerce and art are familiar sparring partners.

When Mitchell hit the backstage scrum at the Shrine that Grammy night, she looked a little shell-shocked. "I'm so stunned," she said. When asked which award meant more—the best album or best artwork—she stared into the middle distance for a while, then answered: "That's a good question . . .

I've been known for making music, but not as a painter. And I think of myself as a painter first, really. I was thinking of quitting music and going into painting—I'm glad I didn't... I'm very proud—maybe more proud of winning prizes for my music."[5]

There was validation in the double-barrelled win. More importantly, it allowed her to re-laminate a part of herself professionally: she could reunite the singer and the artist, at least for one victorious moment in the spotlight, after a lifetime of malingering cleavage.

The original schism—and the critical moment of departure—happened at the inception of Mitchell's career, when she had to drop out of art school as a result of getting pregnant. She says she had no ambition to become a singer but assumed the identity of a folkie in front of the mike and made money. Meanwhile, there was a part she left behind—the lonely painter hiding away in the attic with a box of paints. The musical side "wrote the sorrow" and the "frustration." The unfettered artist "painted the joy." And the human Joan chain-smoked and observed her warring muses.

ART FIRST

Mitchell has always said she was a visual artist first. It's how her brain is wired. Even when she speaks to her session players, because she is not musically trained and cannot explain things clinically, she uses painterly metaphor to get a point across. "I'm a painter, so I tend to think in pictures and store pictorial information," she says, "like an autistic person."[6] She drew and doodled from as early as she can remember— no matter where she was, no matter what the surface or the tool. She would prop up mirrors so she could watch TV and draw at the same time. This constant source of creative expression proved an early coping mechanism and helped the young Roberta Joan Anderson deal with life's irreconcilable equations at a young age. She says *Bambi* was one of her first inspirations: "I always drew, but being a sensitive child, the fire in [*Bambi*] haunted me. The downside of sensitivity is that when you get stuck on a topic, you can't get off it—it's another quality artistic and autistic people share. I was down on my knees for about three days after that movie, drawing forest fires and deer running."

This reaction suggests Mitchell was already adept at administering her own mode of art therapy. The rest of us who were traumatized by *Bambi* simply chewed the sheets and clutched our stuffies hoping the house wouldn't burn down and our mothers wouldn't be shot by faceless hunters. Mitchell painted it and owned it. She revisited the same themes in the 1990s when she painted more forest fires as a gesture of mourning for the planet and, somewhat compellingly, a self-portrait with a deer. The image, titled *In the Park of the Golden Buddha*, features Mitchell in profile on the left side of the frame and a deer on the right. As she describes it in a radio interview with KCSN-FM's Rene Ingle: "Both of the animals—me animal and deer animal here—are calm, but there's a suspension of, you know, like an impending kind of feeling. [The deer is] going to take his cue from me, and so instead of the movement taking place only on the flat surface of the painting, it seems to have a volume that sticks out that I don't recall seeing in another image, because the two eyes belong to two different creatures. I think that…"[7] Mitchell either stops talking, or she's cut off by the host, because the thought is never finished. No matter. She gave us a crucial insight: both eyes belong to different creatures; this is another sign of cleavage—but also creative integration.

The deer looks at Mitchell, but Mitchell looks at the viewer from the corner of her eye, which translates into a hint of editorial detachment. She stands in the foreground while the deer cranes its head into the warping, sun-dappled centre. There is an odd, unspoken recognition as well as a desire for separation. Mitchell does not belong to either world—neither the deer's forest nor the small group of human silhouettes clustered in the distance. Mitchell seems to belong to the world of the canvas itself, the very fabric that supports and carries the creative message. Like a creative Dorian Gray, Mitchell inserts bits and pieces of herself into her self-portraits, giving us freeze-frame glimpses into her evolving sense of identity through works of art.

ARTISTIC IDENTITY

Mitchell says her first sense of personal identity came about as a result of discovering her artistic talent in grade two. She told Camille Paglia there were so many baby boomers cramped into the tight corridors of Queen Elizabeth School in Saskatoon that they dragged a teacher out of retirement and put Mitchell's class in the parish hall. She seated students by academic rank—and Mitchell, never a scholastic standout, was seated with the kids in the C row—the "wrens." She says she didn't like any of the kids in the A row anyway. They were "so smug," she says, adding that she preferred "the ones who were bored and not trying or even the ones who were a little simple."[8] From that time onward, Mitchell has maintained a healthy mistrust of external evaluations. "I have this prejudice against the illusory sense of attainment associated with the educational system on this continent," she says in a 1976 interview with Stewart Brand of the *CoEvolution Quarterly*. "The best you can do is regurgitate what they tell you." Mitchell had a bright moment in that bleak grade two year, however, and it came as the teacher asked the class to draw a three-dimensional doghouse. "I drew the best one, and I drew security from that. At that moment I forged my identity as a visual artist. I also pissed off the educational system by spacing out, squeaking by, and finally flunking chemistry and math in grade 12 and having to repeat it," she told Paglia. "[The doghouse event] gave me the courage to become an artist."[9]

Mr. Kratzman helped Mitchell continue her creative odyssey with encouragement, and a caution against cliché. "He was a great disciplinarian in his own punk style," she told Brand. "He was more a social worker and a renegade priest... I laboured to impress him."

Mitchell says her artistic skills pumped up her self-esteem again in art school: in her first year, the C-row "wren" landed on the honour roll for the first time in her life. She found inspiration in the work of Van Gogh, Gauguin, Matisse, Rembrandt, Picasso, and Georgia O'Keeffe—with the latter two becoming lifetime heroes and personal icons. In fact, they are the only two public personalities Mitchell ever tried to contact as a fan.

In a November 2007 interview, Charlie Rose asks Mitchell if there's anyone—living or dead—she would like to meet: "I would have liked to have met Picasso," she says. Why? "His constant creativity, his restlessness. You know, like Miles [Davis], I met. I knew Miles a little bit. You know, but Picasso and Miles and myself, we were all long-distance runner types. And also, we craved innovation, but we also craved change. You know, [it's] the appetite that makes Picasso interesting to me to have known. Nietzsche: I would have liked to have known Nietzsche. He didn't have many friends, I think." Rose asks Mitchell what she would have asked Nietzsche, and she says it's not like that: "I just think we're kindred... I think we could have gotten along, and he didn't have a lot of friends."[10]

The central thread that runs through Mitchell's inspirations, from Picasso to Nietzsche, is the bulletproof fiber of creative originality—and the frequent consequence of coming under fire for stepping outside the trenches. Mitchell is acutely aware of her otherness, and the fact that so few people really understand her life's work, which is why she's sought communion with her heroes—the same way her fans have sought communion with her.

"I wanted so badly to go and visit Picasso… even with the possibility that I would be turned away," she tells Rose. "Picasso is one of my teachers. Although I never met the man, I have applied some of his philosophy of painting to my songwriting." Picasso pushed a lot of buttons with his work, not only as granddaddy of dada but also as an artist possessed with enough arrogance to do exactly as he pleased. Mitchell found affirmation in stories like Picasso's, because they affirmed her originality, as well as the split between her two creative outlets. She explains, "At art school innovation is everything, but in music, you're just a weird loner. So I have a painter's ego or approach, which is to make fresh, individuated stuff that has my blood in it and on the tracks."

Mitchell never got a chance to meet Picasso, but she did get a chance to meet another hero—actually, heroine—in Georgia O'Keeffe. She and Don Alias took to the road in the flush of their romance and in 1977 headed to Abiquiu, New Mexico, in search of the famed painter of flowers. Even though it was something Mitchell would have been loath to experience in her own backyard after a long history with tenacious stalkers, she took her cues from old buddy Warren Beatty, who used his fame as an entry into others' lives.

The cold call with a famous face "is a wonderful way to do it," says Mitchell of the fame-loves-fame idea. Warren Beatty, she says, "also approaches things that way. He calls people that interest him and flies to meet them. Warren and Marlon [Brando] have that ability. Who's going to turn them away from the door?" she says. "That's why I was hoping Picasso would like my music, and wouldn't turn me away… I lack the chutzpah to just go up and knock at somebody's door."[11]

Mitchell did get to knock on the door of O'Keeffe's estate. A five-thousand-square-foot compound O'Keeffe bought in 1945 and spent three years restoring, the home and surrounding landscape can be found in much of O'Keeffe's work: the patio, black door, cottonwood trees, and the many bleached cattle skulls scattered across the terracotta vastness. Mitchell would have noticed it all as she went through the gate with a small package of gifts, including a copy of her new album *Hejira*, limited editions of her drawings, and a handwritten note that read: "I want you to have this book—it is a collection of growing pains. The work it contains is not quite ripe. Nevertheless—I want you to have it out of my respect, admiration and identification with some elements in your creative spirit."

Joni Mitchell would have identified with O'Keeffe's sense of exile, especially from a gender perspective, given O'Keeffe was doing commissions and public projects no female artist had ever undertaken before. She was a pioneer not only artistically but also socially, as a result of having a public affair with gallerist and photographer Alfred Stieglitz—a married man with children. Mitchell and O'Keeffe were both eager to put their creative growth first, before any man or any contract, and though Mitchell didn't meet her ornery idol that particular trip, she was eventually invited to visit the legendary painter in the home she shared with her younger companion, Juan, who happened to be a big fan of Mitchell's.

The two women apparently shared an awkward introductory dinner, with Mitchell remembering only two points of conversation. "The first was 'Well, Warhol was here. He wasn't much,'" says Mitchell, who felt intimidated by the challenge to be entertaining. The second point that struck

Mitchell was O'Keeffe's insistence on unique vision, and her assumption that a pop star like Mitchell wouldn't see things the same way. "She'd say things like 'Of course, she doesn't see things like we do, does she Juan?' And I'd say, 'Wait a minute, I can see perfectly fine.'"[12] It was O'Keeffe who was legally blind at the time.

Although it was, as Mitchell says, "testy" at first, the two women warmed up to one another and shared something soulful, since O'Keeffe assigned Joni the nickname "Zoni" and later asked Mitchell to be a witness of her will. Shortly before her death, an interviewer from *ArtNews* magazine asked O'Keeffe how she would like to return to earth, should she have the joy of being reincarnated. "I would come back as a blonde soprano who could sing high clear notes without fear," she replied.[13]

Mitchell says their connection was the result of a profound, shared respect for the creative vibration that offers up signs to those who are truly naked and open: "I think in a certain way, synchronistic events and auspicious things mean a great deal. And the more you trust them... the more spectacular the display they seem to put up. For a long time, that's been the colour in my life and kind of my guidepost, and Georgia's too."[14]

Because the women were on a shared platform of professional achievement and creative expression, O'Keeffe was able to push buttons in Mitchell no one else could—especially when it came to the issue of creative cleavage. O'Keeffe believed you could only serve one muse in order to be a master—an idea that made Mitchell recoil. "When I met Georgia O'Keefe she was in her 90s and she said to me, 'Well, I would have liked to have been a musician too, but you can't do both.' And I said, 'Oh yes you can!' And she leaned in on her elbows and said, 'Really? You know, I would have liked to have played the violin.' I said, you know, 'Well, take it up, Georgia,' you know? I mean, you know, start today," Mitchell told NPR's Liane Hansen.[15]

The other big button that O'Keeffe laid into was smoking: she may be the only person on the planet with enough balls to tell Mitchell to butt out. According to Karen O'Brien's Joni Mitchell biography, "As they walked across the arid, stony ground, Georgia spun around to a chain-smoking Mitchell and exclaimed, 'You should stop smoking!' Juan remonstrated with her, only to have Georgia insist on the last word: 'Well, she should live.'"[16]

Mitchell says she's a smoker—period. It's part of her creative persona and a lingering wink at death in the wake of eluding the grim reaper as a kid. Mitchell's early bout with polio actually led to her first cigarette: she had made a deal with the Christmas tree in her room that if she could walk, she'd sing in the choir. When she ditched her crutches, she made good on her promise and starting singing the descant harmonies the other kids didn't hear. "Nobody wanted to sing the descant part," Mitchell explains. "I said 'I'll do it, that's the pretty melody,' the part with the odd intervals, fourths and fifths. Most kids couldn't really hear them; they were lucky to hang in with the triads."[17]

One night after practice, she smoked her first cigarette: a Black Cat king size. Some kid had stolen her mom's butts and brought them to share with her friends, who happily partook, peeling back their woolly mittens to get their little fingers around a tobacco-filled tube. "We all sat by the wintry fish pond in the snow, and passed them around. Some girls choked and some threw up, and I took one puff and felt really smart! I just thought, 'Woah!' My head cleared up. I seemed to see better and think better. So I was a smoker from that day on."[18]

Mitchell has called smoking her "focusing drug" and a "grounding herb."[19] It helps her think. It helps her create in the wee hours of the morning. That's why she makes no apologies for her habit and was a bit taken aback when Georgia O'Keeffe suggested she stop. As Mitchell says, she's been doing it a long time: "I smoked in cars, in saunas, in all sorts of small spaces. If secondary smoke is going to kill me, I would have been dead 20 years ago." It's a gesture of control over the chaos. Mitchell finds cigarettes a bitter nipple, nurturing to her creative soul. "Honestly, I couldn't have gotten through life without it," she admits.[20]

Mitchell seems to find the same creative support when she holds a paintbrush, because it's not for any other purpose than her own enjoyment. As she told Rene Ingle, "I don't paint for galleries, I don't paint for museums... I paint to go with my couch." When Ingle asked whether she would paint over someone else's work so that it matched her couch, Mitchell said, "Oh, I've done that... I mean, after all, they're domestic decorations. That's really what they are."[21]

Mitchell's terminology is suggestive, because "domestic decorations" moves beyond "wall treatment" and pulls us right into the domestic sphere of the home. Moreover, Mitchell has referred to her album cover artwork as contractually obligated "decorations": "[The record company] said, put your picture on the cover... to decorate the space."[22] And so she did. That said, the idea of "decorating" one's internal spaces with artwork from one's own easel of experience sounds like something altogether inspiring—as well as integrating. By creating artwork that wasn't subject to market forces, Mitchell could re-laminate her peeling soul.

In her interview with *CoEvolution Quarterly*, she talks about reading Tom Wolfe's book *The Painted Word*, which helped her understand herself as an artist and inspired a track off

The Hissing of Summer Lawns. "'The Boho Dance' [tells of] that period in an artist's existence when he's a Bohemian, when he's established all of his moral justifications for poverty while still striving for success," she says. "The second stage is the consummation which he has aimed himself toward, when the public says, 'Yes, we like your work, we would like to buy it,' and he is celebrated. He finds himself sucked into a social strata which he deplored as a Bohemian."

As Mitchell explains to Brand, artists react differently to this change. "Picasso went right into it you know and bought himself a Rolls Royce and some little black and white maids, and everybody said, 'Look at Picasso, man, he's going to blow it,' like he sold out. Jackson Pollock said, 'I won't sell out,' went to all of these fancy cocktail parties and pissed in the fireplace and did everything just to show he wasn't going to enjoy it." Mitchell says she found Pollock's words to be stupefying: "I experienced my own understanding of what he was saying so strongly that it almost paralyzed me from reading further."[23]

Mitchell did not want to be resentful of success or pee in the fireplace of fame. And thanks to her passion for painting, she found a more suitable outlet for her many frustrations. In the half-consciousness of creative release, she's able to find a fresh outlook. "An amazing perspective takes place where your brushes are suspended in air and you can see, you know, behind them . . . you hit that point in the painting where your eyes open up, you know exactly where to go. I mean it's almost worth it pushing yourself for fourteen hours to hit a pocket of fatigue just to hit that state," she told Ingle.[24]

Mitchell says painting is not just a pastime or a more sophisticated form of needlepoint. "It's not like a hobby," she maintains. It's a true obsession, and one that's helped her balance the constraints of commerce—because she's never painted for money. There was one exception, where she sold a crop of paintings in Japan "at inflated prices" in order to pay some bills. It was one of the more depressing periods of Mitchell's career and made her particularly bitter about the business. Art has been therapeutic in the sense that it has afforded Mitchell a means of expression without the weight of public judgement. She likened it once to crop rotation, where she leaves her musical fields fallow while she lives in her box of paints to recalibrate and re-energize.

Mitchell still paints in her new and improved house on the Sunshine Coast, as well as her residence in California. She's had career retrospective showings in Los Angeles and at the Mendel Art Gallery in her hometown, Saskatoon. And even though she now calls herself a "bourgeois painter"[25] as a result of abandoning abstractionism and other influences that didn't speak to her, she's still, no doubt, teaching herself new lessons every day. "I'm still experimenting with very personal painting... I haven't taken any formal training but I have discovered my own educational system. I know how I learn best and I know how I learn most rapidly and how to feed myself information for my particular kind of growth, so I'm out of this a self-educator," she says. "Picasso was constantly searching and searching and changing and changing. I thrive on change... That can drive some people crazy, but that's how my life is."[26] Sounds like an artist to me.

nine

SING SHINE DANCE

"And to me also, who appreciate life, the butter-
flies, and soap-bubbles, and whatever is like them
amongst us, seem most to enjoy happiness.

To see these light, foolish, pretty, lively little
sprites flit about—that moveth Zarathustra to tears
and songs.

I should only believe in a God that would know
how to dance."

FRIEDRICH NIETZSCHE, "Of Reading and Writing,"
Thus Spoke Zarathustra

THERE WAS A hint of déjà vu about Grammy night 2008. All
the awards, save one, had been handed out—mostly to Amy
Winehouse, who was being toasted as the femme feral for
Back to Black. Winehouse had been granted a day pass from
rehab in order to play a song via satellite from London, and
she ended up patching into the broadcast to make acceptance speeches for best new artist, song of the year, record
of the year, female pop vocal performance, and pop vocal
album. Everyone expected Winehouse—or at the very least

then-tragedy-stricken Kanye West, who had just lost his mother to surgical complications—to win the final and most prestigious prize for album of the year.

When a breathless Quincy Jones opened the envelope, "there was an audible gasp—at least where I was sitting," said music reporter Joe Levy when interviewed on *The Today Show*.[1] The winning album on the Grammys' fiftieth anniversary was *River: The Joni Letters*, Herbie Hancock's tribute album to Joni Mitchell, explored entirely through jazz progressions. The win was a surprise on a few levels. First, few people had even heard of the record before it picked up the biggest prize of the night. Second, Joni Mitchell's name hadn't been Grammy night currency in more than a decade. Third, it was a jazz record.

"You know it's been forty-three years since the first and only time that a jazz artist got the album of the year award," said Hancock, referring to the 1965 win for Stan Getz and João Gilberto. Hancock, the boundary-breaking musician who rose to fame in the wake of his pioneering 1983 dance hall instrumental "Rockit," thanked his mentors, from his former employer and friend Miles Davis to fellow jazz artist John Coltrane, for their inspiration along the way. "But this is a new day," he continued, "[It] proves the impossible can be made possible. Yes, we can, to coin a phrase."

As Hancock's tip of the hat to Barack Obama ricocheted through the Staples Center in downtown Los Angeles, he thanked the blond ghost who occupied the studio: "My thanks of course to Joni Mitchell, her music and her words, and without the vision of Larry Klein as producer, this could never have happened."

Hancock held it together in the moment, but he later said he was as "shocked" as everyone else by the win. "It's totally out of the blue," he said. Once Hancock had digested the awards-night press, he called Mitchell, who was supportive of Hancock's win but largely indifferent to the Grammy glitz. "She is not enamored with the Grammys, I'll tell you that," said Hancock. "She's all for the things that have the greatest real value, such as the quality of music, honesty, compassion. And she could care less about the media and television."[2]

FULL CIRCLE

From what Hancock tells us, Mitchell is happy in her hermit's cave, where she can sit back and focus on what gives life real meaning: creative honesty. This brings us back to the beginning, because there's a circularity to the unexpected win for *River: The Joni Letters*, and it lends the narrative a beautiful sense of closure—it proves her catalogue is not only enduring; it's capable of being interpreted by others without losing its inherent power. Symbolically, Mitchell's work is no longer falling on deaf ears; her voice is finally what the perpetually misunderstood Zarathustra called the "mouth for these ears."

Creating work that can strike the universal is proof of artistic success, and Hancock's interpretation of Mitchell's music offers us the reverse image of the one we started with: Art Nouveau and *Don Juan's Reckless Daughter*. Instead of a white woman assuming the persona of a black man while recreating jazz in her own image, we get the image of a well-regarded jazz musician reinterpreting the music of a white woman as a genuine black man. Hancock's album proves that Mitchell has achieved "classic" or "standard" status, which in the music world is akin to hanging a painting in the Louvre or the Met.

"Standards are a part of my roots, whether it's visible or not," Mitchell says. "I think people were surprised I'd absorbed standards. People assumed that I didn't understand that. I don't think I proved myself to guys like Herbie Hancock until I did standards."[3]

The Grammy win proves Mitchell's music is like all great art: capable of being recreated, repeated, emulated, and even turned into elevator muzak without losing any of its inherent integrity. Thousands of artists have turned to it for inspiration, and some of the biggest names in pop music cite her as a seminal influence, from Chrissie Hynde, Elvis Costello, P.J. Harvey, and Sarah McLachlan to Stevie Wonder, Sting, Van Morrison, Jack Johnson, Tony Bennett, Prince, and even kids' performer Raffi.

Hancock had known Joni since 1979, when he and fellow Miles Davis backup player Wayne Shorter worked on *Mingus*, but his fandom was no less ardent as a result of the familiarity: "She's like a hero to me. I consider her a Renaissance woman," he said. "I love hanging out with her, conversing with her, and listening to her talk. She talks the same way that she writes the lyrics. I don't think of ["River"] as a tribute. She inspires me, so yes, it is a tribute, but that's not the primary motivation. It's more respect for this friend of mine whom I love as a person and I love as an artist."[4]

Hancock said his compassion and profound respect for the work and the passion didn't hamper him creatively, however, because Mitchell was all about exploration. Hancock's own approach to creation broadened and deepened by working through Mitchell's example.

"Herbie and I have the same problem from two different approaches," Mitchell told *JazzTimes* during a joint interview with Hancock.[5] "He was going too far into pop and I was going too far into jazz. They accused him of commercialism, and they accused me of obscurity."

Hancock nodded. "I learned early on that if I'm feeling what I'm supposed to do, that's all I'm supposed to do—no ifs, ands or buts about it. Who's sitting there behind the piano? Me. Not them. Who has to answer to that? Who's it coming out of? It's coming out of me. I have to be honest with myself. She does the same thing."

Hancock said there was one tune that shook him to the creative core and pushed him to find his own path—a song that would bring Joni Mitchell's oeuvre full circle: "Both Sides Now." "Something happened when I was trying to figure out what to do with that song," he said, splaying his fingers before him. "I started following what I was feeling, and it was getting more and more interesting. I said, 'It would naturally go here, but I want it to go somewhere where it's not expected to go.' I tried something and I said, 'Oh, wow, that's a surprise.' Finally, I said, 'The meaning as I feel it seems to say it's O.K. for me to do this,'" he concluded.

"Yeah," agreed Mitchell, "because it's a discourse on fantasy and reality."

We could say the same thing about Mitchell's body of work, as well as her life: it's a discourse about what is, and what could be. In every undertaking, she has fearlessly addressed the longing and the communion, as well as the emptiness and the exhilaration, of being alive.

THE VOICE WITHIN

We've explored several manifestations of Mitchell as creator, except the obvious: the singer. Voice is the very echo of the soul, which is why German philosopher Martin Heidegger put such an emphasis on using it. It's not enough just to breathe. In order to transcend and realize one's creative potential, one needs to speak and, finally, to sing—because "song is existence." Heidegger sees song as the highest state of being because it represents the urge to utter made into art. Some sing falsely, but the true artists can be identified: "Their singing is turned away from all purposeful self-assertion. It is not willing in the sense of desire. Their song does not solicit anything to be produced. In the song, the world's inner space concedes space within itself. The song of these singers is neither solicitation nor trade." Heidegger says that in singing, one belongs to the realm of the truly living: "To sing the song means to be present in what is present itself. It means *Dasein*, existence."[6] In short, to sing is to be—and not just any garden variety of being, but Being: the holiest of the holy metaphysical grails, in which we are one with the spheres.

Mitchell had a voice, and if we're going to make a distinction between creativity and natural, god-given talent, we can easily assert the notion that Mitchell had a leg up on the rest of the ambitious masses as a result of her three-octave range and pure, almost ethereal singing voice. Singing came naturally to Mitchell, but when she first started to strum and hum at parties, she says, the voice she used wasn't truly her own.

"I found out two years ago that I'm an alto," she said in October of 2002. "My mother was an alto, my grandmother was an alto. And all this time I've been singing sort of soprano just because at the time that I began to sing in art school, I'd imitate Judy Collins and Joan Baez, just to get money to smoke."[7] Mitchell suggested she was almost whoring herself creatively at the genesis of her life as a performer, compromising her truth and her artistic purity for the corporeal satisfaction of tobacco. Yet, like most things in Mitchell's career, it was a calculated risk with significant rewards; it allowed her to assume the folkie stance and play the waify maiden onstage. She could play to expectation with a quiet little smirk that no one could ever see because her audience was dazzled by the appropriate, pretty facade. It was like acting. "I would say [I was] a folksinger from 1963 to 1965," she told William Ruhlmann. "When I crossed the border, I began to write. Once I began to write, my vocal style changed," she said. "My Baez/Collins influence disappeared. Almost immediately, when I had my own words to sing, my voice appeared."[8]

Joni Mitchell has been a singer ever since she sang Christmas carols "real loud" in the polio ward as a child and realized she "was a ham." Having made good on her polio-ward bargain with an almighty power that if she could dance again she would sing in the church choir, she discovered she was a natural.

The assertion of her voice was an act of defiance in the face of death, and from that moment on, Mitchell used her voice as a sort of sonar—a way of orienting herself in the sea of experience. It's this voice that spurred Chrissie Hynde to grab Carly Simon by the neck and proclaim, "That's a REAL singer up there,"[9] but it took a while to bloom. Although Mitchell's voice is automatically recognizable in today's cacophonic mix of generic howlers, it's undergone several transformations—both literally and figuratively. She has gone from the "multi-phrenia" of her early career and arrived at a single, whole, resonating voice that is entirely her own.

Mitchell has sunk from the gliding, ephemeral soprano that marked her first two records in the late sixties to the huskier alto we hear on *Shine*, her last release, from 2007. The descent in range is the result of age as well as her well-publicized nicotine addiction, but Mitchell says the voice we hear later in her career is the one that's closer to her truth—on several levels.

If we look at the vocal evolution as a spiritual voyage unto itself, we can observe the arc of a creator's victory: Mitchell descended the heights of the soprano mountain and bore witness to the changing world below. She got harder, wiser, and "more masculine." As her vocal range condensed, she too began to integrate: the notes of her life began to cluster tighter as she gained self-knowledge and trusted her inner voice.

In the beginning, Mitchell disappeared behind a persona. Her voice was still in the glass-shattering soprano range, and its "girly tone" seemed to match her "ultra-feminine" beginnings, but by the time she made *Blue*, she was already descending the vocal slope—and stripping off the vocal veneer.

As Elvis Costello noted in the précis to his *Vanity Fair* interview with Mitchell:[10] "Joni shifted from the beautiful pure soprano voice of her first records to her more natural alto tones—the opening vocal note of the song 'Blue' sounded like a horn." Costello applied the same critical ideas to the "narrative voice" within Mitchell's music as he described the shift from the commercial, first-person plots woven through *Court and Spark* to the distance she began to find in *The Hissing of Summer Lawns*. Mitchell's voice was changing, whether in her role as a singer, storyteller, or producer and arranger.

"The influence of jazz upon her writing and arranging became more pronounced, and the dense, third person lyrical portraits of damaged and unsympathetic characters in songs such as 'Edith and the Kingpin' and 'Shades of Scarlet Conquering' did not sit well with some of her more starry-eyed listeners," said Costello, pointing out the now-standard Joni theme—and cruel irony—of fan disenfranchisement.

The closer Mitchell came to being true to her voice, the more challenging she became to her hardcore fans. One reviewer even went so far as to write: "Mitchell doesn't always sound like Mitchell." Proving just how potent expectation and predictability can be, the critic felt betrayed by Mitchell's changing vocals on *Both Sides Now*. "She comes across instead like someone who has listened a lot to Billie Holiday and at least a little to Sarah Vaughan," wrote Mark Miller in the *Globe and Mail*. "The strongest of her borrowings can seem studied and sometimes rather strangulated (the untoward mannerisms of 'You're My Thrill' for example) but, these specific points of style aside, Mitchell's singing is remarkable for its absolute certainty of pitch and phrasing."[11]

Compare this "certainty" with a review of a 1966 show at Toronto's Riverboat coffee house:[12] "This wide-eyed girl with long, soft, blond on blond hair is playing a very conscientious acoustic guitar and sometimes missing a note. And it doesn't bother you," wrote Paul Ennis. He went on to say her "soprano is... growing less breathy every day" and "[her voice is] so pure, it is almost a distillate, so clear, so exalted and so simple that somewhere along its enchanting, wondering journey, it approaches the magical."

His language is somewhat fawning, and just a little condescending—describing her work as "childlike"—but he also senses the burgeoning independence and power of the woman before him. He says her voice is "strong and powerful" and has "broken through all the clouds that slow or trap most singers."

We can only assume the writer was referring to clouds seeded by self-doubt, because self-doubt is what gets caught in your throat, and makes it impossible to express yourself. Mitchell not only pushed out the sounds with her diaphragm, but she also kicked out the jams of musical genre to explore character. Whether it's the heartsick lover stripped to the bone in "Blue" or the sage's cool observations spoken in "If I Had a Heart," a song from *Shine* that features Mitchell singing in her lowest register to date, they are accurate reflections of who Mitchell was—at that moment. Her voice is always honest, even if she is in character, which is the central reason why every album feels so whole and thematically unified.

Mitchell is highly aware of her vocal evolution, as well as its symbolic implications. In a 1986 interview, Pete Fornatale of WNEW asks her about her first record, wondering if she'd be capable of making another one in a similar vein. "Well, my voice has changed considerably since then, so—and my sense—I couldn't do it exactly like that because I've assimilated the blues, I've assimilated—I mean this is pretty much British Isles–influenced music," she says. "The blues haven't entered into the picture. It's very—under the rule of Queen Lizzy, you know what I mean?"[13]

In other words, Mitchell says her voice is still that of "the colonized"—she hasn't explored the world, assimilated its sounds, and belted out a new chorus in her unique style. By the time she spoke with Fornatale, shortly after the release of *Dog Eat Dog*, she was already well versed in jazz and African beats. "My rhythmic sense has changed, my voice has deepened. I've lost off the top and gained on the bottom. I have a different sense of expression," she says. "The first two records, I had nearly all of the songs that compose those first two before I started recording. But the second album, the *Clouds* album, my voice changes radically."

Mitchell says this second shift (if we take the first to be from imitative folkie to soul-searching troubadour) took place in the wake of hanging out with Crosby, Stills, and Nash—who started singing together in Mitchell's Laurel Canyon living room one day. Apparently Graham Nash, Mitchell's lover at the time, came downstairs while David Crosby and Stephen Stills were visiting—and when Nash decided to sing a little harmony, the boys realized they had a band. "CSN was just forming at that time and we used to sit around and sing a lot, and in order to blend with them you had to adopt a kind of a vocal affectation to get the blend," says Mitchell, who would go on to draw album artwork for the new band. "They had to develop a common singing style even though their timbre and everything was different. And from singing with them I picked up some of that. So suddenly I have kind of an overt American accent, to my ear anyway, being Canadian, on the second album which kind of dies down by the time you get to the third."

Canadians tend to make good chameleons. It's a survival mechanism for us, since we don't have the biggest teeth in the zoo, and we're too small (population wise) to start a stampede. Mitchell's Canadian accent is evident when she speaks, though somewhere along the line she seems to have restrained herself from using "eh?" as verbal punctuation. She has camouflaged herself and taken on different roles through her vocal performance. Because her songs are like "little plays" that she directs, she has a habit of "casting" the vocals—sometimes as a one-man show, sometimes as an ensemble piece. Check out her nasal-voiced diner waitress in the Miles of Aisles version of "The Last Time I Saw Richard"—you can hear Mitchell's inner Bette Davis scratching to get out. She told Jody Denberg, "I never wanted to be a human jukebox. I think more like a film or a dramatic actress and a playwright. These plays are more suitable to me. I feel miscast in my early songs. They're ingénue roles."[14]

When she was interviewed about those early songs in 1969 by the Globe and Mail, she noted how much she loved hearing a man sing them: "After a song's been written, it becomes a whole different thing: You don't own it anymore. I love to hear men sing my songs, because they're written from a feminine point of view, and men bring totally different things to them."[15] Eventually, Mitchell hired men to perform on the records so she could realize the whole *mise en scène*. The first notable stunt casting was on *Court and Spark* in 1974, when she hired Grammy Award–winning comedy-album kings Cheech & Chong as the babbling rabble. Mitchell had them talking about her in the background when she came to the line, "no [bus] driver on the top": "Man, the chick is twisted, crazy, poop-shoobie, y'hear? Flip city." There's no doubt it added a "je-ne-sais-wha?" to the Lambert, Hendricks & Ross number "Twisted." It was playful and, given the earnestness of what had come before on *Blue*, *For the Roses*, *Clouds*, and *Song to a Seagull*, it might even be said to be "out of character."

Her search for the right external voices to fill out the aural canvas she created in her head began in earnest after her stint with Rolling Thunder. Dylan's gypsy caravan was a bit of a lab agar for the artistic spirit: the musicians were getting into the myriad manifestations of being "a player," performing onstage before a live audience one minute, acting for a movie camera the next, and shagging up a hormonal storm in all the moments in between. Mitchell's refusal to release the footage she shot for *Renaldo and Clara* is an interesting paradox, given she has frequently spoken about her desire to bring her talents to the film world. She's called herself a "frustrated filmmaker,"[16] and she clearly has a talent for performance. So why she decided to pull a Garbo on this occasion really is a mystery. She told Cameron Crowe that Rolling Thunder "was a trial of sorts for me ... What was in it for me hadn't anything to do with applause or the performing aspect. It was simply to be allowed to remain an observer and a witness to an incredible spectacle. As a result, the parts of the film that I was in ... for all I know, it was powerful and interesting footage. But I preferred to be invisible," she added with a nervous laugh. "I've got my own reasons why."[17]

Either Mitchell was serving her ego because she was afraid of what people might say (not in character) or she was seeking to detach from ego, as she described to Crowe. She wanted to be "invisible," and she certainly gets the singer's equivalent of that by the end of the tour: "My voice is gone... I sound like an old spade. I lost like ten notes on this tour. They are just gone forever. I'm just a prisoner of notes. I guess I'll have to do more with the four I have left."[18]

Rolling Thunder coincided with the release of *The Hissing of Summer Lawns*, the album that pushed Mitchell to find a new "voice" for her music by introducing new instrumentation and new beats, thanks in large part to the startling, bone-shaking, sense-tingling warrior drummers of Burundi on "The Jungle Line." The evolution continued with *Hejira*, which pretty much rewrote Mitchell's whole production language—and seems entirely contemporary more than three decades later, predating the same sonic landscapes now equated with Daniel Lanois.

Don Juan's Reckless Daughter featured Mitchell in drag, suggesting the importance of assuming alternative characters in order to fully express yourself. On *Wild Things Run Fast*, she asked Don Henley to sing on "You Dream Flat Tires"—but was "dissatisfied" with the result. It wasn't Henley's vocal performance she had a problem with, per se, it was the register he sang in. "I wanted a female/male contrast," Mitchell explained, "but because of the register I had Henley sing it in, I didn't get any contrast. We were both singing lower than usual, and you'd be a long way into it before you realized the voice had changed." Mitchell recruited Lionel Richie, who was recording across the hall, to fill in. She never told Henley why she'd cut him out. When she called him again to guest-star on *Chalk Mark in a Rainstorm*'s "Snakes and Ladders," he said (according to Mitchell, as quoted by Bill Flanagan):

"You're not gonna take me off and replace me with a Negro this time, are you?" [19] (Zoinks!) Mitchell was happy with the Henley results this time, but *Chalk Mark* also featured some other guests, including Billy Idol, Willie Nelson, Peter Gabriel, and Tom Petty. Nelson was cast as "Old Dan" in the Bob Nolan tune, "Cool Water," and Petty and Idol were cast as street thugs on "Dancin' Clown." "She said she had a song about two street toughs and she wanted me to play one of them… Then she told me Billy Idol was the other one… There's a trio for ya!" said Petty. [20]

As Mitchell tried on different personae, she found the right voices to match. "There are showy, fun songs that will accommodate a certain amount of winky-wink, nod-nod from the stage, but on these intimate things you almost have to sing with a method acting kind of way—you have to find your sincerity like an actor does. Like Meryl Streep. You have to sing from the heart." [21]

In 1994, Mitchell's voice gave out during a video shoot. When the specialists threw a fiber optic camera down her throat, they told her she had a bleeding throat lesion. It didn't look good, and if the doctors were right, it was the same condition that killed Sammy Davis Jr. She would have about five years, they said. Not being one to take the word of any god seriously—even the ones in white lab coats—Mitchell sought a second opinion and consulted Oleta, the Hawaiian mystic: "I said, 'Look in my throat, Oleta. Do you see death there?' 'No,' she said. This sounds so crackpot: she sent me water. The water was electrically charged and commanded to sluice and slowly restore. She fixed me. It's healed up. My voice is fragile, but I do believe I'm singing better than ever in my life. I'm on the brink of being a great singer. I've lost my high end but I don't miss it—you don't need it. I had three and a half octaves, all of that stratospheric stuff was just trying to impress. Billie

Holiday had seven notes. And what she did with it."[22] Even amid the dark coils of cigarette smoke, Mitchell found the lightning in the cloud of nicotine: she responded to the challenge and found a new voice.

This new voice is especially audible on *Shine*, her last and perhaps final album, as it finds Mitchell back where she started—with echoing production and a solo voice, only in a lower register and a higher place. *Shine* may be the Joni Mitchell release that surprised me the most, because I want to crank the title track. I can't think of any other Joni Mitchell tune that's ever inspired me to light up the LEDs on my speakers. It's not a cathartic purge thing, like I get listening to Everclear or Patti Smith, but a spiritual gong thing. I don't care that after the first few bars of pinging synth and sonar-inspired guitar the first lyric feels like homage to E.T., kids' music, and Neil Diamond in the same breath: "Let your little light shine."

The song goes on for another seven minutes, making it by far the longest song on the album, and as the orchestration builds behind Brian Blade's drums, the textures grow more complex and detailed. The big bongs and brushes of percussion weave with deep symphonics created and arranged entirely by Mitchell. She is one of only three musicians credited on the sleeve. The last (in addition to Blade) is James Taylor, whose guitar can be heard in the gaps and crests, bringing an increasing sense of humanity to an ethereal mix. The airiness of the sonic landscape is a beautiful contrast to the earthiness of Mitchell's voice, which has a fragility that it never possessed in her so-called prime as a pristine soprano. It quakes and fades and scratches, but there is unprecedented power in the delivery.

Mitchell's final voice is certain and declarative as she lists the earth's current ails: Wall Street and Vegas, rising oceans and evaporating seas, Frankenstein technologies, mass destruction in god's name, and lousy leadership licensed to kill. It's a litany of human sin, but the tone is not cruel or angry. Mitchell's voice is full of compassion and understanding.

It's the same dynamic tension on every track, from the opening instrumental: "One Week Last Summer," which pulls up Mitchell's clearly produced, and heaving, acoustic piano against Bob Sheppard's alto sax. It feels like quiet waves lapping up against the rocks, and in the liner notes, Mitchell explains it was one of those creative moments that kind of just happened: "I stepped outside of my little house [in B.C.] and stood barefoot on a rock. The pacific ocean [sic] rolled towards me. Across the bay, a family of seals sprawled on the kelp uncovered by the low tide. A blue heron honked overhead. All around the house the wild roses were blooming. The air smelled sweet and salty and loud with crows and bees. My house was clean. I had food in the fridge for a week. I sat outside 'til the sun went down," she writes. "That night the piano beckoned for the first time in ten years. My fingers found these patterns which express what words could not. This song poured out while a brown bear rummaged through my garbage cans. The song has seven verses constructed for the days of that happy week. On Thursday, the bear arrives."

On Thursday, the sax growls a little on the low end while the rest of the sonics spill out in colourful fits and spurts. It's a song of home, and you can feel it in the repeated themes and the routine of the rhythmic piano. She carries the vibe onto the next track, "This Place": "Sparkle on the ocean / Eagle on top of a tree / Those crazy crows always making a commotion / This land is home to me." The laid-back Pacific lifestyle comes through in every subtle motion of Greg Leisz's pedal steel guitar. It's a clear gesture of love to the landscape, but she's no starry-eyed waif. "These lovely hills won't be here for long... here come the toxic spills, when this place looks like a moonscape, don't say I didn't warn ya," she sings, without so much as a hint of judgement.

That's the bizarre thing about *Shine*: it may well be the most political and personally engaged, often enraged, album of Mitchell's career. But that's only the lyrics. Mitchell's voice and instrumentation, as well as the arrangements, are sweetly gentle. It's as though she's accepted every flaw and failing of the human race and found a way to keep going, despite the apparent futility of the endeavour, by coming at it from a loving place.

The record encapsulates Mitchell's oeuvre and her many voices—musician, composer, producer, and singer. *Shine* proves Joni Mitchell has achieved the epitome of the realized creator: integration through art. She has not become, as she predicted, "an ornery old lady."[23] She has become the wise crone. At least, that's what I think. Not everyone would agree with me. The critics weren't entirely kind to *Shine*—some felt the lyrics were a little scolding. As the *JazzTimes* critic noted, "[*Shine*] offers a somber prayer for the planet's healing by asking the sun to shine down on everything from 'Frankenstein technologies' to 'fertile farmland...' But by the second verse she has so much to say that she bursts the bounds of meter to get it all in, relying on Blade's flexibility to make it work."[24]

The point is, it does work—even when she breaks the rules. Mitchell's last album proves she's come a long way from singing into a grand piano with a Byrd on her shoulder—not only because she's got a whole, largely self-created orchestra behind her but also because she twirled all the knobs herself. Ironically, this record also put her back in the coffee houses—the billion-dollar latte franchise Starbucks, which commissioned the work and distributed it next to the chocolate and cinnamon sprinkles.

Speaking to Charlie Rose at the time of the record's release in November 2007, Mitchell said the Starbucks project gave her back her love of music: "They allowed me to do this album and take my time at it. Because I took some time. You know, so I could say this album—let's just say where I'm at now, like my influences are beginning just now to come to fruition. It takes a long time for an artist to ripen. And pop music doesn't let you."[25]

Shine speaks Joni Mitchell's current truth—and the truths of all the versions of her that have gone before. It's the curtain call of albums and the one that articulates the most vocal, thematic, personal, and political integrity in a single package. It's also one of the few Mitchell releases that does not feature a likeness of herself on the cover: it features the troupe of dancers who performed *The Fiddle and the Drum*, which she called the "best project of [my] career"[26] because it incorporated so many forms of creation: music, art, and dance.

I AM THE LORD OF THE DANCE

Before we wrap this odyssey, it's worth addressing the last of Joni Mitchell's talents—and one she's never received a penny for: dancing.

Before we can draw, before we can speak, before we can scrawl our own name in the sand, we can dance. Dancing is more universal than music because it has no scales, no tunings or pitches. It crosses all human boundaries in a bodily act of celebration. It is the great democratic force within the arts, which is why revolutionary anarchist and noted intellectual

Emma Goldman has been commonly paraphrased as saying: "If I can't dance, I don't want any part of your revolution."[27] Even the supposedly bleak Nietzsche understood it was important to shake your booty: "And let that day be lost to us on which we did not dance once! And let that wisdom be false to us that brought no laughter with it!" he writes in *Zarathustra*.

Dancing isn't just fun; it's a language. German filmmaker Wim Wenders says he didn't realize how much the body could speak until he saw modern dance performed by Pina Bausch. His girlfriend dragged him kicking and screaming to a performance and, by the end of it, he was weeping. "It was as though I had learned a whole new language," he says. "In forty-five minutes, Pina Bausch taught me more about the relationship between men and women than I could have ever known. Pina spoke with the language of the human body, and suddenly my body was telling me things my brain could not. Who knew my body knew things I didn't? This was a huge revelation to me."[28]

Joni Mitchell describes herself as a dancer—almost before a musician or a painter. It's a passion she articulates on "In France They Kiss on Main Street," when she sings "I love to dance."

She says she first committed herself to speaking with her body when she came back from the brink of being physically dumb in the wake of polio. "Having my legs taken away and getting them back, by God, when I got 'em back I rock 'n' roll danced my way through my teens," she says.[29] Mitchell says she's always taken advantage of a dance floor if one happens to be lying around. Her love of dance is part of "All I Want": "Alive, alive. I want to get up and jive. I want to wreck my stockings in some juke box dive." She talks about dancing throughout her odyssey. "When I was vacationing on St. Martin, I used to go to a little disco several times a week to dance, and I fell in love with a song by the Police," she says, drifting into a round of "De do do do. De da da da."[30]

Dancing taught her not only to play with rhythm, and to feel, but also to accommodate the shuffle of another. "So there, when it was partner dancing, and every guy was like a different drummer... you learned to play with people who rushed, whose time was inconsistent, who had good time or laid back on the beat and so on," she says. "I think that gave me, you know, a sense of rhythm which I didn't really [have]—my music was always very rhythmic but it had no drums."[31]

To reiterate an observation by Bob Dylan, Joni moves to her own metre—in every element of her life—because she feels the beat deep within her, the beat of creation. This gift of rhythmic improvisation has given Mitchell the literal and figurative moves to dance through life and experience what she's often called "the magic." Early in her career, Mitchell would observe in rehearsal: "The magic has arrived." She believes, to some degree, that being an artist means being in touch with the realm of the inexplicable and the unforeseen. "I try when starting a record to not have too much of a concept," she says. "I think it gets in the way of the magic—magic being those things that occur spontaneously. If you have too much of a roadmap in front of you, you can sleep through the best of the spontaneity."[32]

Mitchell's self-awareness in the face of this creative muddle is astonishing, but it's no doubt one of the reasons why her oeuvre will stand the test of time: she embraces the process, the artifact it creates, but most of all the feeling she gets when she's taken nothing and made it into something. "[Creating] translates your mood," she told Penny Valentine.

You can be in a really melancholic depressive mood, you're feeling downright bad and you want to know why. So you sit down and think, "Why?" You ask yourself a lot of questions. I find if I just sit around and meditate and mope about it all then there's no release at all. I just get deeper and deeper into it, whereas in the act of creating—when the song is born and you've made something beautiful—it's a release valve. And I always try and look for some optimism you know, no matter how cynical my mood may be. I always try to find that little crevice of light peeking through. Whatever I've made—whether it's a painting, a song, or even a sweater—it changes my mood. I'm pleased with myself that I've made something.[33]

Mitchell's limitless creativity is informed by the signs around her. Whether it was a crow flying in front of her windshield that made her look at her odometer reading "88888" or stumbling into a guy who just happened to have some much-needed wolf recordings, she says she believes in creative synchronicity. "I have a lot of voodoo following me around, whether I like it or not," Mitchell recently told an audience at a $175-plate dinner. "I just know that this is a very mysterious place we're in."

Being open to this mystery, and dancing to the magic of the universe, is what the creative process is all about, because it helps us find meaning in the seemingly random unfolding of events. The meaning is self-created, but that only brings the power of the divine back home. Mitchell has mastered the creative waltz. She can dance with her shimmering muse as well as her fragmenting shadow. Most importantly, she can laugh.

"I do have this reputation for being a serious person," she told Cameron Crowe. "I'm a very analytical person, a somewhat introspective person; that's the nature of the work I do. But this is only one side of the coin, you know. I love to dance. I'm a rowdy. I'm a good-timer," she said, proud of her ability to kick up her heels when the world gets a little too dour. "There's a private club in Hollywood that usually is very empty, but on one crowded evening, I stumbled in there to this all-star cast: Linda Ronstadt was running through the parking lot being pursued by photographers, Jerry Brown was upstairs, Bob Dylan was full of his new Christian enthusiasm—'Hey, Jerry, you ever thought of running this state with Christian government?' Lauren Hutton was there, Rod Stewart," said Mitchell, offering an inventory of the glamour factor. "There were a lot of people and this little postage stamp of a dance floor, and nobody was dancing on it. These are all people who dance, in one way or another, in their acts."[34]

Unlike her peers, who no doubt felt too cool to surrender to the primal beat, or too protective of a manufactured image, Mitchell wanted to move her body. "I just wanted to dance. I didn't want to dance alone, so I asked a couple of people to dance with me, and nobody would. They were all incredibly shy," she told Crowe, noting an oft-overlooked truth about most performers. "So I went to the bathroom, and a girl came in and hollered to me from the sink over the wall, 'Is that you? I'll dance with you.' I said, 'Great.' It was just like the fifties, when none of the guys would dance. And it was at this moment that the girl confided to me: 'You know, they all think of you as this very sad person.' That was the first time that it occurred to me that even among my peer group I had developed this reputation. I figured, these guys have been reading my press or something," she said, laughing. "But as far as shattering preconceptions, forget it. I feel that the art is there for people to bring to it whatever they choose."

Mitchell says all her art, even the dance, is designed to address the binary creative forces of life. "That's what I love about [the ballet]... You look at those beautiful kids and think 'what a beautiful animal the human being is,'" she says. "But the words are very critical of [humans]. It's a stupid animal. It hasn't learned anything. It doesn't learn from history. It makes the same mistakes."[35]

We're a deeply flawed species, but through creation we can be redeemed. "Creation—that is the great redemption from suffering," says Nietzsche.[36] "But that the creator may exist, that itself requires suffering and much transformation." Finding "the dancing god within" is a process, because humankind is a work in progress. As Heidegger says: "Being's poem, just begun, is man."[37]

Mitchell the poet, the singer, and the dancer let her life become a living testament to creative courage. The ire and the irritation in the face of humanity's stunted growth is always present in her oeuvre, but thanks to her unflagging creative output, she found a sense of palpable inner peace and wholeness that echoes through her final album as she urges us to "let our little lights shine" on all the good and all the bad. There is integration and acceptance of the human duality and, through this achievement, she can rejoice in her existence. Nietzsche says, "You need chaos in you to give birth to a dancing star,"[38] and Mitchell combusted without compare. Her life lights up the night sky like a continuous big bang. She is a true star, but she's not seeking followers. She's seeking to enlighten, as the last words she utters on a recording make perfectly clear. The final track on *Shine* is an adaptation of Rudyard Kipling's poem "If," and it underscores the potential for all human beings to find the same balance and pulsing heavenly brilliance.

If you can keep your head
While all about you
People are losing theirs and blaming you
If you can trust yourself
When everybody doubts you
And make allowance for their doubting too.

If you can wait
And not get tired of waiting
And when lied about
Stand tall
Don't deal in lies
And when hated
Don't give in to hating back
Don't need to look so good
Don't need to talk too wise.

If you can dream
And not make dreams your master
If you can think
And not make intellect your game
If you can meet
With triumph and disaster
And treat those two imposters just the same.

If you can force your heart
And nerve and sinew
To serve you
After all of them are gone
And so hold on
When there is nothing in you
Nothing but the will

That's telling you to hold on!
Hold on!

If you can bear to hear
The truth you've spoken
Twisted and misconstrued
By some smug fool
Or watch your life's work
Torn apart and broken down
And still stoop to build again
With worn out tools . . .

If you can fill the journey
Of a minute
With sixty seconds worth of wonder and delight
Then
The Earth is yours
And Everything that's in it
But more than that
I know
You'll be alright
You'll be alright . . .

Thus sang Joni Mitchell.

AFTERWORD

THE JONI JOURNEY ends here. But I hope if you came this far, your journey has just begun. This book taught me that the creative drive exists within us all. We're all here to make something, whether it's a family, a great casserole, or a portfolio of masterpieces. Creating is our human purpose, and the more we do it, the more meaningful our lives become. There is no right or wrong way to approach creation; one simply has to move forward with courage and inner strength. The rest, it seems, falls into place—because once we have the vision, we can see the bigger picture. Nietzsche likens the creative endeavour to assembling a puzzle or solving a riddle: "And how could I endure to be a man, if man were not also a poet and a reader of riddles and the redeemer of chance!"[1] The bits and pieces surround us like so many clues and mosaic tiles, and the creative act gives them beauty and order, redeeming the chaos of the human condition.

Many times over the course of piecing this book together, I felt the thrill of creation pulsing within, and it was truly liberating because it opened me to life's mystery. There was no pressure, just a wide-eyed sense of awe at how much beauty surrounds us every second. I think these are innate abilities, and although they've been squelched by our current techno-drone, they are not gone. Great creators live among us at all times—but seldom are they recognized for the gifts they offer. I thank the universe for handing me a book about one of the greatest, because it put me in touch with my own creative will.

The world could use more Joni Mitchells, but we all know she's a one-off. What we can do is follow her lead, the one charted by Nietzsche's *Zarathustra* as a way of overcoming the self. He says, "Man needs to be overcome," and I got a giggle while writing this book when I realized Mitchell was in every way a perfect example of the "Overman" or "Superman": not only is she a true creator, but she is a woman—and, therefore, not man. She is, literally and figuratively, man overcome.

But those were private puzzle games. Everyone will pull what they want from the pieces and arrive at their own private mosaic of meaning. The most important thing is hon-ouring the creative spirit and our potential to make the world a better, more beautiful place through the artistic endeav-our—no matter what form it takes.

My dad went to his fiftieth college reunion at Columbia University while I was researching this book, and he said ninety-seven per cent of the graduates in his 1961 MBA class wanted to start their own business. In 2011, it was the oppo-site: ninety-seven per cent want to be CEOs in someone else's company. No one wants to take entrepreneurial risk any-more: they want the cushy chair and the corner office without creating.

But hope springs eternal: my mother recently rediscovered her passion for music. She bought herself *The Beatles: Remas-tered*. She cranked it loud one Christmas. We all sang along. And we danced.

ACKNOWLEDGEMENTS

I WANT TO thank every writer who's ever written anything about Joni Mitchell. Without you, this book would not have been possible. In the same breath, I would also like to note the invaluable contributions of Les Irvin, the jonimitchell.com webmaster, who made sure this book was as accurate as possible and generously offered kind words of support.

Michelle Benjamin, who for some mysterious reason thought I'd be a good candidate to write a Joni book. Thank you for the opportunity.

Rob Sanders at Greystone, for believing in the underlying idea when it was still a muddle. Thank you for your faith, and the incredible journey.

Marsha Lederman and Melora Koepke, two brilliant writers and true friends who encouraged me every step of the way. Without you, I would have buckled.

Peter Norman, for all the great edits and, mostly, for understanding.

Shirarose Wilensky, for making it tight as a drum.

Lee Crawford, my personal therapist, for listening to me whine about my own creative hurdles and celebrating my strange revelations over the past two years. Lee, who also happens to be an art therapist, was a support emotionally, mentally, and most of all creatively during a rather draining period in my personal life over the course of which this book was created. She also loaned me some great books and let me become acquainted with the theories of Ellen Levine, Melanie Klein, and D.W. Winnicott.

Wally Breese, for originating the jonimitchell.com website, easily the most comprehensive fan site ever created. Your spirit lives on through Les.

Bob Lesperance, my lawyer, for guiding me through the wilds of intellectual property.

Margaret Atwood, because I spoke with you twice over the course of the book, and each time, you gave me a little piece of the larger creative puzzle.

Susan Joy Carroll, because you asked me to thank you… and because you are a great friend and a fantastic reader.

Dave Chesney, who understands the eagle.

Rick Bedell, who understands the snake.

Cynthia Fish, for being the skipper and letting me crew. You changed my life.

My mother and my father, for supporting me without question when I asked you to, and letting me have the captain's room to create in.

My sister, Tracy, for sharing her record player.

Allie and Sam, Pat Leidl, Janet Forsyth, Paul Dodsworth, Joe and Shannon Rotundo, and Lee Majors, for various brands of support that made this book easier (and furrier) to write.

The universe, for arranging all the bizarre synchronicities that made this book what it is. There are too many to mention, but it seems when you write about Joni Mitchell, the spheres cooperate in the most unexpected ways.

The spirit of Joan (all of them), whom I sensed next to me on every leg of the odyssey. Thank you for the inspiration and the magic.

And Stephanie Innes, who has only two rules: "Pull your own weight, and have joy." You make my little light shine brighter than it's ever shone before.

NOTES

INTRODUCTION

1   Friedrich Nietzsche, "Prologue," *Thus Spoke Zarathustra* (Middlesex: Penguin, 1961), 49.
2   Martin Heidegger, "What Are Poets For?" *Poetry, Language, Thought* (New York: Perennial Classics, HarperCollins, 1971), 92.

CHAPTER ONE
LADY LOOKED LIKE A DUDE: IMPERSONATION AND IDENTITY

1   Neil Strauss, "The Hissing of a Living Legend," *New York Times,* October 4, 1998.
2   Alice Echols, "Thirty Years with a Portable Lover," *L.A. Weekly,* November 25, 1994.
3   Angela LaGreca, "Joni Mitchell," *Rock Photo* (June 1985).
4   Patrick Nagle, "...Ssshhhhhh...Listen, Listen to Joni," *Weekend Magazine,* January 11, 1969.
5   Neil Strauss, "Joni with an 'I,'" *New York Times,* October 18, 1998.
6   Barney Hoskyns, "Our Lady of the Sorrows," *Mojo* (December 1994).
7   LaGreca, "Joni Mitchell."
8   Hoskyns, "Our Lady of the Sorrows."
9   Marci McDonald, "Joni Mitchell Emerges from her Retreat," *Toronto Star,* February 9, 1974.
10 Melanie Klein, *The Psycho-Analysis of Children* (London: Hogarth Press, 1932).
11 Carl Jung, "Instinct and the Unconscious," *British Journal of Psychology* 10 (November 1919).
12 Nietzsche, "Of the Despisers of the Body," *Thus Spoke Zarathustra,* 63.
13 Jacques Lacan, *The Mirror-Stage as Formative of the I as Revealed in Psychoanalytic Experience,* translated by Alan Sheridan, *Ecrits: A selection* (New York: W.W. Norton & Co., 1977).

14   Ellen Levine, *Tending the Fire: Studies in Art, Therapy & Creativity* (Toronto: Palmerston Press, 1995), 72–74.

15   Cameron Crowe, "The Rolling Stone Interview," *Rolling Stone* (July 26, 1979).

16   Joni Mitchell's description of her piece is contained in the coffee table book *StarArt*, edited by Deborah Chesher (Alberta: StarArt Productions Limited, 1979.)

17   Quoted in Karen O'Brien, *Joni Mitchell: Shadows and Light* (London: Virgin, 2001), 292.

18   Jenny Boyd, *Musicians in Tune: Seventy-Five Contemporary Musicians Discuss the Creative Process* (New York: Fireside, 1992), 82.

19   *Joni Mitchell: Woman of Heart and Mind*, PBS American Masters documentary, 2003.

20   Timothy White, "Joni Mitchell—A Portrait of an Artist," *Billboard*, December 9, 1995.

21   McDonald, "Joni Mitchell Emerges from her Retreat."

22   Alan Jackson, "Joni Mitchell," *New Musical Express* (November 30, 1985).

23   Crowe, "The Rolling Stone Interview."

24   Sheila Weller, *Girls Like Us* (New York: Washington Square Press, 2008), 430.

25   Kurt Loder, *Rolling Stone* interview transcript, November–December 1987 http://expectingrain.com/dok/int/rs1987.html.

26   Stuart Henderson, "'All Pink and Clean and Full of Wonder?' Gendering 'Joni Mitchell,' 1966–74," *Left History* (Fall 2005). https://pi.library.yorku.ca/ojs/index.php/lh/article/viewFile/5682/4875.

27   Brian Jewell, "John Kelly Brings Joni Mitchell to 'Out on the Edge,'" *Bay Windows* (November 1, 2007).

28   Matt Diehl, "It's a Joni Mitchell Concert, Sans Joni," *Los Angeles Times*, April 22, 2010.

29   Pauline Rose Clance and Suzanne Imes, "The Imposter Phenomenon in High-Achieving Women: Dynamics and Therapeutic Intervention," *Psychotherapy Theory, Research and Practice* 15, no. 3 (Fall 1978): 1. http://www.paulineroseclance.com/pdf/ip_high_achieving_women.pdf.

30   Ibid, 3.

31   Ibid.

32   Ibid, 4.

33   Ibid, 5.

CHAPTER TWO
FACING DOWN THE GRIM REAPER: ILLNESS AND SURVIVAL

1   Charles Mingus, spoken remarks contained in the TV documentary *Charles Mingus: Triumph of the Underdog*, directed by Don McGlynn, 1998. Text version can be found here: learn.bcbe.org/.../jazz%20unit%204%20part%202%20text.pdf?.

2   Johann Wolfgang Von Goethe, *The Maxims and Reflections of Goethe*, translated by Thomas Bailey Saunders, VII, 336 http://www.rodneyohebsion.com/goethe.htm.

3   Charles Mingus to Nat Henthoff, as quoted in *The Nat Henthoff Reader*,
    "Part 2: The Passion of Creation" (Boston: Da Capo Press, 2001), 99.
4   Mary Dickie, "No Borders Here," *Impact* (December 1994).
5   Vic Garbarini, "Joni Mitchell is a Nervy Broad," *Musician* (January 1983).
6   Echols, "Thirty Years with a Portable Lover."
7   Leonard Feather, "Joni Mitchell Has Her Mojo Working," *Los Angeles Times*,
    June 10, 1979.
8   John Rockwell, "The New Artistry of Joni Mitchell," *New York Times*,
    August 19, 1979.
9   Dickie, "No Borders Here."
10 Boyd, *Musicians in Tune*, 82.
11 Ibid, 86.
12 Garbarini, "Joni Mitchell is a Nervy Broad."
13 Feather, "Joni Mitchell Has Her Mojo Working."
14 Nietzsche, "Introduction," *Thus Spoke Zarathustra*, 18.
15 Feather, "Joni Mitchell Has Her Mojo Working."
16 *Details*, "Interview" (July 1996). As cited on jonimitchell.com.
17 Feather, "Joni Mitchell Has Her Mojo Working."
18 Nietzsche, "The Intoxicated Song," *Thus Spoke Zarathustra*, 331.
19 Levine, *Tending the Fire*, 53.
20 *Woman of Heart and Mind* outtakes.
21 Giles Smith, "Joni Mitchell," *Independent*, October 29, 1994.
22 Jim Irvin, "Joni Mitchell," *Word* (March 2005).
23 Jimmy McDonough, *Shakey: Neil Young's Biography* (Toronto: Random House
    Canada, 2002), 45.
24 Ibid, 188.
25 Ibid, 47.
26 Ibid, 46.
27 Ibid, 96.
28 Ibid, 254.
29 Boyd, *Musicians in Tune*, 87.
30 Carl G. Jung, *Flying Saucers: A Modern Myth of Things Seen in the Sky*,
    translated by R.F.C. Hull (Princeton, NJ: Princeton University Press, 1979).
31 McDonough, *Shakey*, 339.
32 Ibid, 96.
33 Echols, "Thirty Years with a Portable Lover."
34 Joni Mitchell speaking on MuchMusic's *Intimate and Interactive*,
    "The SpeakEasy Interview," with Jana Lynne White, March 22, 2000,
    transcript at http://jonimitchell.com/library/view.cfm?id=1388.
35 Diehl, "It's a Joni Mitchell Concert, Sans Joni."
36 Iain Blair, "Poetry and Paintbrushes," *Rock Express* (May 1988).
37 Garbarini, "Joni Mitchell is a Nervy Broad."

CHAPTER THREE
BABY BUMPS: EXPECTING AND EXPECTATION

1   Levine, *Tending the Fire*, 61.

2   D.W. Winnicott, "Transitional Objects," (1951), quoted in Jan Abram,
    The Language of Winnicott (London: Karnac, 1996), 116.
3   Oscar Brand's introduction to Mitchell's first performance on CBC's
    Let's Sing Out, October 1966.
4   Weller, *Girls Like Us*, 243.
5   William Rice, "Joni Mitchell Casts a Spell at Cellar Door," *Washington Post*,
    November 27, 1968.
6   Larry LeBlanc, "Joni Takes a Break," *Rolling Stone* (March 4, 1971).
7   Nagle, "…Ssshhhhhh…Listen, Listen to Joni."
8   Weller, *Girls Like Us*, 274.
9   Michelle Mercer, *Will You Take Me As I Am: Joni Mitchell's Blue Period*
    (New York: Free Press, 2009), 72.
10 Crowe, "The Rolling Stone Interview."
11 Echols, "Thirty Years with a Portable Lover."
12 Carla Hill, "The New Joni Mitchell," *Washington Post*, August 25, 1979.
13 Morrissey, "Melancholy Meets the Infinite Sadness," *Rolling Stone*
    (March 6, 1997).
14 Dickie, "No Borders Here."
15 Bill Higgins, "Both Sides at Last," *Los Angeles Times*, April 8, 1997.
16 Ibid.
17 Ibid.
18 Joni Mitchell to Mary Black, *Both Sides Now*, BBC2, February 20, 1999,
    transcribed by Lindsay Moon, produced and written by Roland Jaquarello
    for BBC2.
19 Higgins, "Both Sides at Last."
20 Black, *Both Sides Now*.
21 David Gardner, "Why Joni Mitchell Has to Find the Little She Gave Away,"
    Daily Mail, December 8, 1996.
22 William Ruhlmann, "From Blue to Indigo," *Goldmine* (February 17, 1995).
23 John J. Miller, "The Superstar Mamas of Pop—Why They're Singing the
    Blues," *Motion Picture* (December 1975).
24 Crowe, "The Rolling Stone Interview."
25 Higgins, "Both Sides at Last."
26 Alexandra Gill, "Joni Mitchell in Person," *Globe and Mail*, February 17, 2007.
27 Higgins, "Both Sides at Last."
28 Reola Daniel, "Adoption—Both Sides Now," *Western Report* (April 21, 1997).
29 Laila Fulton, "Alberta Native Gave Up Daughter," *Calgary Sun*, December
    1996.
30 Crowe, "The Rolling Stone Interview."
31 David Wild, "Joni Mitchell," *Rolling Stone* (October 31, 2002).
32 Steve Matteo, "Woman of Heart and Mind," *Inside Connection* (October 2000).
33 Boyd, *Musicians in Tune*, 59.
34 Jeffrey Pepper Rodgers, "The Guitar Odyssey of Joni Mitchell: My Secret
    Place," *Acoustic Guitar* (August 1996).
35 O'Brien, *Joni Mitchell*, 44.
36 Ruhlmann, "From Blue to Indigo."

37 Phil Sutcliffe, "Joni Mitchell," Q (May 1988).

38 Divina Infusino, "A Chalk Talk with Joni Mitchell," *San Diego Union-Tribune*, April 3, 1988.

39 James Bennighof, *The Words and Music of Joni Mitchell* (Santa Barbara, CA: Praeger, 2010), 10.

40 Before the western scales were "tempered" during the Renaissance, musicians relied on Pythagorean tuning—which tuned in progressions of perfect fifths. The fifths worked fine, but there was always a snag around the major third. It didn't sound right because it wasn't "just" (the term used for pure intonation—in just intonation, the interval between two pitches corresponds to a whole-number ratio between frequencies). The solution was to change the fifth ever so slightly to bring the rest of the notes into tempered harmony. This altered fifth is called a diminished fifth, an augmented fourth, or a tritone—and the resulting diminished triad chord includes a minor third and a diminished fifth above the root. This was called "the devil's interval," because in the Middle Ages that's what tritones were considered: too dissonant to be pure or good, they were labelled "*diabolus in musica*," or what Georg Philipp Telemann called in 1733 "Satan in music." The devil's interval was stigmatized in Western culture until the Romantic movement, but it re-entered the musical vocabulary of the masses through jazz, which makes ample use of tertian harmonies—and was, as a result, branded the "devil's music" by Southern holy rollers looking to stigmatize black music as evil and impure.

41 Jim Bessman, "Mitchell Does Rare Live Show at New York Club," *Billboard* (November 18, 1995).

42 Joni Mitchell to Chris Douridas, "Morning Becomes Eclectic," KCRW-FM broadcast transcribed by Lindsay Moon, March 27, 1998.

43 Bennighof, *The Words and Music of Joni Mitchell*, 27.

44 David Crosby interviewed by Wally Breese for jonimitchell.com, March 15, 1997.

45 Sylvie Simmons, "A Long Strange Trip," *Mojo* (November 2003).

46 McDonough, *Shakey*, 245.

47 In 1934, Crosby the elder had been invited to document the strange odyssey called the Bedaux Expedition. Financed by French millionaire Charles Bedaux, the odyssey had two ambitions: to make a feature film and to test the off-road capabilities of the specially designed Citroën halftrack truck. The journey was supposed to go from Edmonton, Alberta, to Telegraph Creek, B.C., but the crew and the entourage of more than one hundred people turned back at Hudson's Hope at the urging of the Canadian guide. Crosby's footage was considered lost until it was found in a Paris basement more than seven decades later and became the basis for the 1995 documentary by George Ungar.

48 Crosby to Breese, March 15, 1997.

49 Quoted in O'Brien, *Joni Mitchell*, 73.

50 Crosby to Breese, March 15, 1997.

51 David Crosby and Carl Gottlieb, *Long Time Gone: The Autobiography of David Crosby* (New York: Dell, 1988), 130.

52 Quoted in O'Brien, *Joni Mitchell*, 75.
53 Les Brown, "Joni Mitchell," *Rolling Stone* (July 6, 1968).
54 Robert Hilburn, "Both Sides Later," *Los Angeles Times*, December 8, 1996.
55 Timothy White, "Joni Mitchell Interview," March 17, 1988.
    (For *Rock Lives: Profiles and Interviews*, New York: Holt Paperbacks, 1991.)
56 Carla Hill, "The New Joni Mitchell," *Washington Post*, August 25, 1979.
57 Laura Campbell, "Joni Chic," *Sunday Telegraph*, February 8, 1998.
58 Edie Falco to the author at the 2010 Sundance Film Festival in an interview about the film 3 *Backyards*. Unpublished material.
59 Weller, *Girls Like Us*, 226.
60 Dickie, "No Borders Here."
61 Ani DiFranco, "Ani DiFranco Chats with the Iconic Joni Mitchell," *Los Angeles Times*, September 20, 1998.
62 Steven Daly, "Rock and Roll," *Rolling Stone* (October 29, 1998).

CHAPTER FOUR
WOODSTOCK: MYTH AND MYTHMAKING
1 Joseph Campbell with Bill Moyers, *The Power of Myth* (New York: Anchor, 1988), 2.
2 Pete Fornatale, *Back to the Garden: The Story of Woodstock and How It Changed a Generation* (New York: Touchstone, 2009), 4.
3 Ibid, 8.
4 Ibid, 17.
5 *Details*, "Interview."
6 Bill Flanagan, "Lady of the Canyon," *Vanity Fair* (June 1997).
7 Sutcliffe, "Joni Mitchell."
8 Interview for the Dick Cavett DVD collection.
9 Dave Zimmer, *Crosby, Stills & Nash: The Authorized Biography* (Boston: Da Capo Press, 2000), 111.
10 Abraham Maslow, "The Creative Attitude," *Farther Reaches of Human Nature* (New York: Viking, 1971). See also Jenny Boyd, *Musicians in Tune*, 158.
11 Folksinger Jake Holmes claims he wrote "Dazed and Confused" two years before it appeared on Led Zeppelin's debut album in 1969.
12 Scene in the documentary Woodstock, directed by Mike Wadleigh, 1970.
13 Walter Cronkite, quoted in *Back to the Garden*, xviii. "I Can Hear It Now/The Sixties," Columbia/Legacy, 1970.
14 Margaret Mead, quoted in *Back to the Garden*, xix. "Woodstock in Retrospect," *Redbook* (January 1970).
15 Robert Hilburn, "The Mojo Interview," *Mojo* (February 2008).

CHAPTER FIVE
BUSINESS AND BULLSHIT
1 White, "The SpeakEasy Interview."
2 Buffy Sainte-Marie to the author in an interview about the documentary *Buffy Sainte-Marie: A Multimedia Life*. Parts of this interview were published by Postmedia News (then Canwest), May 8, 2010.

3 McDonough, *Shakey*, 244.
4 Wild, "Joni Mitchell."
5 McDonough, *Shakey*, 244.
6 Tom King, *The Operator: David Geffen Builds, Buys, and Sells the New Hollywood* (New York: Random House, 2000), 228.
7 Ibid, xii.
8 James Reginato, "The Diva's Last Stand," W (December 2002).
9 Howie Klein, "2002 Lifetime Achievement Award Recipient—Joni Mitchell," *Grammy* (February 24, 2002).
10 White, "The SpeakEasy Interview."
11 Malka Marom, "Self-Portrait of a Superstar," *Maclean's* (June 1974).
12 Stephen Holden, "The Ambivalent Hall of Famer," *New York Times*, December 1, 1996.
13 Garbarini, "Joni Mitchell is a Nervy Broad."
14 LeBlanc, "Joni Takes a Break."
15 Penny Valentine, "Joni Mitchell Interview," *Sounds* (June 3, 1972).
16 White, "Joni Mitchell Interview."
17 Ibid.
18 Ibid.
19 *Rolling Stone*, "Joni Mitchell" (February 18, 1999).
20 Reginato, "The Diva's Last Stand."
21 Ethan Brown, "Influences: Joni Mitchell," *New York* (May 9, 2005).
22 White, "Joni Mitchell Interview."
23 Valentine, "Joni Mitchell Interview."
24 Christopher Guly, "Music World Courts and Sparks Joni Mitchell," *Globe and Mail*, December 16, 1996.
25 Joe Jackson, "If You See Her, Say Hello," *Hotpress* (January 23, 1999).
26 Ibid: "No doubt this sense of betrayal, which has led to Joni Mitchell undertaking less than 20 interviews during the past 31 years, goes back to those days when *Rolling Stone* described her as a rock 'n' roll groupie—bed-mate of seemingly ever changing lovers such as Graham Nash. Now Joni's back in New York and no, *Rolling Stone* editor Jann Wenner is not on the list of invited guests."
27 *Rolling Stone* (February 4, 1971).
28 McDonald, "Joni Mitchell Emerges from her Retreat."
29 Garbarini, "Joni Mitchell is a Nervy Broad."
30 Flanagan, "Lady of the Canyon."
31 Sybil McGuire, "Both Sides of Mitchell," *Progressive Quarterback* (March 2000).
32 Introduction to the song "Carey" for a performance at the Troubadour, as cited on the website http://crete.wordpress.com/2008/02/26/joni-michell-in-matala-crete.
33 McGuire, "Both Sides of Mitchell."
34 Valentine, "Joni Mitchell Interview."
35 Bill Flanagan, "Joni Mitchell Has the Last Laugh," *Musician* (December 1985).
36 Ibid.
37 Valentine, "Joni Mitchell Interview."

38 McDonald, "Joni Mitchell Emerges from her Retreat."
39 Joni Mitchell to Pete Fornatale, "Mixed Bag: Music and Interview with Pete Fornatale," WNEW, January 12, 1986.
40 White, "Joni Mitchell Interview."
41 Levine, *Tending the Fire*, 69.
42 Garbarini, "Joni Mitchell is a Nervy Broad."

CHAPTER SIX
GODS AND MONSTERS
1   Boyd, *Musicians in Tune*, 11.
2   Paolo J. Knill, Helen N. Barba, and Margot N. Fuchs, *Minstrels of the Soul: Intermodal Expressive Therapy* (Toronto: Palmerston Press, 1995), 71.
3   Hoskyns, "Our Lady of the Sorrows."
4   David Wild, "A Conversation with Joni Mitchell," *Rolling Stone* (May 30, 1991).
5   Brown, "Influences: Joni Mitchell."
6   Stewart Brand, "The Education of Joni Mitchell," *Co-Evolution Quarterly* (June 1976).
7   Mercer, *Will You Take Me As I Am*, 98.
8   Weller, *Girls Like Us*, 236.
9   The story of Bob Dylan going electric at the Newport Folk Festival in 1965 is dramatized in the movie *I'm Not There*, by director Todd Haynes, which features a scene of an irate Pete Seeger trying to drive a hatchet blade through the main power cable. This is conjecture, but Seeger has said in recent years that he didn't like the electric amplification because no one could properly hear Dylan's beautiful poetry.
10 Larry Sloman, *On the Road with Bob Dylan* (New York: Three Rivers Press, 1978), 271.
11 Hilburn, "The Mojo Interview."
12 Susan Gordon Lydon, "Joni's Trek from Canada to Laurel Canyon," *Globe and Mail*, April 29, 1969.
13 Mercer, *Will You Take Me As I Am*, 104.
14 Brand, "The Education of Joni Mitchell."
15 Sloman, *On the Road with Bob Dylan*, 360–83.
16 Ibid, 439–40.
17 Ibid, 383.
18 Crowe, "The Rolling Stone Interview."
19 Mercer, *Will You Take Me As I Am*, 33.
20 Will Elliott, "Painting with Words and Music," *Poetry* (June 2000).
21 Garbarini, "Joni Mitchell is a Nervy Broad."
22 Sloman, *On the Road with Bob Dylan*, 439.
23 Ibid, 375.
24 Ibid, 379.
25 Ibid, 437.
26 Ibid, 436.
27 Ibid, 438.
28 Crowe, "The Rolling Stone Interview."

29   Mary Aikins, "Heart of a Prairie Girl," *Reader's Digest* (July 2005).

30   Mercer, *Will You Take Me As I Am*, 191–94.

31   Levon Helm, "Do It, Puke and Get Out," *Independent*, April 10, 1994.

32   Hoskyns, "Our Lady of the Sorrows."

33   Jody Denberg, "Taming Joni Mitchell—Joni's Jazz," *Austin Chronicle*, October 12, 1998.

34   Edna Gundersen, "The Cat's 'Meow-meow-meow!'" *USA Today*, September 29, 1988.

35   Rene Ingle, "Interview of Joni Mitchell," KCSN, December 21, 1999.

36   Elvis Costello, "Joni's Last Waltz?" *Vanity Fair* (November 2004).

37   Ingle, "Interview of Joni Mitchell."

38   Nietzsche, "Retired from Service," *Thus Spoke Zarathustra*, 275.

39   Nietzsche, "Of the Afterworldsmen," *Thus Spoke Zarathustra*, 60.

40   Nietzsche wanted to replace the dragon of "Thou Shalt" with the "I Will" of human triumph, and therein lies the other major problem with Nietzsche: the Nazis adopted great swaths of his philosophy to sell an agenda of hate—something that (I believe) Nietzsche would have loathed and done his best to prevent by teaching a doctrine that refuses any notion of an all-powerful leader. In "Of the Higher Man" in *Zarathustra*, he talks about the "parasites" who build "a loathsome nest in your grief and dejection" and "the evil falsity of those who will beyond their powers … these fabricators and actors … who are at last untrue to themselves, squint-eyed, white-washed rottenness, cloaked with clever words, with pretended virtues, with glittering, false deeds. Guard yourselves well against that." Those who want further reading on both sides should check out Walter Kaufmann's *Nietzsche: Philosopher, Psychologist, Antichrist* and Bertrand Russell's *History of Western Philosophy*.

41   Denberg, "Taming Joni Mitchell—Joni's Jazz."

42   Nietzsche, "Of the Chairs of Virtue," *Thus Spoke Zarathustra*, 58.

43   Black, *Both Sides Now*.

44   Although I can't document the connection, I think this has to be John Landy, one of the first runners to break a four-minute mile and one of two runners memorialized in my hometown of Vancouver, in a bronze statue that shows him and Roger Bannister in the so-called race of the century during the 1954 British Empire and Commonwealth Games.

45   Nietzsche, "Of Reading and Writing," *Thus Spoke Zarathustra*, 67.

46   Weller, *Girls Like Us*, 296.

47   Flanagan, "Joni Mitchell has the Last Laugh."

48   Ibid.

49   Nietzsche, "Prologue 2," *Thus Spoke Zarathustra*, 40.

50   Nietzsche, "Prologue 5," *Thus Spoke Zarathustra*, 47.

51   Nietzsche, "Prologue 6," *Thus Spoke Zarathustra*, 48.

52   Ibid.

53   Nietzsche, "Prologue 9," *Thus Spoke Zarathustra*, 52.

54   Nietzsche, "Part Two: The Child With the Mirror," *Thus Spoke Zarathustra*, 107.

55   Ibid.

56   Costello, "Joni's Last Waltz?"

57   Nietzsche, *The Birth of Tragedy* (New York: Dover Thrift Editions, 1995), 64.

58   John Mackie, full transcript of Joni Mitchell interview for the *Vancouver Sun*,
     January 15, 2010.

59   Nietzsche, "The Convalescent," *Thus Spoke Zarathustra*, 234

60   Nietzsche, "Of War and Warriors," *Thus Spoke Zarathustra*, 75–76.

61   Denberg, "Taming Joni Mitchell—Joni's Jazz."

62   Nietzsche, "Of the Chairs of Virtue," *Thus Spoke Zarathustra*, 57.

63   In his essay "What Rough Beast? Yeats, Nietzsche and Historical Rhetoric
     in 'The Second Coming'" (from highbeam.com), scholar John R. Harrison
     explores the details of Yeats's relationship and exposure to Nietzschean texts:

> Yeats's interest in Nietzsche was aroused at least as early as September 1902,
> when his American lawyer friend, John Quinn, sent him his own copy of *Thus
> Spake Zarathustra* together with copies of *The Case of Wagner* and *A Genealogy
> of Morals*. The first mention in Yeats's letters is dated by Wade 26 September
> 1902. He wrote to Lady Gregory: "You have a rival in Nietzsche, that strong
> enchanter...Nietzsche completes Blake and has the same roots—I have not
> read anything with so much excitement since I got to love Morris's stories
> which have the same curious astringent joy" (Letters 379). It was shortly after
> this, and not I believe coincidentally, that he began to reconstruct his poetic
> style to give it more "masculinity," more "salt," and to make it more idiomatic.
> Yeats also annotated John Quinn's copy of Thomas Common's *Nietzsche as
> Critic, Philosopher, Poet and Prophet*, which appeared in 1901. Most of his annota-
> tions are on passages from *A Genealogy of Morals, Beyond Good and Evil* and *Thus
> Spake Zarathustra*. According to Professor Donald Torchiana Yeats's library
> contained at least the following texts (the dates of English translations are
> given in brackets): *The Case of Wagner* (1895), *A Genealogy of Morals* (1899), *The
> Dawn of Day* (1903), *The Birth of Tragedy* (1909), *Thoughts out of Season* (1909), and
> *The Will to Power* (1909–10).

64   Daniel Levitin, "A Conversation with Joni Mitchell," *Grammy* (March 1997).

65   Mercer, *Will You Take Me As I Am*, 62.

66   Ibid, 42.

67   Hilburn, "The Mojo Interview."

68   Mercer, *Will You Take Me As I Am*, 27–32.

69   Nietzsche, "Prologue," *Thus Spoke Zarathustra*, 42–43.

70   Nietzsche, "Of the Priests," *Thus Spoke Zarathustra*, 114–17.

71   Nietzsche, "The Sorcerer," *Thus Spoke Zarathustra*, 264–70.

72   Hoskyns, "Our Lady of the Sorrows."

73   Nietzsche, "Of Poets," *Thus Spoke Zarathustra*, 151.

74   Flanagan, "Joni Mitchell Has the Last Laugh."

75   Tim Murphy, "Joni Mitchell Gets Angry, Hugs it Out," *New York*
     (September 26, 2007).

76   Nietzsche, "Of the Old and New Law Tables," *Thus Spoke Zarathustra*, 218.

CHAPTER SEVEN
LOVE: THE BIG PRODUCTION

1   Morrissey, "Melancholy Meets the Infinite Sadness."
2   Weller, Girls Like Us, 415.
3   Hilburn, "Both Sides Later."
4   Breese, "A Conversation with David Crosby."
5   Crosby and Gottlieb, Long Time Gone, 130.
6   Boyd, Musicians in Tune, 139.
7   Weller, Girls Like Us, 277–78.
8   Susan Gordon Lydon, "In Her House, Love," New York Times, April 20, 1969.
9   Crowe, "The Rolling Stone Interview."
10 Helen Brown, "Jackson Browne: Legendary Californian Singer-Songwriter," Independent, December 14, 2005.
11 Steve Pond, "Wild Things Run Fast," Rolling Stone (November 25, 1982).
12 Malka, "Self-Portrait of a Superstar."
13 Dickie, "No Borders Here."
14 Weller, Girls Like Us, 413.
15 Sloman, On the Road with Bob Dylan, 384.
16 Robert Hilburn, "Out of the Canyon," Los Angeles Times, February 24, 1991.
17 Weller, Girls Like Us, 435.
18 Wild, "A Conversation with Joni Mitchell."
19 Bill Flanagan, "Secret Places," Musician (May 1988).
20 Larry LeBlanc, "Industry Profile: Larry Klein," celebrityaccess.com, March 2012.
21 Weller, Girls Like Us, 438.
22 Pond, "Wild Things Run Fast."
23 Iain Blair, "Joni Mitchell," Chicago Tribune, December 1, 1985.
24 Ibid.
25 Ibid.
26 Infusino, "A Chalk Talk with Joni Mitchell."
27 Hilburn, "Out of the Canyon."
28 Costello, "Joni's Last Waltz?"
29 Geoffrey Himes, "Music and Lyrics," JazzTimes (December 2007).
30 Ibid.
31 Hoskyns, "Our Lady of the Sorrows."
32 Himes, "Music and Lyrics."
33 Ingle, "Interview of Joni Mitchell."
34 Ibid.
35 Diehl, "It's a Joni Mitchell Concert, Sans Joni."
36 Garbarini, "Joni Mitchell is a Nervy Broad."
37 Robert Hilburn, "No Longer Speaking for the Rest of Us, Joni Mitchell Got Herself Back to the Garden," Los Angeles Times, September 20, 2004.

CHAPTER EIGHT
I'M OKAY, YOU'RE O'KEEFFE

1 Liane Hansen, "Music Icon Joni Mitchell Discusses Her Music," NPR Weekend Edition, May 28, 1995.
2 Charles Gandee, "Triumph of the Will," *Vogue* (April 1995).
3 O'Brien, *Joni Mitchell*, 284.
4 Benjamin Weissman, "Amy Adler Curates Joni Mitchell," *Frieze* (March 3, 2000).
5 This is from the author's scrum with Mitchell at the Grammys, February 28, 1996.
6 Camille Paglia, "The Trailblazer Interview," *Interview* (August 2005).
7 Ingle, "Interview of Joni Mitchell."
8 Paglia, "The Trailblazer Interview."
9 Brand, "The Education of Joni Mitchell."
10 Charlie Rose, *The Charlie Rose Show*, PBS, November 15, 2007.
11 Brand, "The Education of Joni Mitchell."
12 Quoted in O'Brien, *Joni Mitchell*, 300.
13 Quoted in Clifford Chase, "Trouble Child (Joni Mitchell and the History of My Sadness)," jonimitchell.com, June 17, 1996.
14 Quoted in O'Brien, *Joni Mitchell*, 302.
15 Hansen, "Music Icon Joni Mitchell Discusses Her Music."
16 Quoted in O'Brien, *Joni Mitchell*, 301.
17 Aikins, "Heart of a Prairie Girl."
18 Irvin, "Joni Mitchell."
19 Gill, "Joni Mitchell in Person."
20 Ibid.
21 Ingle, "Interview of Joni Mitchell."
22 Ibid.
23 Brand, "The Education of Joni Mitchell."
24 Ingle, "Interview of Joni Mitchell."
25 Ibid.
26 Wild, "A Conversation with Joni Mitchell."

CHAPTER NINE
SING SHINE DANCE

1 Joe Levy on *The Today Show*, February 11, 2008, http://video.today.msnbc.msn.com/today/23110632#23110632.
2 Greg Burk, "He's Still Full of Surprises," *Los Angeles Times*, February 24, 2008.
3 Brown, "Influences: Joni Mitchell," and http://www.gettyimages.ca/detail/video/herbie-hancock-at-the-2008-grammy-awards-press-room-at-news-footage/80159632.
4 Siddhartha Mitter, "To Pay Tribute to an Old friend, Hancock Adopts a New Approach," *Boston Globe*, September 23, 2007.
5 Himes, "Music and Lyrics."
6 Heidegger, *Poetry, Language, Thought*, 135.

7   Wild, "A Conversation with Joni Mitchell."

8   Ruhlmann, "From Blue to Indigo."

9   Hilton Als, "Birthday Suite," *New Yorker* (December 11, 1995).

10 Costello, "Joni's Last Waltz?"

11 Mark Miller, "Mitchell's Jazz Plaintively Mimes Arc of Modern Love,"
    Globe and Mail, March 30, 2000.

12 Paul Ennis, "So Joni Misses a Note—So Who Cares?" *Toronto Telegram*,
    November 9, 1966.

13 Joni Mitchell to Pete Fornatale, "Mixed Bag: Music and Interview
    with Pete Fornatale," WNEW, January 12, 1996.

14 Denberg, "Taming Joni Mitchell—Joni's Jazz."

15 Lydon, "Joni's Trek from Canada to Laurel Canyon."

16 Brown, "Influences: Joni Mitchell."

17 Crowe, "The Rolling Stone Interview."

18 Sloman, *On the Road with Bob Dylan*, 440.

19 Flanagan, "Secret Places."

20 Ibid.

21 Levitin, "A Conversation with Joni Mitchell."

22 Smith, "Joni Mitchell."

23 LeBlanc, "Joni Takes a Break."

24 Himes, "Music and Lyrics."

25 Charlie Rose, *The Charlie Rose Show*.

26 Notes on the packaging of Joni Mitchell's *The Fiddle and the Drum*, DVD, Koch,
    2007. Mitchell talks about her enjoyment in creating the piece on the extras
    with co-creator and Alberta Ballet artistic director Jean Grand-Maître.

27 Emma Goldman, *Living My Life, Volumes One and Two* (New York: Knopf, 1934),
    56. The actual quote is much longer: "I did not believe that a Cause which
    stood for a beautiful ideal, for anarchism, for release and freedom from
    convention and prejudice, should demand the denial of life and joy. I insisted
    that our Cause could not expect me to become a nun and that the movement
    would not be turned into a cloister. If it meant that, I did not want it. I want
    freedom, the right to self-expression, everybody's right to beautiful, radiant
    things."

28 Author interview with Wim Wenders, Toronto International Film Festival,
    September 2011, for *Pina*. Published by Postmedia News, February 15, 2012.

29 Hoskyns, "Our Lady of the Sorrows."

30 Stephen Holden, "High Spirits Buoy a Joni Mitchell Album," *New York Times*,
    November 7, 1982.

31 Barney Hoskyns, "Joni Mitchell in Conversation with Barney Hoskyns,"
    tape transcript of interview, September 14, 1994. Unpublished.
    http://jonimitchell.com/library/view.cfm?id=2143&from=search

32 Lynne Shuttleworth, "Joni Gets a Little Help From Her Friends,"
    Smash (April 1, 1988).

33 Valentine, "Joni Mitchell Interview."

34 Crowe, "The Rolling Stone Interview."

35 John Mackie, "Full Transcript of Joni Mitchell's Interview with *The Sun's* John Mackie," January 15, 2010, http://jonimitchell.com/library/ view.cfm?id=2203&from=search.
36 Nietzsche, "On the Blissful Islands," *Thus Spoke Zarathustra*, 111.
37 Heidegger, *Poetry, Language, Thought*, 4.
38 Nietzsche, "Prologue 5," *Thus Spoke Zarathustra*, 46.

AFTERWORD
 1 Nietzsche, "Prologue 7," *Thus Spoke Zarathustra*, 49.

BIBLIOGRAPHY

BOOKS:

Augustine of Hippo (Saint Augustine). *Confessions*. Translated by Rex Waner. New York: Signet Classics, 2009.

Bangs, Lester. *Psychotic Reactions and Carburetor Dung*. Edited by Greil Marcus. New York: Vintage, 1988.

Barfe, Louis. *Where Have All The Good Times Gone?: The Rise and Fall of the Record Industry*. London: Atlantic, 2005.

Barron, Frank. *Creativity and Personal Freedom*. New York: Van Nostrand Reinhold, 1968.

Bego, Mark. *Joni Mitchell*. New York: Taylor Trade Publishing, 2005.

Bennighof, James. *The Words and Music of Joni Mitchell*. Santa Barbara, CA: Praeger, 2010.

Boyd, Jenny. *Musicians in Tune: Seventy-Five Contemporary Musicians Discuss the Creative Process*. New York: Fireside, 1992.

Butler, Judith. *Gender Trouble: Feminism and the Subversion of Identity*. New York: Routledge, 1990.

Campbell, Joseph with Bill Moyers. *The Power of Myth*. New York: Anchor, 1988.

Collins, Judy. *Trust Your Heart*. New York: Houghton Mifflin, 1987.

Crosby, David and Carl Gottlieb. *Long Time Gone: The Autobiography of David Crosby*. New York: Dell, 1988.

Echols, Alice. *Shaky Ground: The Sixties and Its Aftershocks*. New York: Columbia University Press, 2001.

Fetherling, Douglas. *Some Day Soon: Essays on Canadian Songwriters*. Kingston, ON: Quarry Press, 1991.

Fornatale, Pete. *Back to the Garden: The Story of Woodstock and How It Changed a Generation*. New York: Touchstone, 2009.

Freud, Sigmund. *Beyond the Pleasure Principle and Other Writings*. Translated by John Reddick. London: Penguin Books, 2003.

Goethe, Johann Wolfgang von. *Sämmtliche Werke*. Leipzig: Karl Prochaska Neue Ausgaben, 1870.

Heidegger, Martin. *Nietzsche: Volumes One and Two*. Translated by David Farrell Krell. San Francisco: HarperSanFrancisco, 1979.

___. *Poetry, Language, Thought*. New York: Perennial Classics, HarperCollins, 1971.

Henderson, Stuart. "'All Pink and Clean and Full of Wonder?' Gendering 'Joni Mitchell', 1966–74." *Left History* (Fall 2005).

Heylin, Clinton. *Bob Dylan: The Recording Sessions (1960–1994)*. New York: St. Martin's Press, 1995.

Hinton, Brian. *Joni Mitchell: Both Sides Now, the Biography*. London: Sanctuary, 2000.

Homer. *The Odyssey*. Translated by Robert Fitzgerald. New York: Doubleday, 1963.

Jennings, Nicholas. *Before the Gold Rush*. Toronto: Penguin Canada, 1998.

Jung, C.G. *Flying Saucers: A Modern Myth of Things Seen in the Sky*. Translated by R.F.C. Hull. Princeton, NJ: Princeton University Press, 1979.

___. "Instinct and the Unconscious." *British Journal of Psychology* 10 (November 1919).

___. *Man and His Symbols*. New York: Doubleday, 1964.

___. *Memories, Dreams, Reflections*. Edited by Aniela Jaffe. Translated by Richard and Clara Winston. New York: Vintage, 1989.

Kaufmann, Walter. *Nietzsche: Philosopher, Psychologist, Antichrist*. New Jersey: Princeton University Press, 1974.

King, Tom. *The Operator: David Geffen Builds, Buys, and Sells the New Hollywood*. New York: Random House, 2000.

Klein, Melanie. *The Psycho-Analysis of Children*. London: Hogarth Press, 1932.

Knill, Paolo J., Helen N. Barba, and Margot N. Fuchs. *Minstrels of the Soul: Intermodal Expressive Therapy*. Toronto: Palmerston Press, 1995.

Lacan, Jacques. *The Mirror-Stage as Formative of the I as Revealed in Psychoanalytic Experience*. Original publication 1949 in Ecrits. Translated by Alan Sheridan. *Ecrits: A selection*. New York: W.W. Norton, 1977.

Levine, Ellen. *Tending the Fire: Studies in Art, Therapy & Creativity*. Toronto: Palmerston Press, 1995.

Luftig, Stacy, ed. *The Joni Mitchell Companion: Four Decades of Commentary*. New York: Schirmer Books, 1999.

Maslow, Abraham H. *Religions, Values, and Peak-Experiences*. New York: Viking Penguin, 1987.

278 | JONI

___. *The Farther Reaches of Human Nature.* New York: Viking, 1971.

McDonnell, Evelyn and Ann Powers, eds. *Rock She Wrote: Women Write About Rock, Pop, and Rap.* New York: Delta, 1995.

McDonough, Jimmy. *Shakey: Neil Young's Biography.* Toronto: Random House Canada, 2002.

Mercer, Michelle. *Will You Take Me As I Am: Joni Mitchell's Blue Period.* New York: Free Press, 2009.

Mingus, Charles. *Beneath the Underdog: His World as Composed by Mingus.* Edited by Nel King. New York: Vintage, 1971.

Mitchell, Joni. *Joni Mitchell: The Complete Poems and Lyrics.* Toronto: Random House Canada, 1997.

Nadel, Ira B. *Various Positions: A Life of Leonard Cohen.* New York: Pantheon, 1996.

Nelson, Sean. *Court and Spark 33⅓.* New York: Continuum, 2007.

Nietzsche, Friedrich. *Thus Spoke Zarathustra: A Book for Everyone and No One.* Translated by R.J. Hollingdale. Middlesex, UK: Penguin Classics, 1961.

___. *Twilight of the Idols and The Anti-Christ.* Translated by R.J. Hollingdale. Middlesex, UK: Penguin Classics, 1968.

O'Brien, Karen. *Joni Mitchell: Shadows and Light.* London: Virgin, 2001.

O'Brien, Lucy. *She Bop: The Definitive History of Women in Rock, Pop & Soul.* New York: Penguin, 1995.

Richards, Keith with James Fox. *Life.* New York: Little, Brown, 2010.

Rilke, Rainer Maria. *Letters to a Young Poet.* Translated by Stephen Mitchell. New York: Random House, 1984.

___. *Späte Gedichte.* Leipzig: Insel-Verlag, 1934.

Sloman, Larry "Ratso." *On the Road with Bob Dylan.* New York: Three Rivers Press, 1978.

Sontag, Susan. *Illness as Metaphor and AIDS and Its Metaphors.* New York: Picador, 2001.

Weller, Sheila. *Girls Like Us.* New York: Washington Square Press, 2008.

White, Timothy. "Joni Mitchell Interview." March 17, 1988. (Research for *Rock Lives: Profiles and Interviews.* New York: Holt Paperbacks, 1991.)

Whitesell, Lloyd. *The Music of Joni Mitchell.* New York: Oxford University Press, 2008.

Wilkinson, Alec. *The Protest Singer: An Intimate Portrait of Pete Seeger.* New York: Knopf, 2009.

Winnicott, D.W. *The Maturational Process and the Facilitating Environment.* New York: International Universities Press, 1965

___. *Playing and Reality.* London: Penguin Books, 1971.

___. *Therapeutic Consultations in Child Psychiatry.* London: The Hogarth Press, 1971.

Zimmer, Dave. *Crosby, Stills & Nash: The Authorized Biography.* Boston: Da Capo Press, 2000.

The following magazines, journals, newspapers, wire services, and other periodicals were consulted or used as source material:

Acoustic Guitar, Advertising Age, The Age, All About Jazz, Art Issues, The Arts in Psychotherapy, Austin Chronicle, Bay Windows, Being There, Berkeley Monthly, Billboard, Black and White, Border Crossings, Broadside, Calgary Herald, Calgary Sun, Canadian Press, Chatelaine, Chicago Sun-Times, Chicago Tribune, Christian Science Monitor, Circus, CoEvolution Quarterly, Crawdaddy, Cue, Daily Mail, Denver Post, Details, Detroit News, Downbeat, Edmonton Journal, Elm Street, Entertainment Weekly, Esquire, Express, Forbes, Frieze, Gadfly, Globe, Globe and Mail, Goldmine, Grammy Magazine, Guardian, Guitar Player, Hot Press, Impact, Independent, Inside Connection, Interview Magazine, Irish Times, Ithaca New Times, Jam!, JazzTimes, L.A. Weekly, Left History, Life, Listener, Look, Los Angeles Times, Maclean's, Mail on Sunday, Melody Maker, Miami Herald, Mirabella, Mix, Mojo, Musician, National, New Music Express, New York, New York Post, New York Times, New Yorker, Newsweek, Ottawa Citizen, Parade, People, Philadelphia Inquirer, Pittsburgh Post-Gazette, Playboy, Postmedia News, Progressive Quarterback, Pulse, Q, Reader's Digest, Record Collector, Record Guide, Redbook, Regina Leader-Post, Rock Express, Rock Photo, Rock's Backpages, Roland Users Group, Rolling Stone, San Diego Union-Tribune, Saskatoon Star-Phoenix, Scanners Blog, Sounds, Spin, Stereo Review, Sunday Telegraph, Telegram, Time, Toronto Star, Toronto Telegram, TV Guide, Us Weekly, USA Today, Vancouver Sun, Vanity Fair, Variety, Vibe, Village Voice, Vogue, W, Washington Post, Weekend, Western People, Western Report, Word, ZigZag.

RADIO BROADCASTS AND TRANSCRIPTIONS:

BBC1, BBC2, CBC, CBC Newsworld, CNN, The Dick Cavett Show, Fox News, KCSN-FM, MuchMusic, NPR, PBS, WDAS, WMMR, WNET, WNEW, WXPN.

MOVIES, CD-ROMS:

The Fiddle and the Drum, Joni Mitchell: Shadows and Light, Joni Mitchell: Refuge of the Roads, Joni Mitchell: Painting with Words and Music, Joni Mitchell: Woman and Painting, Joni Mitchell: Woman of Heart and Mind, The Last Waltz, The Kids are All Right, Rolling Stone: Cover to Cover, Woodstock.

WEBSITES:

1heckofaguy.com, thecanadianencyclopedia.com, dagbladet.no, fpinfomart.ca, gonzo.org, highbeam.com, jonimitchell.com, plosone.org, salon.com, wikipedia.org, youtube.com.

INDEX

Page numbers followed by "n" and a note number are references

27 Club, the, 111

"A Case of You" (song), 22, 145–46, 147–48
"After the Gold Rush" (song), 42
Alberta Ballet, 180, 274–26
album covers
  black man persona, 3, 5–6, 10, 13, 21, 23
  with cat, 164
  as contractual obligation, 229
  Grammy award, 218–19
  horse's ass image, 117
  Mitchell/Dylan comparison, 152
  photographic, 11, 12–13, 133
  self-portraits, 3, 10, 11, 13, 164, 215–16, 219–20
  Van Gogh spoof, 219–20
Alias, Don, 206, 208–9, 215, 225
  painting of, 19
aliens, outsider experience, 41–43
"All I Want" (song), 105, 193, 202, 250
Amchitka concert, 102
"Amelia" (song), 208
American Idol (television), xiv–xv
amyotrophic lateral sclerosis (ALS), 27
Andersen, Eric, 68, 69
Anderson, Bill (father), 17, 18
Anderson, Myrtle McKee (mother), 17, 64–66
Anderson, Roberta Joan. See Mitchell, Joni
appearance
  "childlike," 13, 208, 240
  folk persona, 4–5, 86

hippie makeover, 75-76, 81-83
    and identity, 54, 55
    and music industry, 52, 121
Arcade Fire, 104
artistic expression. *See also*
    creative process
    and audience expectations, 112,
    113, 239-40
    and creative control, xiv, 3, 77
    in dance, 249-51, 253
    experimenting with, 155-56,
    189-90, 212-13
    external evaluation, 223, 231
    frustrated filmmaker
    remark, 243
    and maturity, 149
    Mitchell on, 31, 54, 62, 117-18
    and outsider experience, 10,
    39, 41-43, 225
    in photography, 220
    Starry Nights metaphor, 126, 148
    and women, x, 66-67, 226
ArtNews (magazine), 227
Art Nouveau, (Mitchell persona),
    5-6, 9, 13, 234
art school, 65, 221, 224, 225, 237
artwork. *See* album covers;
    painting
Asher, Betsy and Peter, 4
Asylum Records, 108, 150
Auden, W.H., 47
Augustine, St., 183-84, 190
Austin Chronicle, 161
authenticity. *See* originality
awards and honours
    Billboard Century Award, 93
    Grammy Award (lifetime
    achievement), 109-10
    Grammy Awards, xvii, 127, 214-
    15, 218-19
    "Guitar Gods," 117
    Hancock tribute album, 233-34
    Rock and Roll Hall of
    Fame, 124
    Time (magazine cover), 124

Back to Black (album), 232
Back to the Garden (Fornatale),
    91
Baez, Albert, 143
Baez, Joan, 143-44, 237
Baez, Joan Bridge (Senior),
    143-44
Balin, Marty, 94
ballet, 180, 249, 274n26
Band, the, 90, 160
Barba, Helen, 138
Barbie dolls, 50
Bausch, Pina, 250
Bay Windows (newspaper), 21
BBC, 60, 167
Beatles, the, 91
Beatty, Warren, 85, 225
Beck, Jeff, 90
Bedaux, Charles, 75, 266n47
Bedtime Stories (album), 218
beer, Canadian, 147-48
Beethoven, Ludwig van, 41,
    210, 228
Bening, Annette, 202
Bennett, Tony, 235
Bennighof, James, 71, 73
Bernstein, Joel, 11, 220
Berosini, Estrella, 77
Bessborough Hotel
    (Saskatoon), 10
Beyond the Pleasure Principle
    (Freud), 35, 36
Biblical references
    Corinthians, 231
    Job, 186-87
    Lilith, 183
Big Sur celebration, 97
Billboard (magazine), 12, 83, 98
    rankings, 197
Billboard Century Award 1995,
    Mitchell's acceptance speech,
    93-94
Birth of Tragedy, The (Nietzsche),
    174, 175
Black, Mary, 60, 167

black man persona, 1, 2–4,
    5–6, 9, 13, 19, 23, 27, 28–29,
    234
Blade, Brian, 246, 248
Blair, Iain, 46, 210, 211
Blakley, Ronee, 143, 169, 170
Blonde on Blonde (album), 153
Blood, Sweat & Tears, 90, 142
Blue (album)
    cover art, 11
    public perception of, 202–3
    themes, 62, 129, 130–31, 193
    vocal style, 239
"Blue" (song), 111, 239, 240
Bluebird (Mercedes car), 86–87
blues, 241
    chording, 71–72, 266n40
    guitar tunings, 69
Blues Project, the, 142
Blumenfeld, Roy, 141–42
"Boho Dance, The" (song), 230
Bonli, Henry, 15
Bono, 175
Both Sides Now (album), 215–16,
    239–40
"Both Sides Now" (song)
    Collins's version, 11, 76, 83,
        142, 153
    Hancock's version, 236
    Mitchell singing, 74, 216
    other versions, 56, 153
    themes of, 197–98, 208
Bowie, David, 5
Boyd, Jenny, 14, 31, 67, 135, 200
    on God, 137–38
Boyd, Joe, 51
"Boys of Summer, The" (song), 31
Brand, Oscar, 51
Brand, Stewart, 223, 224, 230
Brando, Marlon, 225
Brecht, Bertolt, 59
Breese, Wally, 63, 74, 78, 79
Brown, Jerry, 253
Brown, Les, 80
Browne, Jackson, 108, 114, 204–5

Buffalo Springfield, 40, 78
Butler, Judith, 20
Byrds, the, 73–74
Byrne, David, xvii

"Cactus Tree" (song), 198
Cafe au Go Go, 106
Calgary Sun, 83
"California" (song), 69
Campbell, Joseph, xv, 88
Camus, Albert, xii, 12, 141
Canadian
    beer, 147–48
    First Nations issues, 57
    politics, 95
    psyche, 15, 110, 144
    view of U.S. media, 153
Capote, Truman, 125
car, stolen, 86–87
career. *See also* life experiences
    choice over marriage, 200–201
    coffee houses, 105, 110–11
    establishing, 50–52
    first record deal, 3, 77
    as journey, 126
    media impact on, 120
    obtaining U.S. work visa, 61, 197
    retirements, 104, 105, 111, 118,
        126, 131
    vocal style changes, 237–38
"Carey" (song), 127–28
Carey, Mariah, 218
"Car on a Hill" (song), 204
Carter, Rubin "Hurricane,"
    156–57
Casey, Patrick, 55
Cash, Johnny, 153, 154
Cashbox (magazine), 12
Castaneda, Carlos, 182
cats, 162–64, 169
Cavett, Dick, 91, 94–96
Cavolina, Robbie, 219
CBC television, 51, 105
Chalk Mark in a Rain Storm (album),
    176, 212, 244–45

Champagne Safari, The (film), 75, 266n47

Chapman, Tracy, 178

Charles, Ray, 83

Cheech, Marin, 4, 243

Cheech & Chong, 4, 243

"Chelsea Morning" (song), 11, 142

Cher, 150

"Cherokee Louise" (song), 57

Chicago Tribune, 210

childhood experiences
    of choir, 228, 238
    as described by Mitchell, 16–17
    of fashion, 52–54
    of gender stereotyping, 18–19
    illness, 36–38
    piano lessons, 67
    poetry writing, 115, 167–68, 224
    of the prairies, 144
    of school, 223–24
    of smoking, 228

children
    gender stereotyping, 24–25
    Mitchell on, 62
    mother-daughter reunion, 63–64
    psychology of, 7–8, 35–36, 48–49

Cholodenko, Lisa, 202

Chong, Tommy, 4, 243

"Circle Game, The" (song), 56, 68, 84, 125

Clance, Pauline Rose, 23, 25

Clark, Gene, 91

Clarke, Michael, 73

classical music, 196, 210

clothing. *See* fashion

Clouds (album), 153, 201
    cover art, 10
    liner notes, 17
    promotion of, 83
    success of, xvii, 10–11, 127
    vocal style, 241, 243

cocaine, 125, 159–60, 213

Cocker, Joe, 90

CoEvolution Quarterly, 223, 229

Cohen, Leonard
    background, 139, 148
    "Hallelujah" (song), 105, 141, 145
    as mentor to Mitchell, 140–41, 149
    Mitchell's "superficial" remark, 141, 147
    referenced in Mitchell songs, 145–46, 147–48, 185
    relationship with Mitchell, 144–49, 198, 201

Collins, Judy
    "Both Sides Now" version, 76, 83, 197
    "Chelsea Morning" version, 11
    meets Mitchell, 142–43, 144
    and Mitchell comparison, 80, 237
    on *Seagull* vocal style, 79

Coltrane, John, 233

"Comes Love" (song), 215

composition method.
    See also song writing;
    studio production
    chording, 71–72, 73
    as described in "Hallelujah," 145
    scale and harmony, 68–69, 71–72, 74, 266n40
    use of Picardy third, 73

concept albums, 157, 241

concerts
    cancelled, 104, 127
    formal setting of, 110, 115
    live recordings, 12, 170

Confessions (St. Augustine), 183–84

Considine, Tim, 11

"Cool Water" (song), 245

Cornyn, Stan, 83

Costello, Elvis
    Mitchell interview, 162, 163, 174, 177, 178, 213, 239
    Mitchell's influence on, 235

Cotten, Elizabeth, 68
Court and Spark (album)
  cover art, 12
  success of, 120, 150, 151
  tour, 108
  vocal style, 4, 195, 239, 243
cover art. *See* album covers
"Coyote" (song), 148, 207
creative process. *See also*
  artistic expression
  and art therapy, 134–35
  cycle of recreation, 125, 181
  and destiny, 13–14
  Freud's theory, 35–36
  and the god concept, xvi, 32,
    136–37, 165–67, 180–82
  and the inner child, 117–18
  inspiration, 138–39, 224, 225
  of mother-infant bonding,
    48–49
  and multiple identities, 6–7
  and near-death experience, 40
  and outsider experience,
    41–43
  and self, 7–10, 181
Cronkite, Walter, 100
Crosby, David, 121, 169, 200
  "humble as Mussolini" remark,
    33–34
  as mentor to Mitchell, 73–77,
    89
  and Mitchell, 195, 198–200
  recording of *Clouds*, 201
  on relationship with Mitchell,
    77–78
  and *Song to a Seagull* (album),
    77–80
  and Woodstock, 93, 95, 97
Crosby, Floyd Delafield, 75,
  266n47
Crosby, Stills & Nash (album), 169
Crosby, Stills & Nash: The Authorized Biography (Zimmer), 96
Crosby, Stills & Nash (CSN),
  241–42

Crosby, Stills, Nash & Young
  (CSNY), 40, 79, 90, 91, 92–93,
  94–95
  "Woodstock" version, 98
Crowe, Cameron, 18, 19, 53, 62,
  65, 86, 151, 154, 158, 202, 203,
  243, 244, 252, 253
Cryst, Art, 78, 79
culture
  Canadian, 147–48
  consumerist, x, 176–78
  decadent, 174–77
  of greed, 102–3, 105
  and patriotism, 177

Daily Mail, 61
Dale, Kelly. *See* Gibb,
  Kilauren (daughter)
Daly, Steven, 86
dance, 249–51, 253
  ballet, 180, 249, 274n26
"Dancin' Clown" (song), 245
Daniel, Reola, 65
Darin, Bobby, 115
da Vinci, Leonardo, 41
Davis, Bette, 242
Davis, Miles, 16, 224, 233, 235
Davis, Sammy, Jr., 245
"Dawntreader, The" (song), 199
"Day After Day" (song), 56
Daydream (album), 218
"Dazed and Confused" (song),
  98, 267n11
de Beauvoir, Simone, 50
Dee, Sandra, 115
Déjà Vu (album), 98
Demme, Jonathan, 40
Denberg, Jody, 161, 166, 178,
  242
depression, 133, 134, 204
  Mitchell on, 251–52
Depression, The (coffee house),
  52
Details, 34, 93
Detroit, home, 60, 68

Detroit News, 171
Dick Cavett Show, The (talk show),
    91, 94–96
Dickie, Mary, 28, 55, 85
Diehl, Matt, 21, 23, 216
DiFranco, Ani, 86
Dion, Celine, 125
Dog Eat Dog (album), 177
    literary references, 175, 179
    production, 210–12
    response to, 180, 212
    vocal style, 241
Dolby, Thomas, 210, 211, 212
*Don Juan's Reckless
    Daughter* (album)
    and black community, 28–29
    cover art, 3, 5–6, 10, 13, 21, 23,
    234, 244
    jazz influence, 5, 170
Doobie Brothers, the, 212
Douridas, Chris, 72
dragon metaphor, 179, 180,
    270n40
drugs
    cocaine, 125, 159–60, 213
    marijuana, 76, 84, 85, 106
    and Mitchell, 125
dulcimer, 128
Dylan, Bob (Bobby), 105, 253
    background, 139, 152–54
    comparison with Mitchell,
    149–52, 161
    and Geffen, 108, 150, 160
    on god concept, 181
    going electric, 46, 142, 269n9
    Great Music Experience
    concert, 160–61
    influence on Mitchell, 139, 152
    Last Waltz, The (film), 160
    Mitchell's "plagiarist" remarks,
    22–23, 55–56, 141, 150
    relationship with Mitchell,
    154–55, 156, 157, 158, 160–61
    remarks on Mitchell, 19–20,
    154–55, 251

Renaldo and Clara (film), 158
Rolling Thunder Revue (1975),
    143, 146, 157, 158

Eagles, the, 108, 218
Earth Day, 102
Echols, Alice, 2, 30, 43, 54
"Edith and the Kingpin" (song),
    239
education
    art school, 65, 221, 224
    lack of formal, 140
    piano lessons, 67
    school experience, 223–24
    self-taught, 42, 141
Elbing, Peter, 52
Elektra/Asylum, 150
Eliot, T.S., 29–30
Elliot, Mama Cass, 52
Elliott, Ramblin' Jack, 143
Ennis, Paul, 240
environmental movement, 102

Falco, Edie, 82, 85
fame
    experience of, 184, 230
    Mitchell on, 110–16
    Richards on, 88, 112
family
    dynamics, 24–25, 48–49
    grandmothers, 66–67,
    200–201
    motherhood, 57–67, 182
    parents, 17, 18, 64–66
Farina, Mimi, 143
fashion
    and the folk persona, 4–5, 86
    hippie makeover, 75–76, 81–83
    and performance, 52, 86
    punk, 55
    as self-expression, 18, 54–56,
    65–66
Feather, Leonard, 30, 32, 33, 34
Feminine Mystique, The (Friedan),
    83

feminism
  and love relationships,
    198, 205
  Mitchell on, 85–86
Fez (nightclub), 22
"Fiction" (song), 177–78
Fiddle and the Drum, The (ballet),
  180, 249, 274n26
"Fishbowl, The" (Mitchell poem),
  115
Flanagan, Bill, 124, 125, 130, 131,
  166, 170, 188, 209, 244
Flying Saucers: A Modern Myth of
  Things Seen in the Sky (Jung), 41
folk persona
  appearance, 4–5, 86
  audience expectations,
    239–40
  of Dylan, 23
  "female Bob Dylan," 149
  hippie makeover, 75–76, 81–83
  Mitchell's discomfort with,
    86–87
  vocal style, 236–37
Fonda, Peter, 76
"For Free" (song), 113–14, 115–16
Fornatale, Pete, 91, 133, 241
fort-da game, 35–36, 48
For the Roses (album), 203, 243
  cover art, 11, 117, 133
"For the Roses" (song), 113, 115
Fort Macleod, AB, 16, 52
Four Quartets (Eliot poem), 29
Fourth Dimension (coffee house),
  39, 43
"Free Man in Paris" (song),
  108
Freewheelin' Bob Dylan, The
  (album), 152
Freud, Sigmund, xv, 7, 8,
  35–36, 48
Friedan, Betty, 83
Friedman, Kinky, 143
Fuchs, Margot, 138
Fulton, Laila, 65

Gabriel, Peter, 245
Gandalf Publishing, 60
Gandee, Charles, 219
Garbarini, Vic, 29, 46, 112, 123,
  154, 217
Garbo, Greta, 44, 125
garden, metaphysical, 90, 117, 119,
  151, 177
Gardner, David, 61
Gaslight South (nightclub), 73,
  169
Gauguin, Paul, 219, 224
Geffen, David
  and concept albums, 157
  and Dylan, 108, 150, 160
  and Mitchell, 90–91, 108, 109,
    150–51, 204
  and Roberts, 107–8
  and Young, 40
Geffen Records, 108
gender
  alienation, 18–19
  black man persona, 1, 2–4, 5–6,
    9, 13, 19, 23, 27, 28–29, 234
  drag impersonator, 21–22
  as function of performance,
    20–21, 242–43
  and identity, 1–7, 18–22
  and the media, 118, 121–25
  and self-esteem, 23–26
  stereotyping, 18, 19, 24–25,
    49–50, 85–86
"Gendering Joni Mitchell"
  (Henderson), 21
Gender Trouble (Butler), 20
Getz, Stan, 233
Gibb, Kilauren (daughter)
  birth of, 57–59
  and Mitchell, 63–64
Gilberto, João, 233
Ginsberg, Allen, 148
Girls Like Us (Weller), 19, 169, 204
Globe and Mail, 120, 144, 240, 242
"God Must Be a Boogie Man"
  (song), 136

Goethe, Johann Wolfgang von, 1, 27
Goldman, Emma, 250, 274n27
Gorge, the (amphitheatre), 161
Graham, Bill, 108
Grammy Awards
    Clouds (album), xvii, 127
    Hancock tribute album, 232–34
    lifetime achievement, 109–10
    Turbulent Indigo (album), xvii, 214–15, 218–19
Great Music Experience concert, 160–61
Greenpeace, 102
Grossman, Albert, 105–6
Guerin, John, 30, 69, 206–7
"Guinnevere" (song), 199
guitar
    chording, 71–72, 73
    electric, 72
    influences, 67–68
    tunings, 68–69, 72, 74, 266n40
"Guitar Gods," 117
Guly, Christopher, 120
Guthrie, Woody, 56, 152

Haeny, John, 79
"Hallelujah" (song), 105, 141
    and Mitchell, 145
Hancock, Herbie, 233–34, 235–36
Hannah, Daryl, 205
Hansen, Liane, 228
Harvey, P.J., 235
Havens, Richie, 92, 100
health issues
    depression, 133, 134, 204
    hypoglycemia, 115
    insomnia, 166
    polio, 36–39, 182, 228, 250
    skin condition, 44–45
    smoking, 228, 229
    throat lesion, 245
Heart of Gold (film), 40
Heidegger, Martin, xii, xvi, 236–37, 254

Hejira (album)
    cover art, 13
    jazz influence, 148, 170, 244
    themes, 208
Hell Freezes Over (album), 218
Helm, Levon, 160
"Help Me" (song), 12
Henderson, Stuart, 21
Henderson the Rain King (Bellow), 197
Hendrix, Jimi, 90, 111, 122
Henley, Don, 31, 212, 244, 245
"Hey, That's No Way to Say Good-bye" (song), 142
Higgins, Bill, 64
High Noon (film), 75
Highway 61 Revisited (album), 153
Hilburn, Robert, 102, 182, 213, 217
Hill, Carla, 54, 81
Hillman, Chris, 73
Hinitt, Robert, 52
Hinton, Christine, 169
Hissing of Summer Lawns, The (album), 230
    cover art, 12–13
    jazz influence, 148, 239, 244
    reaction to, 13, 33, 189
Hoffman, Abbie, 98
Holiday, Billie, 169, 240, 245–46
Hollies, the, 200
Holmes, Jake, 267n11
Hoskyns, Barney, 5, 6, 138, 187
Hotcakes (album), 150
Howe, James Wong, 75
How to Play Folk-Style Guitar (Seeger), 67
Hutton, Lauren, 253
Hynde, Chrissie, 235, 238

I Can Hear it Now/The Sixties (radio), 100
I Ching, 141
identity
    Cohen on, 147
    and conformity, 2, 15, 110

and the creative process, 7–10
and fashion, 54, 55
and gender, 1–7, 18–22
Mitchell on, 147
and painting, 221–25, 229–31
self-creation of, 1–7, 15–18, 147,
184
Idol, Billy, 245
"If" (Kipling), 180, 254
"If" (song), xvii, 180
text of, 254–56
"If I Had a Heart" (song), 240
"I Had a King" (song), 60, 200
illness. See health issues
Illness as Metaphor (Sontag), 47
imagery. See also song
writing; themes
circle of life, 125–26, 137, 176
dragon metaphor, 179, 180,
270n40
garden, metaphysical, 90, 117,
119, 151, 177
lion metaphor, 165, 173, 179,
180
mirror metaphor, 8–9, 140, 149
river metaphor, 190–92
spaceman, 42–43, 45–46, 100
Imes, Suzanne, 23, 25
I'm Not There (film), 269n9
Impact (magazine), 28
impersonator, drag, 21–22
"Impostor Phenomenon in High-
Achieving Women, The"
(Clance and Imes), 23
impostor syndrome, 23–26
"In France They Kiss on Main
Street" (song), 250
Infusino, Divina, 71, 212
Ingle, Rene, 162, 222, 229, 230
Ingram, Bobby, 169
Inside Connection, 66
"Instinct and the Unconscious"
(Jung), 8
In the Park of the Golden Buddha
(painting), 222–23

Intimate and Interactive
(television), 43
Iron Butterfly, 90
Irvin, Les, 63
"I Shall Be Released" (song), 160,
161
Isle of Wight Festival, 90, 128

Jahn, Mike, 92
Janes, Loring, 59
jazz
collaboration with Mingus,
29–31, 32–33, 46
Hancock tribute album,
233–34
influence of, 30–31, 33, 34, 239
scale and harmony, 266n40
style, 148, 170–71
JazzTimes, 214, 235, 248
Jefferson Airplane, 94
Jewell, Brian, 21
John, Elton, 5
Johnny Cash Show, The (televi-
sion), 153
Johnson, Jack, 235
Jones, Brian, 111
Jones, Quincy, 233
Jones, Rickie Lee, 178
Joni Mitchell: Shadows and Light
(O'Brien), 68
Joni Mitchell: Woman of Heart and
Mind (documentary), 14
Joplin, Janis, 111, 122, 124, 217
journalists. See media
Jung, Carl, xv, 6, 8, 31, 41, 42, 48,
166
"Jungle Line, The" (song), 244
"Just Like Me" (song), 51
"Just Like This Train" (song),
195

Katz, Steve, 141–42
KCRW, 72
KCSN-FM, 162, 222
Ke$ha, 119

Kelly, John, 21–22
Kerouac, Jack, 159
Kershaw, Doug, 153
Kids are All Right, The (film), 202
King, Carole, 86
King, Tom, 108
Kipling, Rudyard, 141, 180, 254
Klein, Howie, 109–10
Klein, Larry, 63, 69
  marriage, 209–10, 213–15
  as record producer, 210–13, 233
Klein, Melanie, 7, 48
Knill, Paolo, 138
Kooper, Al, 142
Kratzman, Arthur, 80, 167–68,
  169, 179, 188, 189, 224
Kristofferson, Kris, 130
Kunkel, Leah Cohen, 52
Kunkel, Russ, 52, 76, 206

Lacan, Jacques, 8–9, 10
Ladies of the Canyon (album), 11, 83,
  84, 127, 145, 202
Ladies of the Canyon (band), 77
Lady Gaga, 54
L.A. Express, the (band), 206
LaGreca, Angela, 4, 6
Lambert, Hendricks & Ross, 16,
  243
Landy, John, 167, 270n44
Langer, Barbara, 169
Lanois, Daniel, 244
Lapidus, Joellen, 128
"Last Time I Saw Richard, The"
  (song), 242
Last Waltz, The (film), 160
Laurel Canyon, 11, 52, 76
  home in, 133, 144, 200, 241
L.A. Weekly, 2, 30
"Lead Balloon" (song), 119–20
LeBlanc, Larry, 113
Led Zeppelin, 98, 119, 267n11
Leisz, Greg, 247
Lennox, Annie, 218
Let's Sing Out (CBC television), 51

"Let the Wind Carry Me" (song),
  203
Levine, Ellen, xv, 9–10, 36, 49, 134
Levitin, Daniel, 181, 182
Levy, Joe, 233
Lewis, Furry, 70–71
Lewy, Henry, 210
Life (magazine), 127
life experiences. See also career
  depression, 133, 134, 204
  of gender stereotyping, 18–19
  illness, 36–38, 182, 228, 250
  Mitchell on, 128–30
  and music, 200
  and originality, 168, 189
  poetry writing, 167–68, 224
  of school, 223–24
  skin condition, 44–45
"Like a Rolling Stone" (song), 142
Lilith Fair, 183
lion metaphor, 165, 173, 179, 180
"Little Green" (song), 61–62, 196
Loder, Kurt, 19
Lorca, Federico Garcia, 141
Lord of the Rings, The (Tolkien), 60
Los Angeles, 44, 231
  Bel Air home, 63, 108, 163
  Hollywood, 4, 77, 122, 271
  Laurel Canyon, 11, 52, 76, 133,
    144, 200, 241
  Malibu, 211
  music scene, 76
Los Angeles Times, 21, 22, 30, 44, 59,
  60, 64, 81, 86, 216
Lou Gehrig's disease, 27
Louis Riel café, 123
Love Parade (Germany), 100
Lucas, George, 125

Machiavelli, Niccolò, 103
Mackie, John, 175
Macklam, Steve, 120
Maclean's, 111, 129
Mademoiselle Oink (Mitchell
  persona), 69–70

Madonna, 65, 120, 141, 218
Magdalene laundries, 182
Major, Phyllis, 204
"Man from Mars" (song), 162,
    163–64
"Man to Man" (song), 184, 205
"Marcie" (song), 112, 145
marijuana, 76, 84, 85, 106
Mariposa Folk Festival, 56, 144
Marom, Malka, 111, 205
marriages
    Chuck Mitchell, 15–16, 39,
        59–61, 83, 107, 140, 197
    Larry Klein, 63, 69, 209–15, 233
Maslow, Abraham, xv, 97
Matala, Greece, 127–29
Mathis, Johnny, 92
Matisse, Henri, 224
Matteo, Steve, 66
Matthews Southern Comfort, 98
McCartney, Paul, 154
McDonald, Marci, 7, 16, 123, 133
McDonald, Michael, 212
McDonough, Jimmy, 38, 39, 40,
    43, 106
McGuinn, Roger, 73, 143,
    146, 148
    and Mitchell conversation,
    207
McKee, Myrtle. See Anderson,
    Myrtle McKee (mother)
McKee, Sadie (grandmother),
    66–67
McLachlan, Sarah, 178, 183, 235
McLaren, Malcolm, 55
McLuhan, Marshall, 96
McMath, Brad, 56, 57–58, 195,
    196
Mead, Margaret, on Woodstock,
    101–2
"Me and Bobby McGee" (song),
    130
media
    and Canadian psyche, 153
    coverage of mother-daughter

reunion, xi, 64
    coverage of sex life, 121–25
    and limiting of interviews,
        118–25, 268–26
    Wenner/Mitchell feud, 119,
        121, 124
Medusa (album), 218
Melody Maker (magazine), 3
Memories, Dreams, Reflections
    (Jung), 42
Memphis, trip, 70
men
    appreciation of love songs, 202
    and self-esteem, 23–24
    undervaluing of female talent,
        93–94, 118, 121–25, 226
Mercer, Michelle, 52, 131, 140, 141,
    152, 159, 183
Mercury, Freddie, 5
"Michael from Mountains" (song),
    74, 200
Miles of Aisles (album), 12, 125, 242
Miller, Mark, 240
Mingus (album), 32–33, 34, 35, 136,
    235
Mingus, Charles, Jr., 27–28
    collaboration with Mitchell,
        29–31, 32–33, 46
Minstrels of the Soul (Knill, Barba,
    and Fuchs), 138
mirror metaphor, 8–9, 140, 149
"Miss Gee" (Auden poem), 47
Mitchell, Chuck
    on ex-wife, 83
    marriage, 15–16, 39, 59–61, 107,
        140, 197
Mitchell, Joni
    autobiography, 1
    biographies of, xi
    and Charles Mingus, 27–34, 46
    and dance, 249–51, 253
    daughter of, xi, 57–59, 63–64
    family of, 17, 18, 64–67, 200–201
    first marriage, 15–16, 39, 59–61,
        197

on her music, xvii, 54, 81, 135
on herself, 16–17, 53, 55–56,
    138–39
and identity, 1–7, 10–13
legacy, ix, xiv, xvii, 109–10,
    234–36, 254
musical influences, 16, 29, 68,
    170–71, 196
mythology of, viii, 16–17, 93,
    121, 194
personal traits, xii–xiii, 15–22
relationships, 121–22, 193–217
reputation, 109–10, 235–36,
    253
second marriage, 63, 69,
    209–15, 233
stage name, 15, 61
website, 74
and the Woodstock genera-
    tion, 102–3
Mojo, 5, 74, 102, 160, 182, 187
Monterey Pop Festival, 91
Moore, Julianne, 202
Morgellons syndrome, 44–45
Morris, John, 91
Morrison, Jim, 11, 111
Morrison, Van, 124, 161, 235
Morrissey, 54, 194
motherhood
    giving up the baby, 57–59, 60,
        62, 64–67
    Mitchell on, 62, 64
    mother-daughter reunion,
        63–64
    unwed mother stigma, 58–59,
        65, 182
Motion Picture (magazine), 61
Mountain Loves the Sea, The (paint-
    ing), 13
"Mr. Tambourine Man" (song),
    59, 74
MuchMusic, 43
Murphy, Tim, 189, 190
musical styles
    blues, 69, 71–72, 241, 266n40

folk, 236–37
jazz, 30–31, 33, 34, 148, 170–71,
    239, 266n40
world beat, 28, 148, 166, 241,
    244
music festivals. See specific
    festivals
Musician (magazine), 29, 130, 188
Musicians in Tune (Boyd), 14, 31,
    137
music industry
    audience expectations, 6, 108,
        171, 219, 239–40
    and concept albums, 157, 241
    disillusionment with, 11, 117
    Geffen Records, 108
    managers, 105–9, 150–51
    marketing, 78, 83–85, 105, 107,
        117, 249
    Mitchell on, 85, 116–18, 146
    Mitchell's reputation, 109–10,
        235–36, 253
    pop music, xiv–xv, 85, 110, 119,
        235, 249
    publishing rights, 60, 106–7
    Reprise Records, xiv, 3, 77,
        83–85, 107, 117
    resistance to innovation,
        72–73, 225
    sale of song rights, 105
    self promotion, 16–17, 112
myth and mythology
    27 Club, the, 111
    and meaning, xv, 41, 42, 88–89
    self-creation of, 16–17
    of Woodstock Festival, 90, 92,
        93, 101–2

Nash, Graham
    and CSN, 241–42
    and CSNY, 79, 94
    and Mitchell, 93, 121, 129, 144,
        169, 200–202
    and Neil Young, 40
"Nathan La Franeer" (song), 145

Naylor, Dave, 196
Nelson, Sean, 151
Nelson, Willie, 245
New College Physics, The: A Spiral
    Approach (Baez), 161
New Musical Express, 18
Newport Folk Festival (1965), 91,
    92, 141, 142, 269n9
Newport Folk Festival (1967), 91,
    92
    Mitchell at, 141–44, 149
New Victoria Theatre
    (London), 3
New York
    Geffen apartment, 90, 92
    music scene, 141–42
New York (magazine), 189
New York Times, 2, 92, 111, 201
Nicholson, Jack, 85, 212
Nietzsche (the cat), 162–64
Nietzsche, Friedrich Wilhelm. See
    also Thus Spoke Zarathustra
    about, xiii, xvi, 164–65
    as inspiration, 139, 164, 166–67,
        168, 224
    misuse by Nazis, 139, 165–66,
        270n40
    Mitchell quoting of, 156, 170, 188
    the performed "I," 8–10, 20
    philosophy of, 8, 10, 165–66,
        177–78
    referenced in Mitchell songs,
        174–80
"Night in the City" (song), ix
Noga, Helen, 92
Nolan, Bob, 245
"Not to Blame" (song), 204
NPR (radio), 228
Nyro, Laura, 108

O'Brien, Karen, 68, 77, 228
O'Donnell, Rosie, 12
O'Keeffe, Georgia, 218, 224, 225,
    226–28, 229
Old Man and the Sea, The (film), 75

Oleta, 245
"One More Cup of Coffee" (song),
    154
"One Week Last Summer" (song),
    247
"Only Love Can Break Your Heart"
    (song), 201
On the Road with Bob Dylan (Slo-
    man), 146
Operator, The (King), 108
originality
    and authenticity, 23, 224–25
    and the collective unconscious,
        42
    Mitchell on, 55–56, 145, 168, 189
    and music industry, 148, 225
Ostin, Mo, 71
"Our House" (song), 201–2
outsider experience
    and childhood illness, 39
    of creative people, 41–43
    otherness, 10, 225

Page, Jimmy, 98
Paglia, Camille, 223, 224
Painted Word, The (Wolfe), 229
painting. See also album covers
    of cat, 163, 164
    of Cohen, 145
    of deer, 222
    of Don Alias, 19
    and identity, 221–25, 229–31
    influences, 15, 224
    lessons in, 145
    Mitchell on, 219–21, 230
    Mountain Loves the Sea, The, 12
    visual imagery and music, 221
"Paprika Plains" (song), 29, 154
Parker, Dorothy, 124
Pastorius, Jaco, 170–71
PBS documentary, 32
Pender Harbour, B.C. (home), 11,
    126, 132–33, 247–48
Penny Farthing, the (nightclub),
    59

performance
and appearance, 52
and audience response, 115
and gender, 20-21, 242-43
and vocal style, 242, 245
personae
black man, 1, 2-4, 5-6, 9, 13, 19,
23, 27, 28-29, 234
folk, 4-5, 23, 75-76, 81-83,
86-87, 149, 236-37, 239-40
Mademoiselle Oink, 69-70
Petty, Tom, 245
philosophy
creator-creation equation, 125,
165, 181
destiny, 14, 66, 165
Nietzschean, xiii, xvi, 165-67,
171-80
and singing, 236-37
photography, 11, 12-13, 133, 220
Piaf, Edith, 187
piano
lessons, 67
singing into, 79, 199
Picasso, Pablo, 224, 225, 226, 230,
231
Pine Knob Music Theater, 12
plagiarism, 22-23, 141
Planet Waves (album), 150, 151
Plant, Robert, 98
Plath, Sylvia, 153
poetry writing
first-person, 239
Mitchell on, 11, 144, 168
third-person portraits, 239
poets, xvi, 170, 187-89
Polanski, Roman, 83
Police, the, 251
police and Mademoiselle Oink
(Mitchell persona), 69-70
polio, 36-39, 43, 69, 182, 228, 250
Pollock, Jackson, 230
Pop, Iggy, 98
pop music
industry, xiv-xv, 110, 119

Mitchell on, 249
Mitchell's influence on, 85,
235
Port, Donna, 38
"Positively 4th Street" (song),
152, 153
Power of Myth, The (Campbell), 88
pregnancy
and art school, 14, 196, 221
and giving up of child, 57-59,
60, 62, 64-67
miscarriage, 63
unwed mother stigma, 58-59,
65, 182
press. *See* media
"Pretender, The" (song), 204
"Priest, The" (song), 180, 184-85
Prince (singer), 13, 235
Psycho-Analysis of Children, The
(Klein), 7-8
psychology
of children, 7-8, 48-49
creative process, xvi, 7-10,
35-36
fort-da game, 35-36, 48
impostor syndrome, 23-26
Jungian theory, 42
the mirrored self, 8-9
public image of Mitchell.
See also personae
and album covers, 3
and appearance, 13, 199, 208,
240
and effort to change style, 6, 31,
189, 209
escape from, 4-5, 86-87
experimenting with, 155-56
fan adulation, 112, 113
fan disenchantment, 239
female stereotype, 5, 49-52
and identity, 54, 55
and mythmaking, viii, 16-17,
88-89, 93, 121, 194
self-penned press releases, 16
punk movement, 54-55

Q (magazine), 70
Quinn, John, 180, 271n63

race
  and identity, 2–7
  and Mitchell's music, 3, 6,
    28–29, 252
Rachmaninoff, Sergei, 196
Raditz, Cary, 127–28
Raffi, 235
"Rainy Night House" (song), 185
Reader's Digest, 159, 168
"Ready to Start" (song), 104
record industry. See music
  industry
Redbird, Duke, 57
Redford, Robert, 125
Reed, B. Mitchell, 76
Reginato, James, 109, 117
religion. See also spiritual
  well being
  and creativity, 32, 125, 136–37,
    165–67, 180–81
  organized, 179, 181–82, 185
  priests, 184–85
  theology, 183–84, 190
Renaldo and Clara (film), 148–49,
  156, 158, 170, 243
"Reoccurring Dream, The" (song),
  176–77, 178–79
Reprise Records
  ad campaign, 83–85, 117
  first record deal, xiv, 3, 77, 107
  Mitchell on, 117
Rhapsody on a Theme of Paganini
  (Rachmaninoff), 196
Rice, William, 51
Richards, Keith, 69, 88, 112
Richie, Lionel, 244
Riefenstahl, Leni, 166
"River" (song), 190–92
Riverboat coffee house, 240
river metaphor, 190–92
River: The Joni Letters (Hancock
  album), 233, 234, 235

Roberts, Elliot
  as Mitchell's manager, 75, 76,
    106–7, 133, 211, 212
  and Woodstock, 90, 91
  and Young, 40, 79, 108
Robertson, Robbie, 160
Rock and Roll Hall of Fame,
  124
Rockefeller, Nelson, 101
Rock Express, 46
"Rockit" (song), 233
Rock Lives (White), 81
Rock Photo, 4
Rocky Horror Picture Show, The
  (film), 5
Rodgers, Jeffrey Pepper, 68
Rolling Stone (magazine), 126
  album review, 12, 80
  Dylan interview, 19
  "Guitar Gods," 117
  interviews, 18–19, 53, 86, 139,
    194, 201, 209, 210
  love chart, 121–22, 216–17,
    268n26
  Wenner/Mitchell feud, 119,
    121, 124
Rolling Stones, the, 105
Rolling Thunder Revue (1975),
  143, 146, 154, 156–57
  Mitchell's experience of, 148,
    155, 158, 159, 207–8, 243
romantic love
  Mitchell on, 206, 207–8, 213
  theme of, 11, 194, 202–3, 213
Ronstadt, Linda, 42, 253
Rose, Charlie, 224, 249
Rosemary's Baby (film), 83
Rosenthal, Mort, 145
Rotten, Johnny, 54, 55
Ruhlmann, William, 69, 237
Rush, Tom, 68–69

Sainte-Marie, Buffy, 56, 69, 106
"Same Situation, The" (song), 43
San Diego Union-Tribune, 71

Saskatoon
on *Clouds* album cover, 10
growing up in, 52–54
Louis Riel café, 105
Mendel Art Gallery, 231
Queen Elizabeth Public
School, 167, 223
St. Paul's Hospital, 36, 37
Saskatoon Star-Phoenix, 153
Seagull. *See Song to a Seagull*
(album)
"Second Coming, The" (Yeats),
179–80, 271n63
Second Sex, The (de Beauvoir), 50
Seeger, Pete, 67, 142, 269n9
"See You Sometime" (song), 203
SEX (boutique), 55
"Sex Kills" (song), 160
Sex Pistols, 54, 55
Sexton, Anne, 153
sexuality
in artwork, 19
Mitchell on, 194–95
and music marketing, 85
and personal empowerment,
19, 50, 75, 82–83
sex life and the media, 121–25
"Shades of Scarlet Conquering"
(song), 239
Shadows and Light (album), 170
Shepard, Sam, 148, 158, 207
Sheppard, Bob, 247
Shine (album), 131, 189, 254
vocal style, 238, 240, 246–49
"Shine" (song), 246
Shipley, Mike, 210
Shorter, Wayne, 235
"Short Shorts" (song), 142
Simmons, Sylvie, 74
Simon, Carly, 150, 238
Sinatra, Frank, 107, 153
singer-songwriter
and album sales, 78, 107
movement, 151, 157
Siquomb Publishing, 106

"Sire of Sorrow, The" (song), 180,
186, 187
"Sisters of Mercy" (song), 142
Slick, Grace, 94, 122, 217
Sloman, Larry "Ratso," 143,
146, 147, 148, 149, 154, 155,
158, 207
"Slouching Towards Bethlehem"
(song), 179–80
"Smokin' (Empty, Try Another)"
(song), 212
"Snakes and Ladders" (song), 244
"Song for Sharon" (song), 125
song genres. *See* themes
Song to a Seagull (album), ix, 60,
153, 243
cover art, 10, 11, 152
dedication, 80, 168
Mitchell on, 78, 80, 81
recording of, 77–80
"Song to a Seagull" (song), 56
song writing. *See also*
imagery; themes
composition method, 68–69,
71–74, 145, 266n40
crediting sources, 141, 156
first-person, 239
impact on vocal style, 237–38
influences, 139, 144, 152
labelled as confessional, 152,
182, 194
literary references, xii, 117, 122,
141, 174–80
as little plays, 242
and maturity, 149
melody, 178–79
Mitchell on, 11, 31–32, 54
and Nietzschean philosophy,
174–80, 187–90
originality, 168, 206–7, 224
poetry, 11, 144, 170, 187–89,
239
process, 31–32, 135, 168
singer-songwriter, 78, 107,
151, 157

third-person portraits, 145, 239

universals of experience, 146, 199

Sontag, Susan, 47

Souther, J.D., 4

spaceman imagery, 42–43, 45–46, 100

SpeakEasy (television), 105, 110

spiritual well being

and cocaine use, 159–60

and the concept of God, 136–39

in consumerist culture, 176–78

and the creative experience, x, 138

creator-creation equation, 125, 165, 181

and fame, 113

and inner peace, 251–54

and self-pity, 186–90

Starbucks project, 249

"Stay in Touch" (song), 213

Steiger, Rod, 178, 212

Stewart, Rod, 253

Stills, Stephen, 79, 122, 259

and Woodstock, 92–93, 94, 95

Sting, 235

Strauss, Neil, 2

Stravinsky, Igor, 46

studio production. See also composition method

of Clouds, 201

and creative control, xiv, 3, 77

of Dog Eat Dog, 210–12

experimentation, 213–14, 251

instrumentation, 210–12, 244

producer credits, 201, 210

rhythms, 166, 213–14, 241, 244, 251

singing into a piano, 79, 199

use of male voices, 244–45

Summer Lawns. See Hissing of Summer Lawns, The (album)

Sunday Telegraph, 81

Sunset Sound (studio), 77, 78

Sutcliffe, Phil, 70

"Suzanne" (song), 145

Tabu (film), 75

Taming the Tiger (album), 72, 119, 213

cover art, 164

Taylor, James, 212, 246

and Mitchell, 102, 114, 122, 206

"Tea Leaf Prophecy, The" (song), 17

Tending the Fire (Levine), 36, 134

"That Song About the Midway" (song), 145, 185

themes. See also imagery; song writing

Bohemian, 230

disillusionment, 117, 197, 215

escape, 175–76, 191, 209

freedom, 198, 204, 208

home, 247–48, 265

identity building, 205

inability to love, 203, 208

nihilist, 177

romantic love, 11, 194, 202–3, 213

self-isolation, 132, 181, 208

sexual abuse, 57

social critique, 246–47, 248

"This Flight Tonight" (song), 113

"This Place" (song), 247

"Three Great Stimulants, The" (song), 174–76

Thus Spoke Zarathustra: A Book for Everyone and No One (Nietzsche)

about, xvi, 8, 164–66, 171–74

on dance, 250, 254

on eternal recurrence, 176

"Intoxicated Song," 34

"Introduction," 33

and Job's story, 187

Mitchell motto from, 168, 169

"Of Poets," 187–88
"Of Reading and Writing," 168,
169, 232
"Of the Afterworldsmen," 165
"Of the Chairs of Virtue," 166,
179
"Of the Despisers of the Body,"
8
"Of the Old and New Law
Tables," 191
"Of the Priests," 185
"Of War and Warriors," 177–78
"On the Blissful Islands," 48,
140, 254
"On the Flies in the Market
Place," 118
"Prologue," xiii, 171, 184, 254
"Retired from Service," 164
and river metaphor, 190–92
on the state, 178
"The Child With the Mirror,"
172–73
"The Convalescent," 176
"The Sorcerer," 187
"Tik Tok" (song), 119
Time (magazine), 124
Times They Are a-Changin', The
(album), 153
"Tin Angel" (song), 68, 73, 142
TMZ (television), 123
Today Show, The, 233
Tork, Peter, 74
Toronto, 38, 39, 57, 74
Mariposa Folk Festival (1964),
56
Penny Farthing, the, 59
Riverboat coffee house, 240
Yorkville, 56, 86–87, 153
Toronto Star, 7, 16, 122
Trans (album), 108
Triumph of the Will (Riefenstahl),
166
"Trouble Child" (song), 179
Trudeau, Pierre, 95
Trungpa, Chögyam, 159

Turbulent Indigo (album), 138, 204,
214
success of, xvii, 164, 218–21
Twilight of the Idols (Nietzsche), 27
"Twisted" (song), 4, 243

ukulele, 50, 67
"Universal Soldier" (song), 56
Uren, John, 52
"Urge for Going" (song), 68

Valentine, Penny, 114, 118, 127,
129, 132, 189, 198, 251
Vancouver, Stanley Cup riot,
100–101
Vancouver Sun, 175
Van Gogh, Vincent, 117, 126
as inspiration, 145, 219–20,
224
Vanguard Records, 106
Vanity Fair, 124, 162, 166, 174, 239
Van Ronk, Dave, 141
Vaughan, Sarah, 240
Vega, Suzanne, 178
visual art. See album covers;
painting
vocal style
Canadian accent, 242
changing, 238–41
of Dylan, 23
folksinger, 236–37, 240
new sound, 246–49
and performance art, 242, 245
throat lesion, 245
Vogue, 219

W (magazine), 109
Wadleigh, Mike, 99
Washington Post, 51, 54
Watts, Michael, 3, 63
Weill, Kurt, 59
Weller, Sheila, 19, 76, 83, 142,
169, 196, 200, 201, 204, 206,
208, 209
Wenders, Wim, 250

Wenner, Jann, 119, 121, 124
West, Kanye, 233
Western Report, 65
"What Are Poets For?" (Heidegger), xvi
White, Jana Lynne, 43, 110
White, Timothy, 15, 81, 115, 116, 118, 133
Wild, David, 66, 139, 209
Wilde, Oscar, 41
Wildflowers (album), 142
Wild Things Run Fast (album), 184, 205, 210, 214, 244
Will You Take Me As I Am (Mercer), 52
Winehouse, Amy, 111, 232
Winnicott, D.W., 48, 49
Winnipeg, 39
WNEW, 241
women
    gender alienation of, 18–19
    and identity, 1–7, 18–22
    impostor syndrome, 23–26
    and Judeo-Christian dogma, 183–84
    and love relationships, 198, 205
    media coverage of, 118, 121–25
    Mitchell on, 18–19, 85–86
    in music industry, 93–94, 123–24
    role models, 83
    sexuality of, 50, 82–83, 123
    stereotyping of, 18, 24–25, 49–50, 85–86
    talent undervalued, x, 93–94, 226
    unwed mother stigma, 58–59, 65, 182
Wonder, Stevie, 235
Woodstock (film), 90, 99
"Woodstock" (song)
    cover versions, 98
    garden metaphor, 90, 98, 99, 101, 151
    legacy, 97, 99

lyrics, 43, 90, 92, 99, 100
Wikipedia entry, 93
writing of, 93–94
Woodstock Festival
    event, 89–93, 98–99, 100, 101
    and Mitchell, 90–91, 94, 96–97
    mythology of, 88–89, 101–3
    post-event interview, 94–96
Words and Music of Joni Mitchell, The (Bennighof), 71
world beat, 28, 148, 166, 241, 244

Yeats, W.B., 141, 179–80, 271n63
Yogi Joe, 128
"You Dream Flat Tires" (song), 244
Young, Neil
    background, 38–40
    and CSNY, 40, 79, 94
    and Geffen, 108
    Last Waltz, The (film), 160
    and Nash, 201
    relationship with Mitchell, 39–40, 43, 208
    and Roberts, 40, 79, 108
    spaceman imagery, 42
    at Woodstock, 91, 94
"You're My Thrill" (song), 215, 240
youth
    counterculture, 75
    role models, 83
    violence today, 100–101
Woodstock generation, 98, 102–3
"You've Changed" (song), 215

Zappa, Frank, xvii, 11
Zarathustra. See Thus Spoke Zarathustra (Nietzsche)
Zimmer, Dave, 96

AUTHOR BIO

AN ACCLAIMED national critic for Postmedia News Services, Katherine Monk is the author of the bestseller *Weird Sex & Snowshoes: And Other Canadian Film Phenomena*.